OWNERS AND OCCUPIERS

AUP Titles of Related Interest

FIT FOR HEROES?
Land Settlement in Scotland After World War I
Leah Leneman

CROMARTIE: Highland Life 1650–1914
E Richards and M Clough

THE ELGINS 1766–1917
S Checkland

EMIGRATION FROM NORTH–EAST SCOTLAND
Volume 1: Willing Exiles
Volume 2: Beyond the Broad Atlantic
Margery Harper

PATRONAGE AND PRINCIPLE
A Political History of Modern Scotland
Michael Fry

THE SHAPING OF SCOTLAND
18th century patterns of land use and settlement
R J Brien

OWNERS AND OCCUPIERS

Changes in Rural Society in South-West
Scotland before 1914

R H Campbell

ABERDEEN UNIVERSITY PRESS
Maxwell Macmillan Publishing Corporation

First Published 1991
Aberdeen University Press

©R H Campbell 1991

British Library Cataloguing in Publication Data

A catalogue record for this book
is available from the British Library

ISBN 0 08 041218 1

Typeset by Bookman Ltd, Bristol
Printed by
Bookcraft, Midsomer Norton

Contents

Maps

Acknowledgements

Much of the unpublished material used in this study is held in the Scottish Record Office and appears with the approval of the Keeper of the Records of Scotland. I am grateful to the Keeper and to the entire staff of the Scottish Record Office for their customary kindness and co-operation.

I acknowledge with thanks the kindness of the following in giving me permission to use unpublished material. In two cases (GD148, Cunninghame of Craigends MSS and GD307 Heron of Heron MSS) attempts to trace the present owner proved unsuccessful.

> The Late Mrs Elizabeth Murray Usher (GD10 Murray of Broughton and Cally);
> The Rt. Hon. Viscount Melville (GD51 Melville Castle MSS);
> Mrs Daphne C Watson (GD99 Vans Agnew of Barnbarroch MSS);
> Col. the Rt. Hon. the Earl of Stair (GD135 Stair MSS);
> The Trustees of the Earl of Galloway (GD138 Galloway MSS);
> Sir Crispin Agnew of Lochnaw, Bt. (GD154 Agnew of Lochnaw MSS);
> W F E Forbes of Callendar (GD171 Forbes of Callendar MSS);
> Sir Ian Abercromby, Bt. (GD185 Abercromby of Forglen MSS);
> Admiral Sir Julian Oswald (GD213 Oswald of Auchincruive MSS);
> Director, Scottish Landowners Federation (GD325 Scottish Landowners Federation MSS).

Dr A J Durie and Mr W Orr made helpful comments on my work and, once again, Miss Margaret Hendry prepared my typescript with her usual skill. I thank them all.

R H Campbell

Introduction

In his inaugural lecture as professor of economic history at Cambridge in 1929 Sir John Clapham distinguished between the contributions of two groups of Scottish historians: the accumulators and dictionary makers, who gathered much factual material but did not always organise it well or direct it to a systematic analysis, and the philosophic historians, who made economic and social philosophy out of unassorted observations.[1] The two traditions have undergone much change since the time of which Clapham wrote, but they may still be distinguished and also the regrettable gap and the suspicion of each other which keep them apart. In his inaugural lecture ten years later, Clapham's successor, Sir Michael Postan, hinted at an explanation of the suspicion when he pointed out that, 'To a true antiquary all past facts are welcome, to an historian facts are of little value unless they are causes, or parts of causes, of the phenomena which he studies'.[2] The historian cannot dispense with the facts the antiquary may provide. He will err if he offers causal explanations of the phenomena he studies without seeking the facts for himself if others have not provided them.

Unfortunately, there has been a tendency for economic and social historians in particular, nurtured as they are in the theoretical approaches of economic and social theory, to dismiss, or even to denigrate, the work of modern accumulators and dictionary makers, especially those who engage in local studies. They may once have had some justification for their suspicion in Scotland but it has diminished greatly in recent years. On the other hand, those who engage in local studies can easily forget the greater world which impinges even on a remote rural community, as Galt portrayed so brilliantly in the *Annals of the Parish*. If they do so, local studies can become mere compendia of every reference to a locality uncovered by the prodigious industry which is frequently devoted to their compilation. Far too often in the past, if there was selection, it led to the neglect of anything off familiar paths and periods, a tendency helped by the nature of the records which were available locally. Many parish histories written two or three generations ago are largely forgotten today, even by those who live in the parishes studied, simply because they failed to link parochial experience adequately to wider issues. Even those which had a wider vision have not retained a wider readership as the questions and problems of interest to historians have changed. The emergence of greater interest in more recent history, and particularly in social and economic affairs, instead of the older stress on the minutiae of ecclesiastical disputes, means that it is unusual to find a local history from earlier years which is of great interest to many modern historians. Fortunately, changes are afoot. The increasing number of local historians in Scotland and the fascination of many with oral history show a change from the past. Their methods, their period and their topics will be neglected by more general historians to the detriment of their own work. There are, however, still barriers to a complete assimilation of local history by general historians because there are still important gaps in the work of local historians. Consequently, there are many historians around who are far from being contemptuous of the facts collected by the antiquaries, who are indeed only too ready to incorporate local studies in their wider work, but who find that the facts, or the local studies, pertinent to the field in which they work are not available.

The present study has its origin in an attempt to fill one such gap. To that extent it is a piece of local history. It is also an attempt to investigate a topic which throws some light on matters of major historical significance which have been neglected and which can only be analysed satisfactorily by more such local studies. In short, it is an attempt to provide a bridge, though only a small and narrow one, among many that are needed between the two traditions of historical writing.

Superficially, it may seem strange to suggest that the agricultural history of Scotland suffers from the failure of the two traditions or approaches to converge. Agricultural history has benefited from many local studies, and historical geographers in particular have contributed a great deal to an understanding of the evolution of much of the landscape by their local studies. However, more serious gaps remain than in Scotland's industrial history, to the filling of which a great deal of attention has been directed. Admittedly, Scotland has become an urban and industrial society but, until modern times, a large proportion of those living in Scotland gained their livelihood from working the land and large areas, if not large numbers of people, are still dependent on agriculture for economic prosperity. Filling gaps in agricultural history warrants attention from anyone who seeks to understand the background to modern Scotland and to the life of many of its inhabitants today.

Two aspects of that neglect show why it is hoped the present study will go some way to providing a remedy, though its main contribution may be to stimulate more local studies in this and in similar fields rather than, or, to be less controversial, in addition to still further work in traditional areas.

Firstly, one difficulty faced by any agricultural historian is that the physical diversity of the land and the climatic variations make any generalisations hazardous. There are significant differences even in quite small areas. Marginal hill land can often be found with good quality arable land in one holding and, as the area widens, so do the contrasts. The opportunities and problems of one area are not those of another. In the south-west of Scotland there are a few, very restricted areas of grade I land where a wide range of crops may be grown with little difficulty,[3] and not far away are bleak hillsides exceeding 2,000 feet in height. These differences are evident in the detailed parochial analysis of agricultural operations which can be derived from the agricultural statistics for the last century and earlier, though in a rougher and much less exact form, from the First and Second Statistical Accounts.

An obvious distinction lies in the contrasting specialisation between livestock and arable husbandry, but the distinctions may be taken further. Livestock may be sheep or cattle. The livestock may be kept for its own products or fattened for market. If the cattle were kept for their own products, as they were in much of the south-west, there were local differences between those who reared the cattle not only for their own dairies but to supply to districts where they did not rear the livestock and between the dairy products in which districts specialised. In some production was chiefly for the liquid milk market; in others butter-making was important and some had a ready sale of buttermilk as well; in other districts the production of cheese dominated. The greater the variety, the less easy to generalise. Any generalisation can become a deceptively attractive way of suppressing the confusion. Doing so is also deceptively misleading for, if the variety is not recognised, or if the detailed work has not been carried out to reveal it, the generalisation is likely to be biassed towards whatever topic is of greatest concern at the moment or simply the one which happens to be readily available.

The attention paid to the experience of different districts in the study of Scottish agriculture has given rise to such bias and the experience of one district has been applied to others without the necessary qualification. The bias is evident in the way in which social background and the consequences of agricultural change have been examined in more detail for the Highlands whereas limited attention has been given to comparable problems in the Lowlands. Even in the Lowlands attention has been directed to the arable operations of the eastern, and frequently of the south-eastern counties, so that the agricultural history of Scotland is often portrayed as chiefly a variant on what took place in these regions. The nature of the labour force, its conditions of engagement and living are then assumed to apply more generally. Ian Carter drew attention to this characteristic in a robust comment some years ago on an alleged conflation of 'Lothian' and 'Lowland' in the work of Edinburgh-based historians.[4] Perhaps he was a shade unfair as he went on to admit that the fault lay not only with local chauvinism but with historiography. Carter himself and others, notably Malcolm Gray, have drawn attention to the special characteristics of the north-east and so have widened the geographical basis for generalisation, but often the eastern counties are still taken as the norm. One illustration will suffice. From the early nineteenth century the growing of turnips became 'the very hinge of the farm-work of the north-east',[5] and so 'the crop which more than any other rules the fortunes of our whole system of Scottish agriculture',[6] but turnips were not grown extensively in the south-west and practically not at all in some of its main dairying districts. The conclusion is obvious and is the first justification offered for this study and for its regional bias. The south-west and its peculiarities, derived from its unique concentration on dairying, need to be recognised and integrated more fully into the history of Scottish agriculture.

The second justification is also based on the nature of much existing work. Studies of the Highlands have proved readier to take account of modern times and in so doing the historian has had the unusual experience of being able to contribute, for good or ill, to the discussion of current policy. By contrast, most studies of the Lowlands are still firmly based in the eighteenth and early nineteenth centuries. The improvers still hold the stage, with one qualification. It has come from the attention paid in recent Scottish agricultural history to earlier periods and to the emergence in them of some of the changes usually associated with later periods. This fruitful work has placed the improvers in a longer-term perspective. The period which has been neglected most of all in the Lowlands is, however, more modern times. So much of the history of Scottish agriculture simply fades out about 1850, so that little is known of some of the special characteristics of the later nineteenth century. To deal with this later period adaptations are sometimes made of English experience which might not fit any of the regional experiences in Scotland. This does not represent a refusal to use Scottish material. Much of it is simply not readily available as the local sources have not been examined or are only beginning to be. Yet it is a period when much documentary material is available to assist local historians. It includes official statistics from the 1860s, the fourth series of the Transactions of the Highland and Agricultural Society and estate records, which, though voluminous, are less used to illuminate this period in the Lowlands than in earlier years. More attention should be directed to the years before 1914, not merely because it is a period which has been neglected but for two special reasons.

The first is that in the years before 1914, in Scotland as elsewhere, agriculture was having to adapt to a new pattern of world trade and to the acceptance in the increasingly urban and industrial society which it served, of the assumption that food should be obtained as cheaply as possible from newly developing countries as more efficient and more specialised transport facilitated its movement throughout the world. It was not merely a case of more imports, for Scotland had never been a major producer of the grain which came from overseas, but of new ones when refrigeration enabled perishable foodstuffs to be brought from distant producers. Given the varied nature of this competition and the varied nature of Scottish agriculture, perhaps more varied than the writings on its history often imply, enterprises and areas were affected differently. It was in the livestock, and especially in the dairying districts, that the contrasts with the depressed conditions which are often assumed to have been common experience of agriculture in the late nineteenth century were most marked. These districts were able to use their skills and to accept sheer hard work to exploit the opportunities offered by the demands of the industrial regions, a tougher task in days before marketing boards, price support and milk quotas.

The second reason, and perhaps one less recognised by modern commentators, is that among the many aspects of life which came to an end in 1914 was the social and tenurial structure which had been common in the nineteenth century. After 1918 a new social structure began to emerge as the great landed estates which had dominated the countryside began to be broken up. The age of the owner occupier dawned. A few statistics illustrate the change. By the outbreak of the First World War over 10 per cent of the acreage under crop and grass in Scotland was owner occupied; by 1919 it was under 10 per cent. By 1939 it was 29 per cent; in 1959 over 50 per cent; in 1987 over 60 per cent. Failure to recognise the radical implications of this silent revolution in the countryside has

contributed to the failure to accord adequate recognition to the
characteristics of the new social structure which emerged. The result
has been the perpetuation into the twentieth century of conceptions
of rural social and economic relationships which were under strain
and breaking down even before the end of the nineteenth century
and before their formal demise in the twentieth. Adverse economic
conditions, restrictive legislation, and sometimes unwise as well as
ostentatious expenditure were forcing landowners to sell up, often to
sitting tenants or to those who meant to work the land themselves.
The result was the growth of the pattern of owners and occupiers
with some unexpected consequences on the social structure of the
countryside through new barriers being placed in the path of social
mobility. The agricultural history of the south-west of Scotland
shows how in the past farm labourers moved to be tenants, some
of whom survived to become owner occupiers in the mid twentieth
century. Such movement, while never widespread, is now rare
indeed. Free tenancies are few and far between and any move to
owner occupation is ruled out for agricultural workers unless they
have an improbable access to substantial capital resources or have
the good fortune to inherit a holding. The paradox in the countryside
is that, as the position of the landowners has been restricted and
become less secure, that of the owner occupiers has been confirmed
and strengthened. Often it receives a degree of public approbation
and sympathy which is withheld from the landowner, against whom
it is easy to whip up popular indignation, even if it has to be over the
sins of several generations back rather than because of the reality of
the present. In many ways the owner occupier has assumed the cloak
of public sympathy which used to belong to the tenant. It is notable
that comparable public sympathy has not been extended to the
agricultural worker, still deemed unskilled in the utterly erroneous
interpretation of his activities which only an urban and industrial
community could produce. Consequently, while public discussion
of changes in agricultural policy give priority to the need to ensure
a livelihood for the owner occupier and the diminishing band of
tenants, or compensation for any loss, any effects on the agricultural
worker are neglected even more than those on the landowner. Roles
have been reversed in the silent revolution.

This study sets out to examine the beginning of these changes in
an area which has often been neglected by agricultural historians.
It suggests that, for all the apparent stability before 1914, the roots
of the social change were well established before the war. It cannot
provide a definitive study for all Scotland. It is merely an attempt
to fill in the mosaic of the complex picture of Scottish agriculture.

To understand these changes before 1914 it is necessary to set the discussion of the south-west in a wider context to see the detailed evolution and change that took place: firstly, in the links between agriculture and the wider economic development of the area; secondly, in the details of the agricultural practices of the area; and thirdly, in the relations of owner and occupier which show how the old order was disintegrating before 1914. These are the three parts of the present study.

No study of any one area can be applied generally. Doing so, it has been suggested, is a fault to be avoided, but it can be avoided only through local studies of the regional diversity of Scottish rural life. Reliable generalisations, though always with their inevitable qualifications, will become more plausible and the two traditions of historical study outlined at the beginning will be merged more easily.

Map 1   South-west Scotland

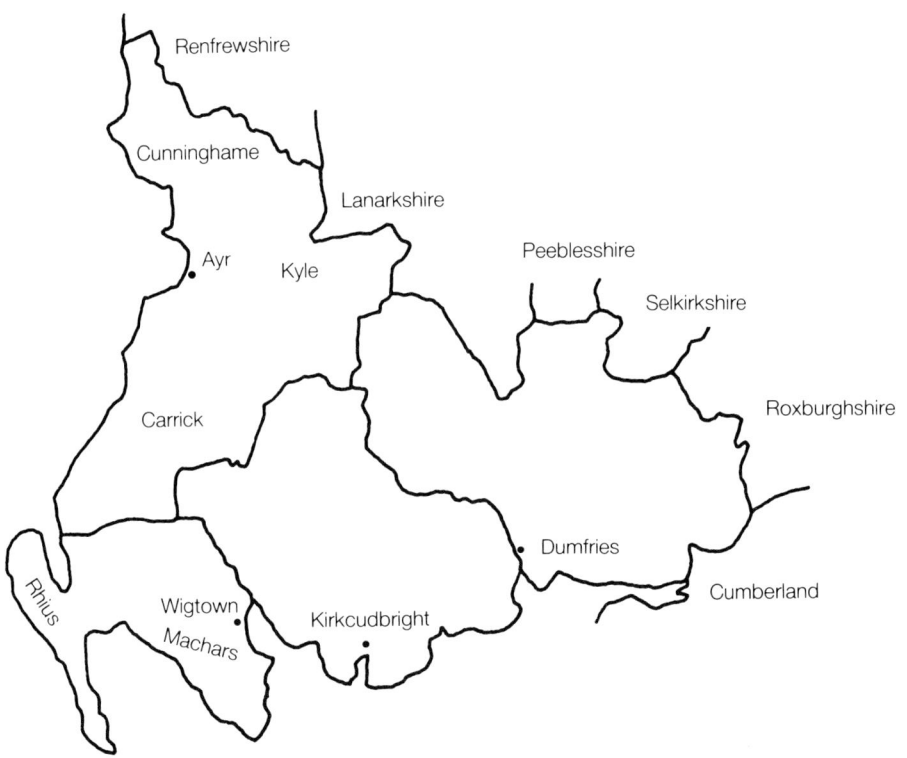

Map 2   Parishes in Ayrshire

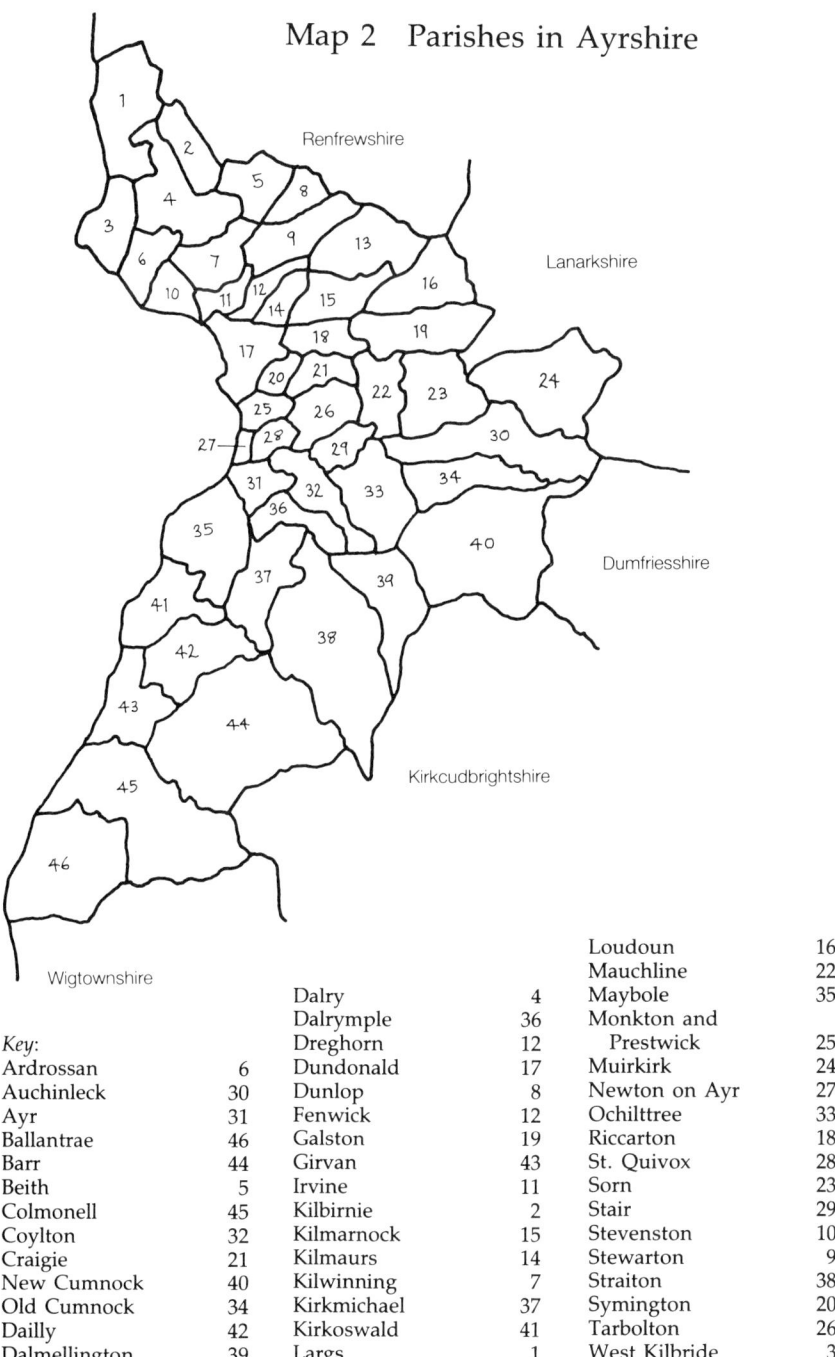

Renfrewshire

Lanarkshire

Dumfriesshire

Kirkcudbrightshire

Wigtownshire

Key:

Ardrossan	6	Loudoun	16
Auchinleck	30	Mauchline	22
Ayr	31	Maybole	35
Ballantrae	46	Monkton and	
Barr	44	Prestwick	25
Beith	5	Muirkirk	24
Colmonell	45	Newton on Ayr	27
Coylton	32	Ochilttree	33
Craigie	21	Riccarton	18
New Cumnock	40	St. Quivox	28
Old Cumnock	34	Sorn	23
Dailly	42	Stair	29
Dalmellington	39	Stevenston	10
Dalry	4	Stewarton	9
Dalrymple	36	Straiton	38
Dreghorn	12	Symington	20
Dundonald	17	Tarbolton	26
Dunlop	8	West Kilbride	3
Fenwick	12		
Galston	19		
Girvan	43		
Irvine	11		
Kilbirnie	2		
Kilmarnock	15		
Kilmaurs	14		
Kilwinning	7		
Kirkmichael	37		
Kirkoswald	41		
Largs	1		

Map 3 Parishes in Dumfriesshire

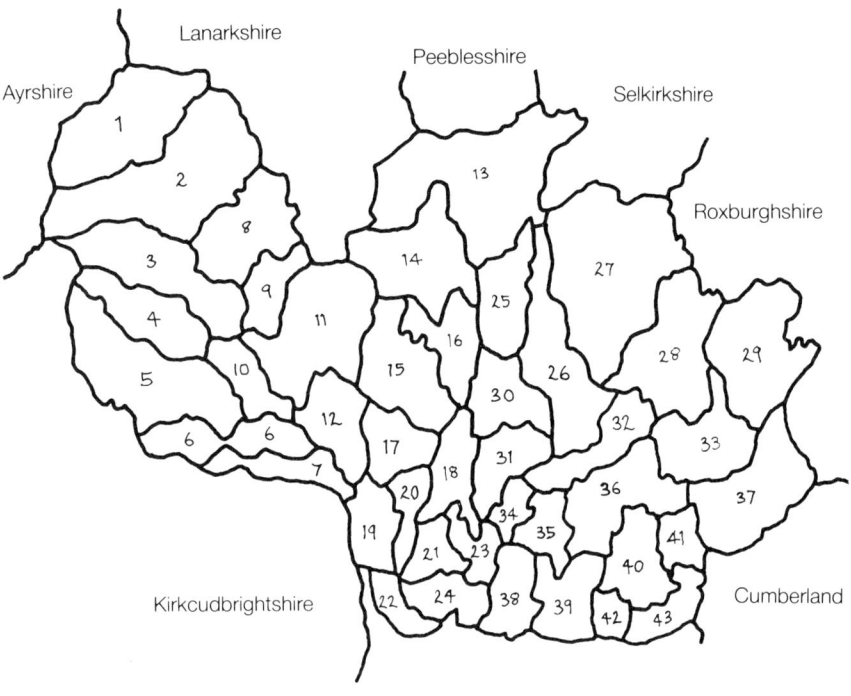

Key:

Annan	39	Glencairn	5	Middlebie	36
Applegarth	30	Gretna	43	Moffat	13
Caerlaverock	22	Halfmorton	41	Morton	9
Canonbie	37	Hoddom	35	Mouswald	21
Closeburn	11	Holywood	7	Penpont	3
Cummertrees	38	Hutton and Corrie	26	Ruthwell	24
Dalton	23	Johnstone	16	St. Mungo	34
Dornock	42	Keir	10	Sanquhar	2
Dryfesdale	31	Kirkconnel	1	Tinwald	17
Dumfries	19	Kirkmahoe	12	Torthorwald	20
Dunscore	6	Kirkmichael	15	Tundergarth	32
Durisdeer	8	Kirkpatrick-Fleming	40	Tynron	4
Eskdalemuir	27	Kirkpatrick-Juxta	14	Wamphray	25
Ewes	29	Langholm	33	Westerkirk	28
		Lochmaben	18		

Map 4   Parishes in Kirkcudbrightshire

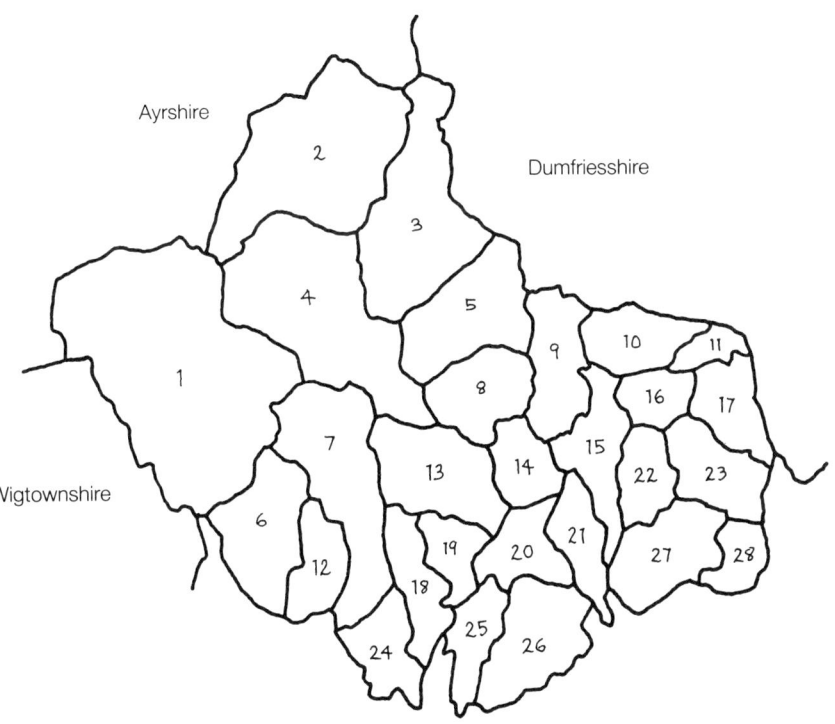

Key:

Anwoth	12	Kirkgunzeon	22
Balmaclellan	5	Kirkmabreck	6
Balmaghie	13	Kirkpatrick-Durham	9
Borgue	24	Kirkpatrick-Irongray	10
Buittle	21	Lochrutton	16
Carsphairn	2	Minnigaff	1
Colvend	27	New Abbey	23
Crossmichael	14	Parton	8
Dalry	3	Rerrick	26
Girthon	7	Terregles	11
Kells	4	Tongland	19
Kelton	20	Troqueer	17
Kirkbean	28	Twynholm	18
Kirkcudbright	25	Urr	15

Map 5   Parishes in Wigtownshire

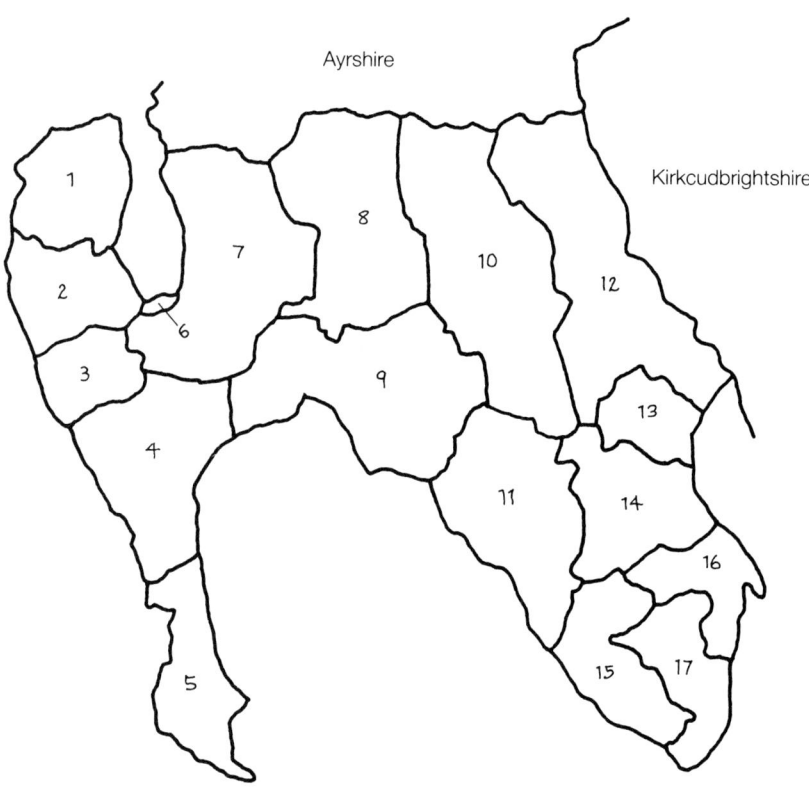

Key:

Glasserton	15	Old Luce	9
Inch	7	Mochrum	11
Kirkcolm	1	Penninghame	12
Kirkinner	14	Portpatrick	3
Kirkmaiden	5	Sorbie	16
Kirkcowan	5	Stoneykirk	4
Leswalt	2	Stranraer	6
New Luce	8	Whithorn	17
		Wigtown	13

Part I

A PERIPHERAL REGION

Chapter 1

A Staging Post

The south-west of Scotland has often seemed remote and isolated from the rest of Scotland. Hemmed in on the west and the south, the hills rise to their highest level in the south of Scotland, culminating in the ranges on the borders of Kirkcudbrightshire and Ayrshire to the east and north. Movement in all directions was impeded. Even as the crow flies, Glasgow is over 110 kilometres from Stranraer and Edinburgh is over 150, the same relative distances from Fort Augustus in the north.

These natural boundaries help to define the south-west geographically: all land to the west of the natural physical boundary from Ayr to Dumfries through Nithsdale suggests a broad but useful grouping for some purposes. If some more modern statistical information is sought, as from civil and agricultural censuses, the four counties of Ayr, Dumfries, Kirkcudbright and Wigtown provide interesting internal comparisons and help to delineate a wider area for discussion.

The inclusion of Ayrshire is particularly important because its experiences provide an illuminating contrast with other parts of the south-west. Its apparently unrepresentative area of industrialisation in the north complements its broad industrial structure. More importantly, Ayrshire was increasingly linked to the economic and social life of Galloway because in the nineteenth century its northerly parishes in its ancient division of Cunninghame were the scene of pioneering industrialisation and gave rise to agricultural enterprises which spread to the neighbouring counties and further afield.

Although the south-west was far from the populous central belt, and peripheral to much of Scotland, the area still provided a link in a wider network of communications. The improvement of this network brought change. New economic opportunities were introduced to the area and in time these influenced both its social life and structure.

In the eighteenth century the importance to the south-west of trade by sea was evident in its many harbours, often little more than creeks, along the coast. Most have gone out of use. On the west coast south of Ayr the exposed nature of the coastline provided only rocky inlets where there were no safe moorings from the prevailing south-west wind. Dunure, Maidens, Girvan, Ballantrae, Portpatrick and Port Logan—formerly Port Nessock—all suffered from the same disadvantages, as their generally ruinous harbours now show. The protracted tribulations in the building of Portpatrick were only a dramatic example of the difficulties of establishing safe harbours on an inhospitable coastline. Loch Ryan offered better shelter but had its own difficulties of access when the winds were from the north-west. Along the southern seaboard harbours proliferated and were more successful. It was more sheltered and had the additional advantage that its river system provided a wider network of communications inland from the ports. The main rivers flowing to the west—the Doon, Girvan and Stinchar—offered no navigable attractions. By contrast, some of the estuaries formed by the main rivers which flowed from the north to the south were navigable for a short distance at least, and so allowed access to the interior. Furthest to the west was the Luce; it was not navigable but its mouth was only a few miles distant from Stranraer and Portpatrick, so that, with the small harbour at Stairhaven, the triangle of land between these three places was adequately served. Similarly provided was the southern Rhins of Galloway from Port Logan and Drummore on the west and east sides of the peninsula. Near the mouth of the Cree was the ancient port of Wigtown, with a new harbour built in the early nineteenth century, while small vessels penetrated a few miles further up the estuary to Creetown, Palnure and Carty. Gatehouse at the mouth of the Fleet and Kirkcudbright at the mouth of the Dee were among the relatively larger ports. The Urr and the Nith had still more extensive groupings of small harbours. On the Urr, Dalbeattie, or the Dub o' Hass, was the main and most northerly port; downstream were quays at Oldland and Steadstone before the main port at Palnackie on the west bank and, of lesser importance, Kippford and Rockcliffe on the east. Dumfries was the objective on the Nith. Improvements which took place on it, especially in the 1830s, encountered difficulties caused by silting, and the importance of the harbours on the Nith other than Dumfries—Castledykes, Glencaple, Kingholm and Laghall—changed.

Though the southern seaboard had good communications by sea, access to the north was restricted by the hills which rose to form the watersheds to the north and east, so confining the life of the more remote south-west to the southern seaboard and directing many of its contacts out of Scotland. An attempt to provide better access to the north had limited success in the only direction where topography made improvement possible, the long arm of low-lying ground—the Glenkens—which ran north from Kirkcudbright along the valley of the Dee with Loch Ken a major natural feature giving access to the interior, but progress along it met with increasing difficulty as the land rose to the watershed between the Deugh and the Doon. The possibility of navigation from the sea was obstructed at Tongland and further upstream, but Sir Alexander Gordon of Culvennan attempted improvement with two cuttings, for which the description of canal usually given to them is too grand. The first, in 1765, was a canal from Carlingwark Loch to the river Dee, and the second, some fifteen years later, was a cut further north below Glenlochar Bridge to allow access to Loch Ken and so provide the means of navigation towards the north end of the loch. A much more ambitious project followed in an Act of 1802 for the construction of a Glenkens Canal, which was to run from the tidal water of the Dee to Loch Ken and for three miles at the loch's north end to bring it to Dalry. The canal was a visionary project which was never constructed.[1]

Until well into the nineteenth century and to a lesser extent even into the twentieth century the mass of hills which bordered the north of Galloway hindered communications from the string of settlements on the north shore of the Solway to central Scotland where most of the new industrial developments were taking place. Such contacts as the southern parishes had with the central belt of Scotland were often based on the need to maintain administrative links with Edinburgh rather than on any possibility of easy contact with the developing economy of Glasgow and the west of Scotland. Yet the most southerly parts of Galloway were not isolated. They had major economic links by sea to the Isle of Man, Ireland, and most importantly of all, to the north-west of England, with Liverpool their major market and the destination of those Gallovidians who sought their fortunes in the industrial north-west of England, a number following the recognised path of a Scotch draper. Coal and lime were imported from Cumberland. Agricultural surpluses were sent there and to Liverpool much more frequently than to ports on the Clyde. The imports of coal were of special significance. The long-standing tax on coastwise shipments brought a flood of bitter complaints, since most of the remoter south-west was cut off from access to supplies from the nearest indigenous resources in the Doon and Girvan valleys or in Nithsdale. The complaints appeared in the *Old Statistical Account* from Anwoth, Borgue, Crossmichael, Kirkcudbright, Kirkpatrick-Irongray, Minnigaff, Rerrick, Tongland and Urr in Kirkcudbrightshire and from Sorbie and Stranraer in Wigtownshire. A few of the more optimistic ministers believed that only the imposition of the duty stood in the way of the successful progress of their parish to industrial achievement. The removal of the duty in 1793 was welcomed by many of those who wrote accounts after the change, as at Buittle, Kirkbean, Twynholm, Whithorn and Wigtown. Coal certainly came across the Solway more readily, though complaints were then transferred to the Cumberland coalmasters who were thought to be the beneficiaries as they raised their prices when the duty was removed. The remoter south-west was to learn that more than cheap coal was required to effect an industrial transformation.

The trade across the Solway, and further afield to the Isle of Man and Ireland ensured that the geographical orientation of the economic life of the remoter south-west was different from that of its administrative or legal life. The link with the north-west of England, and the importance of Liverpool as the most accessible urban centre, can easily be neglected because of its decline in the twentieth century. The perpetuation of the link with Ireland has ensured that it is less likely to be underestimated. It gave rise to unique social tension through immigration, whereas the links with England and the Isle of Man led to emigration and trade. The link with Ireland was encouraged by government action in the eighteenth and nineteenth centuries, comparable to some in the Highlands, but attempts to improve the link with Ireland did not have the objective, which assumed major importance in the Highlands, of trying to stem the flow of emigrants from its surplus population. Thomas Telford's report on the Highlands offers a much wider justification for government intervention than his report on communications with Ireland, though they were both written about the same time. Government's desire to improve the link with Ireland had strategic or even wider political objectives and consequently, it had less direct effect on the economic life of the south-west. The link with the north-west of England had such effects until the middle of the nineteenth century at least, when economic links with the rest of Scotland became easier and more frequent.

The main stages in developing the line of communication with Ireland show how the political and strategic objectives took precedence over any economic disadvantages which might arise. The route to Ireland was well established by the droves of cattle which came from Ireland. The legal ban on their importation was removed in 1765 but, as with so many similar restrictive measures of the time which were then being repealed, the effectiveness of the ban is questionable. The trysts along the route show the direction the Irish cattle traversed, roughly as they would today: Glenluce, Newton Stewart,

Gatehouse, New Galloway, Kelton Hill and Crocketford, before the main collecting one at Dumfries. The route was well established therefore before it was substantially reconstructed between 1763 and 1765. The initial survey clearly stated the military objectives of the renovation: '... the intention of the proposed Road is chiefly with a View to open a speedy, and certain communication between Great Britain and Ireland; especially with regard to the passage of the Troops from one Kingdom to the other, whenever the Exigency of Affairs may require it'.[2] Later, between 1780 and 1782, a spur was added from Stranraer to Ballantrae at the instigation of the then commander-in-chief.

The strategic situation at the time, allied to the Union with Ireland in 1801, gave an added impetus to the military requirements, and were reflected in attempts to construct the harbour at Portpatrick. The first, when John Smeaton carried out a survey of the harbour in 1768, followed the completion of the military road. Ten years later his improvements, with two piers at the entrance to provide shelter from the heavy swell, were finished at a cost of double his estimate. They proved ineffective and did not last, even with repairs and additional supports. The second phase began after Trinity House favoured the Donaghadee to Portpatrick route in 1818. In 1820, authority was given to proceed on a plan of John Rennies, which followed the main features of Smeaton's, and which was carried out on his death by his son. Its fate was not far different from Smeaton's: costs were much higher than expected and the piers no less subject to damage. The history of Portpatrick is a saga in itself, which may be used to illustrate many matters of recurring significance: how the estimates of the greatest of engineers were usually exceeded by substantial margins; how governments had to intervene, as Adam Smith had always said they should, in public works which could never be in the interest of private citizens to undertake; how they tried—without success—to pass work to private contractors; how costs continued to escalate with little to show for the expenditure until, to use a much-quoted, but realistic assessment, 'Portpatrick offers the minimum amount of shelter for the large amount of money that had been laid out upon it'.[3] Portpatrick continued on its disastrous course until 1849 when the Irish mail service was removed. The final, but by then only the formal end to Portpatrick's position as a staging post came in 1873 with the repeal of the Portpatrick Harbour Acts. The link with Ireland continued between Stranraer and Larne, but it too was often only part of a longer journey and the subsequent movement of passengers and goods through Galloway was of limited importance.

While the construction of Portpatrick was absorbing so much public money, two investigations into roads leading to it were undertaken.[4] The first surveys and discussions of the routes to Carlisle and the south came while the Napoleonic Wars were still in progress. In the reports, and in examination by parliamentary committees, arguments were based on the advantages for mails and for military purposes. However, by the early 1820s, when the war was over, and the reconstruction of Portpatrick harbour had been started, Telford examined the route to Glasgow, in assessing which he had the support of John McAdam, who had local knowledge.[5] The examination of the Glasgow route is important, first, because it was an investigation of a line of communication from Ireland through the south-west to other parts of Scotland, and not of one to Carlisle and the south, which had been the concern of earlier studies, and second, because the reasons given for improving this route were often economic and not administrative, and were supported by evidence and petitions from merchants and commercial interests in both Glasgow and Dublin. They argued that only if this route were improved would the expenditure at Portpatrick be effective and prove beneficial by meeting an economic need. They were ready to withdraw support from its reconstruction if the road between Girvan and Stranraer was left in its 'present barbarous condition'.[6]

The economic benefits of the links with Glasgow lay in the future. Those which followed the improvements in the links with Ireland were limited, because the early lines of communication were generally aimed at enabling whoever traversed the roads and bridges to pass through what was generally regarded as an inhospitable area as easily and as quickly as possible. To troops, goods, Irish cattle, or Irish vagrants the south-west was a staging post. To contemporaries the problems they brought in their passage through the region were often more evident than the benefits. The troops were resented unless steps were taken to mollify the inhabitants. When building the military road, the Deputy Quartermaster-General in Scotland arranged terms for billeting which he considered 'not very cheap' but 'convenient'—'22 pence a week and their meal'—but still he was anxious to finish the stretch of road 'that the inhabitants may not be burthened a third season with the quartering of soldiers, which they do not consent to with good will'.[7] The Irish cattle and their drovers had their uses, but also their disadvantages. They abused those whom they passed, grazed where they were not wanted, and broke the Sabbath. Irish migrants were even more objectionable and the major aim of those with whom they came into contact, and especially those who had some responsibility for them—moral or legal—was to pass them on to others as quickly as possible. The way in which they followed the lines of the roads is obvious from the frequency of the complaints from the parishes which lay along them.

The troops and the cattle left their own marks, often their own problems, but their route from Ireland lay through Galloway, often through Scotland, to England. The Irish migrants, vagrant or otherwise, were different. When the military and the drovers faded from the road from west to east, the vagrants and many near vagrants persisted and by the nineteenth century they moved in increasing numbers to central Scotland and its new industrialising regions. The connection with Ireland was still one which led many to move through the south-west, but economic opportunities elsewhere drew migrants to other parts of Scotland. The perpetuation of an unsettled and rootless group in the community was the main consequence of the link with Ireland.

Since the south-west did not offer many indigenous advantages for those who came from Ireland other than being an adjacent part of Great Britain, any changes which introduced quicker, more reliable, or more economical ways of reaching their ultimate destinations were likely to be welcomed by those who passed through. These changes came with the innovation of steam propulsion. Its advent lay behind much of the industrialisation which was to give new opportunities and provide new challenges. More directly and immediately, steam navigation helped to increase the external trade of the area and to take it into new channels; in due course the railways penetrated the land mass which had been the barrier to communications with other parts of Scotland. The result was to loosen some of the old links with Ireland and with England and to strengthen those with Scotland.

Three examples of the changes which grew from the application of steam navigation, taken in order of increasing importance, provide illustrations. The first was the effect on the various small harbours, creeks and safe beaches along the Solway coast. They continued to be used, but with the increase in the size of trading vessels, which accompanied but was not caused solely by the adoption of the steam engine, they gradually fell out of use. With this decline the trade became concentrated on those with better handling facilities. Steam vessels had greater freedom to choose their ports as they were not dependent on favourable winds. The second illustration is a special case of the first. It is the way in which Portpatrick lost its importance to Stranraer. Expensive attempts to ensure a safe anchorage were unnecessary when the safer port of Stranraer could be used as steam navigation reduced the dependence on favourable winds. The first and second examples merely led to the trade and external contacts of the south-west being redistributed throughout the area. The third drew trade away from the south-west. The predictability of steam navigation, even on a longer journey, led to Irish cattle being taken direct to Liverpool, where, if not destined for local consumption, the railways ensured easier dispatch to London.[8]

The evolution of the railway network provides a detailed example of the reorientation of communications. Some of the less accessible parts of the south-west, especially in the Machars of Wigtownshire, found that they were able to exploit both sources of supply and markets, which, though physically close, had often been beyond the reach of economic exploitation. These links were to become more important as the south-west specialised increasingly in dairying. The railways gave access to parts of Scotland which had previously been largely out of reach: to Glasgow and Edinburgh from Dumfries and then later from Stranraer.

The lack of economic attractions in the south-west is confirmed by the reluctance of the major railway companies to enter it. The route to Ireland was the prize, but hardly a glittering one when the Irish mail was diverted to the Holyhead crossing in 1848 and the mail service through Portpatrick was discontinued in 1849. On the other hand, once local initiative was determined to have the railways, the larger companies could not afford to stand by idly and possibly allow a rival to enter the area. Above all, the arch enemies, the Caledonian and the Glasgow and South Western Railways, could not see the other gain the advantage. Since local enterprise could not readily work the lines, for both technical and financial reasons, the major railways companies were drawn into the south-west, often reluctantly, leading to cases of bitter rivalry. This confused and impeded the progress and working of the railways, but it may have given the south-west a more extensive network than could ever have been justified on any rational economic grounds.

The structure of the railway network in the remoter south-west was much less complex than in the northern district of Ayrshire, where the greater population, and above all the mineral potential of the area, led to a criss-cross of lines. This became even more extensive in the later nineteenth century, once again through the rivalry of the Caledonian and the Glasgow and South Western Railways, particularly through their rivalry centred on the port of Ardrossan. The network became sparser further south. In the area between Ayr and Dumfries it consisted simply of the two principal lines from Dumfries to Stranraer and Portpatrick and from Girvan (and so from Ayr and Glasgow) to Stranraer; and two minor spurs, the Kirkcudbrightshire Railway from Castle Douglas to Kirkcudbright and the Wigtownshire Railway, which ran from Newton Stewart through the Machars to Whithorn.

The first move towards the construction of the main line from east to west came with the Castle Douglas and Dumfries Railway, authorised in 1856 and opened in 1859. The stretch from Castle Douglas to Portpatrick was authorised to be built by the Portpatrick Railway in 1857, and was opened to Stranraer in 1861 and to Portpatrick in 1862. The two spurs which complemented this main line were built before the other chief line from north to south along the western seaboard of the area was completed. The Kirkcudbrightshire Railway was authorised in 1861 and opened in 1864; the Wigtownshire Railway was authorised in 1872 and opened in stages between 1875 and 1877.

The early history of the line from north to south, the Girvan and Portpatrick Junction Railway, was interrupted and chequered. It has survived as the others have closed, for very good reason. It proved that, as the nineteenth century progressed, the importance of the south-west's links between Ireland and Carlisle and the south were declining in favour of those with the north as the south-west became more integrated with the industrial west for its prosperity. In that respect its experience was the same as the road to the north. Initially the old attraction of the established route to Ireland brought railway promoters from outside the area. The route stretching from Glasgow and Ayr through Girvan to Stranraer was used by impecunious Irish immigrants who sought work in the central belt. They did not offer an attractive market to railway promoters, and were in any case more likely to take the steamboats on the longer direct passage to Glasgow unless they hoped to pick up some employment, usually of a temporary nature in agriculture in Ayrshire on the way there. It is not surprising that the route was neglected by outside interests and the line was built through local persistence and initiative. Thus the Girvan and Portpatrick Junction Railway was first authorised in 1865, but subsequent approval for extending the period of construction had to be obtained before it was finally opened in 1877.

Subsequently, these various railways were amalgamated or absorbed. In 1865 the Castle Douglas and Dumfries Railway became part of the Glasgow and South Western Railway, which had operated it, and the Kirkcudbrightshire Railway followed. The major change in the ownership of the two other railways which made up the network along the southern seaboard—the Portpatrick and the Wigtownshire—came in 1885, and was effective from the beginning of 1886, when they became the Portpatrick and Wigtownshire Joint Railways. This amalgamation was brought about through four large companies with interests in the route to Ireland. They took the railways over in equal shares, guaranteeing the original shareholders a dividend of 3½ per cent. As well as the two old rivals of the Caledonian and the Glasgow and South Western Railways, the newcomers were the London and North Western Railway and the Midland Railway. The arrangement remained until the railway was merged into the London Midland and Scottish Railway in 1923.

Once again the Girvan and Portpatrick Junction Railway had an unusual career. It was bought by a new company, the Ayrshire and Wigtownshire Railway Company in 1887, only ten years after it was opened, and was then taken over by one of the directors in 1890 before coming into the hands of Glasgow and South Western Railway in 1892.

Though its physical remoteness kept the south-west and its more remote parts in particular peripheral to so much of the life, and especially the economic life, of Scotland, its wider contacts by sea with the north-west of England and with Ireland ensured that it was never as isolated as other parts on the periphery of Scottish life. Even when the south-west was merely a staging post, to be passed through as quickly as possible, the contacts which followed gave it unusual opportunities which moulded its social and economic life.

Chapter 2

On the Industrial Frontier

The improved communications which the south-west established with both the north-west of England and with the central belt of Scotland gave easier access to areas which were experiencing marked industrialisation and urbanisation. In the south-west only parts of Ayrshire—in Cunninghame and Kyle—experienced any significant industrial growth. Generally the south-west was on the periphery of the industrial change. Fortunately, the First and Second Statistical Accounts, for all their faults, give an invaluable insight into what was happening at a parochial level. On these topics the Accounts suffer less from the moralising reflections which can determine and so mar comment on matters of more direct concern to ministers anxious to present the spiritual state of their parishes in a favourable light.

The Statistical Accounts, which were written at the beginning and end of what has been regarded as the first phase of modern industrialisation with the expansion of textile production, and especially the early growth of cotton manufacture, confirm the need to take care not to exaggerate the extent of change. Even in that early phase, when the availability of coal was much less important both as a source of power, and as a raw material in further manufacture than it was to become in the middle of the nineteenth century, its absence in the remoter south-west was recognised as a major limitation to industrial expansion. Only north Ayrshire was well-endowed, and parts had the added advantage of good supplies of iron ore as well. Some other districts had good but concentrated supplies. Others realised their potential only slowly, but the favoured areas were few. Most of the south-west had none, which explains the strength of the complaints against the tax on coal shipped coastwise.

The initial spread of coalmining in the later eighteenth century should not be misrepresented. It was not the large-scale exploitation to meet the demand from the ironworks which was to characterise the major expansion of the north Ayrshire coalfields in the mid nineteenth century. Rather it was a steady growth to meet the general needs of both industrial and domestic markets.

The expansion was greatest in north Ayrshire, as in Stevenston, which had long had major coal enterprises, and in parishes adjacent to Irvine, from which coal was exported. In the eighteenth century there was nothing comparable in the southern valleys of the Doon, Girvan and Nith, even though the potential of their coal-bearing strata was recognised. Dalmellington suffered from its land-locked isolation and the exploitation of collieries at Dailly in the Girvan valley was impeded because of the high cost of conveying their output to the harbour at Girvan. Kirkconnel in the Nith valley had a mere 16 colliers in the 1790s; Sanquhar had only 40, though it had the distinction of a steam engine designed by William Symington to drain its mines. Coal still went overland from these coal workings: it went as far as 30 miles from Dalmellington to the parishes of Kells and Crossmichael; from Kirkconnel it went even further to the parishes of Morton and Kirkpatrick-Irongray; somewhat surprisingly, it went from both to Kirkpatrick-Durham. Since 12 miles was taken to be as far as coal could be transported profitably overland, most coal was transported by sea. The parishes on the southern coast were supplied from across the Solway, generally from Whitehaven. Coal from Ayrshire became more competitive on the western seaboard as it did not need to be taken round the Mull of Galloway. In the remoter south-west coal proved to be expensive and so long as the duty on coal inhibited the use of more accessible supplies from Cumberland, it was ruled out for most uses. Coal from Dalmellington, was 'used by the better sort', in the parish of Kells in the Glenkens,[1] but in Wigtown even they were forced to use peat in their kitchens and could afford coal only in their rooms. At Kirkpatrick-Durham, indifferently situated for supplies from Dalmellington, Sanquhar and Whitehaven, coal was used only by 'gentlemen' and by smiths at their forges.[2] In New Abbey only a few families used English coal but at Tongland it was 'quite beyond the reach of the common people'.[3]

Fortunately, the south-west did not suffer from any general scarcity of fuel for domestic purposes. Peat was an alternative fuel, for domestic if not for industrial purposes, and was plentiful in many parishes. In north Ayreshire, even where coal was so readily available that farmers worked small outcrops, peat was a cheaper fuel and was used for heating milk for cheesemaking and for drying grain. In Kirkcudbrightshire and Wigtownshire, which had no indigenous alternative, peat had to be used extensively wherever it was found, above all in those inland and upland parishes which were furthest from good communications by sea. Though the south-western counties were generally well-endowed with peat, it could be as expensive as imported coal in some places. In Nithsdale it had to be brought six or seven miles to Glencairn; in Keir there was little; at Holywood it was of poor quality and was scarce and expensive. Peat was also scarce in Kirkcudbrightshire in the parishes of Parton, Rerrick, Terregles and Tongland, and in New Abbey its use was restricted. Outsiders were attracted to parishes with good supplies. Its plentiful supply in Urr was taken to explain the increase of its population, when decreases were being registered nearby. In such parishes—specifically in New Abbey, Parton and Twynholm—whin and furze were used by the poor, though, as at Kirkmabreck, the poor also used such fuel even when peat was good and plentiful.

Insufficiency of coal restricted industrialisation more directly in the mid nineteenth century when it was essential for the growth of the heavy industries than in the eighteenth century. In the late eighteenth century water remained the common source of power. Even the more dramatic, but often unrepresentative, examples of early modern industrialisation—the cotton mills and their supporting communities which emerged in the eighteenth century—used water for power as of old. Their dependence on good supplies often took them to locations where they would not have been otherwise and kept them there even when some of the initial attractions had gone. They have often been given more attention by historians than they should have received. Their impact on contemporary society was dramatic rather than penetrating or pervasive.

The major representative of this new industrial era in the south-west was at Catrine in Ayrshire. Similar ventures further south at Gatehouse and elsewhere were too peripheral to the main concentration for success. The exact location of each was determined by the availability of water power: from the river Ayr for Catrine and from Loch Whinyeon and the Fleet valley generally for Gatehouse. Though the elaborate tapping of the water supplies impressed contemporaries less than the buildings, which were on an innovatory scale for the time, the engineering feats required to bring water over long distances are perhaps more impressive to subsequent generations. Cotton spinning was soon the main industry in Gatehouse, but, unlike Catrine, it had also a heterogeneous collection of other activities, symptomatic of the diffuse nature of the town's economic life, an excessive diversification when specialisation was becoming the way to economic success. In addition, markets for black cattle had vessels trading out of the port, one even going 'constantly' to London. All provided the background to the parish minister's hope that: 'the cotton works, which have swelled it to its present size and population, promise soon to give it a rank among the towns distinguished for industry and commerce'.[4]

Of the activity in Gatehouse then there was no doubt; of its failure to realise the expectations of the parish minister there could be no knowledge. Catrine was a very different enterprise. It showed much greater physical evidence of an industrial community planned for one specialisation at the start, with the promise of a long-term stable future. Landed proprietors were behind both ventures. James Murray of Broughton and Cally was an established proprietor, whose encouragement of Gatehouse was part of the general policy of estate development; Catrine was brought into being by a partnership of Claud Alexander, one of the nabobs so disliked by some Scottish intellectuals, who, home with a fortune after service with the East India Company, bought nearby Ballochmyle in 1786, and David Dale, the self-made, Ayrshire-born, linen merchant, who came to dominate the new manufacture of cotton. Their massive five-storied cotton twist mill, built in the 1780s, dominated the village from its setting in a square from which subsidiary streets led out at right angles. Catrine was a company town in a way Gatehouse was not. Characteristic of this was the decision that the town's brewery, built in 1793 by the proprietor of the village should be 'let to a very respectable gentleman in Kilmarnock, with a view to introduce malt-liquor in place of whisky, which has so baneful an effect on the morals of the people'.[5]

Catrine and Gatehouse have had too much written about them. They attracted, and still attract attention because they were dramatic examples of the new forms of industrialisation. More representative of the new industrial life, especially on its periphery was the small-scale adaptation of buildings to new methods of spinning, and more widespread still, the growth of outworking. They were less common in districts some distance from the hub of industrial change around Glasgow and Paisley where the increased output of yarn from the mills generated a demand for weavers over a wide area and for the specialised tambouring work which became so characteristic of Ayrshire. The parishes of Cunninghame and of the Irvine valley were affected most of all and the links from Glasgow and Paisley spread into Carrick, though hardly reaching Wigtownshire and Kirkcudbrightshire. They were too remote.

A culling of the *Old Statistical Account* shows the contrasting experiences of different parishes. Most of those in north Ayrshire, apart from the few in the more upland north-east of the county, reported the general move which had taken place from the working of linen cloth—which encouraged some to a long-term cultivation of flax—to the weaving of silk gauze for Paisley merchants, and then on to cotton weaving. By the 1790s Beith had a bleachfield and, in addition to 32 weavers engaged in 'country work', 44 were weaving silk gauze, 70 were weaving muslin and 63 making thread, besides 'many females' employed sewing and tambouring muslin. The neighbouring inland parish of Dalry had 36 silk weavers with 8 women preparing the silk for the loom and 107 cotton weavers, with 127 women and children preparing the yarn for the loom. Kilwinning had 56 weaving silk gauze and 146 muslin and also 24 tambours. Along the north Ayrshire coast Stevenston had about 70 weavers; West Kilbride merely 17 weaving linen, 19 cotton, and three silk; Ardrossan had nearly 90 in both silk and cotton, though in its case it was thought distance from Glasgow and Paisley had impeded progress, since those at a distance 'are always the first who feel the disadvantages arising from a stagnation of trade, and the last who are benefited by its revival'.[6] Largs, virtually as remote from Paisley, had 66 weaving silk for the merchants there.

The position in the Irvine valley was similar. It had its own urban centre in Kilmarnock, which added cotton spinning to the shoe and carpetmaking, which it was long to retain, though some 200 of its complement of weavers were thought to be employed by manufacturers in Glasgow and Paisley. Increasingly the parishes in the upper Irvine valley came to be dominated by weavers: Loudoun had 344 in total, most of them—241 males and 25 females—were in Newmilns and 58 males were in Darvel. In Galston the domination was less: it had only 55 weavers and 22 stocking weavers, but was moving from its own concentration on making shoes for Kilmarnock merchants to weaving linen and gauze, and the minister felt that, 'if a little money were laid out in establishing these manufactures, while Paisley and Glasgow flourish, this parish might expect to thrive'.[7] The demand for the services of weavers was most conspicuous in these two areas but filtered through Ayrshire, even into Carrick, showing that the fear that even Ardrossan was too far away from Glasgow and Paisley to rely on their demand was unrealistic. The three parishes of Girvan, Kirkmichael and Maybole soon established a position they were to retain. Girvan had over 100 looms at work and the business growing; at Kirkmichael—still without the village of Crosshill which was to become a weaving centre—the old woollen manufacture was in decline due to 'the weavers being employed in weaving muslins sent from Glasgow, the muslin being both a lighter and more lucrative work'.[8] At Maybole the weaving of blankets, at which 80 looms employed 300 persons, overshadowed the 24 looms which had just started to weave cotton.

Further south conditions were markedly different and Gatehouse continued to be exceptional. At the end of the eighteenth century Wigtownshire and Kirkcudbrightshire had high hopes of a new industrial structure but there was little substance behind the expectations. Wigtownshire had one of the rivals to Gatehouse, promoted by Sir William Douglas, who, after making his fortune in the American trade, bought estates in Galloway and withdrew from his commercial activities to devote his attention to their development in the 1780s.[9] In 1793 in partnership with others he built a mill on the west bank of the Cree in Newton Stewart, which was given the new but ephemeral name of Newton Douglas. It was small and unsuccessful and faded out of existence shortly after Douglas's death in 1809. Generally the industrial ventures were of the traditional form to be found in such urban communities as there were. The economic structure of Stranraer, the most important town in Wigtownshire, was more aptly portrayed as, 'being the chief town of the district, [it] is resorted to by the inhabitants of the neighbouring parishes for such necessaries and comforts of life, as their farms cannot furnish, their fancies may demand, or their purses afford'.[10] Of the other parishes, Stoneykirk had the most impressive array of activities with a bleachfield, four flax mills, a pot or pearl barley mill; some kelp was also made and exported to Ireland, and salt had been made at two places but put out of business by produce smuggled from Ireland. Coarse yarn, spun by old women, was sold to be made into osnaburg for the West Indian market. Other parishes vaguely hoped that some industrial undertakings may be started, generally to exploit the local resources of wool and water. At Sorbie, the hopes were high:

> If a spirit of manufacture were once excited, wool, of which the high part of this country produces a vast quantity; flax, which might be cultivated with great advantage on the deepest of the lands; and other raw materials, might be wrought up into articles of commerce; and a Leeds or an Halifax would perhaps grow out of one of our small villages.[11]

At Wigtown the comment gave a more reliable indicator of the possibilities:

> Something of a manufacturing spirit, however, having lately arisen in this part of the country, two small manufactures, the one of wool and the other of cotton, were introduced into this town, about a year and a half ago. In the former of these, which employs between 30 and 40 persons, the wood is manufactured into plaiding and flannel, especially the former, and sent mostly to the English market. The

latter, which would have employed about 20 persons, was soon hurt after its commencement, and is now almost entirely ruined, by the iniquity of the times.[12]

Kirkcudbrightshire had as little to offer. It had Sir William Douglas's second major industrial venture, a more adventurous project than at Newton Stewart. He bought the estate of Carlingwark in 1789, had it erected into a burgh of barony, renamed it Castle Douglas in 1790 and built a cotton mill in 1795. This time the name remained, but the cotton mill was no more successful than at Newton Stewart, hardly surprisingly since both mills originated more from the social ambitions of the proprietor than from his sound economic judgement. At Castle Douglas, as at Gatehouse, though not at Catrine, in addition to the cotton manufacture, there was a range of other small-scale activities indicative of the lack of successful specialisation: a soapwork, a brewery, a tannery, and a woollen manufacture. At Creetown in the parish of Kirkmabreck, which was later to flourish on the basis of exporting its granite, there was a similar variety of enterprises: cotton spinning, which employed about 30 people, a tanwork and a lead shot mill. Though most of its menfolk still went to sea, it was hoped that one day it would be 'an opulent place'.[13] These were the exceptions in Kirkcudbrightshire. In most other parishes there was nothing worth recording by way of manufacturing, in the past, the present or even in a rosy future, except where its absence was explained through the lack of fuel, which provided the cue for an onslaught on the iniquities of the tax on the coastwise shipment of coal. Parishes as diverse as Dalry, Kells, Kirkcudbright and Tongland made this complaint. The last may have had 'many fine situations for erecting cotton-mills'[14] but comments from two other parishes show the wishful thinking about any development of manufacturing industry. Kirkpatrick-Durham reported an extraordinary range of activities, both social and economic, so impressive to make the account seem suspiciously inaccurate. There were apparently many plans for the economic and moral welfare of its inhabitants. The village had been started within the decade before the *Old Statistical Account* appeared and already some 50 dwelling-houses with as many planned. 'But, as villages will always become nurseries of dissipation and profligacy, when the inhabitants are idle, plans have been formed to give them honest and creditable employment.'[15] To that end three copartneries had been formed—for the manufacture of cotton, of wool, and one 'of trade and commerce'.[16] All were tiny and, as the *New Statistical Account* recorded somewhat sadly some years later, they 'have long since died a natural death, and now there are neither artisans nor manufacturers within our boundaries, whose services are required beyond the immediate neighbourhood'. The experiences of 'a remarkable mechanical genius', under the patronage of Lord Daer at Twynholm, should be regarded as typical of the fate which awaited many entrepreneurs in the area. First, he set up a distillery, which was given up because of alterations in the laws relating to distilling. He then planned a conversion to cotton manufacture, but that was brought to an end at once because of the stagnation of trade. It was converted instead into a woollen manufacture but on the small scale of one teasing and one carding machine, driven by water, and several hand jennies. The minister's vision was not limited by observing such reverses. Near the woollen mill was a creek in the Dee 'that might easily be turned into a good harbour, sheltered from every storm. The adjacent field is commodious for wet and dry docks, such as they have at Liverpool'.[17]

Changes in north Ayrshire were marked when compared with those further south, but even the emergence of some spinning and much weaving did not transform the economic lives of its parishes. They were far from being turned into towns comparable to Catrine or Gatehouse. Their parochial economies remained firmly agricultural with the new industrial activities tagged on to a collection of rural craftsmen. The occupational structure of the small burghs of Ayrshire was different from the rural parishes and, therefore, those parishes with Ayr, Irvine and Kilmarnock within their bounds should all be excluded from any rural study. This leaves fourteen in Cunninghame and twenty in Kyle and for nine parishes in each district reasonably comprehensive information remains concerning the inhabitants' occupations.

The majority of six basic occupations—masons, carpenters (widely interpreted), weavers, shoemakers, smiths, tailors—were to be found in each parish. In Cunninghame, West Kilbride had no masons, and Fenwick had no blacksmiths; in Kyle, Symington had no smiths, while Auchinleck, Galston, Newton-on-Ayr and St Quivox had no tailors, though the last three were sufficiently close to Kilmarnock or Ayr to be able to draw on their more extensive resources. Numbers ranged widely from one mason in Symington to 22 in Beith; from two carpenters in West Kilbride to 37 in Newton-on-Ayr; from three weavers in St Quivox to 171 in Kilwinning; from two shoemakers in West Kilbride to 33 in Old Cumnock; from two smiths in Monkton to 15 in Old Cumnock, and from two tailors in Monkton to 15 in Old Cumnock. The size of the total population of a parish affected the absolute numbers but not the distribution of crafts, though some of the parishes had larger numbers in certain occupations for special reasons. The 37 carpenters in Newton and the 29 in Largs were to be explained by the special needs of shipping. The most striking distinction between parishes was in the number of weavers, showing the penetration of outworking into north Ayrshire by the 1790s, even though it had still not displaced the old pattern of rural craftsmanship. The increased number of weavers added to the existing demand from the agricultural community for their services. Thus in the populous parish of Beith, as well as having 146 weavers manufacturing different textile fabrics, 63 making thread, 11 yarn merchants, and many families engaged in sewing and tambouring muslin, there were also more in the traditional occupations than in most parishes.

Information in the *Old Statistical Account* on the situation in the remoter south-west is sufficiently reliable to be used comparatively in 24 of the 66 parishes in Carrick, Nithsdale, Kirkcudbrightshire and Wigtownshire. As is to be expected from the spread of outworking, the parishes of Carrick and Kirkconnel in Nithsdale had more weavers. The difference is too small to be of any great significance and so it is possible to present a common pattern. Each of the six occupations—masons, carpenters, weavers, shoemakers, smiths, tailors—were represented in most of the 24 parishes. The exceptions were Kirkinner and Kirkoswald without masons; Kirkinner without a smith; Keir without a shoemaker. As in Kyle and Cunninghame the numbers in the different parishes varied but within a fairly limited range: from one mason in Balmaclellan to 16 in Dailly; from one carpenter in Kirkconnel to 16 in Wigtown; from five weavers in Crossmichael to 28 in Kirkconnel; from two shoemakers in Barr, Holywood and Twynholm to 14 in Wigtown; from one smith in New Abbey to seven in Kelton and Dailly; from three tailors in Straiton to 15 in Wigtown. The total population in each of the 24 parishes did not differ substantially from each other, and so did not lead to any major differences in the incidence of the tradesmen.

The nature of the parish, especially the existence in it of some town which acted as the centre for the activities of the district was more likely to lead to the appearance of more tradesmen than its size alone might justify. Kelton was a case in point and so was Wigtown which, with a total population of 1,350, had 87 in the six trades, the highest total of any of the parishes, or 6.4 per cent of its total population. As in the more northerly parishes of Ayrshire, some parishes had high representation for special reasons. Kirkcudbright, which is not one of the 24 examined because of inadequate classification, listed 14 ship's carpenters and 88 sailors. Similar parochial specialisation appeared in many coastal parishes: Girvan had 22 seamen and Colvend 52; Kirkoswald had 18 fishermen, though they were not always able to work at their trade. Troqueer, which is not included in the sample of 24 because of failure to distinguish apprentices in its list, had 84 shoemakers in the village of Bridgend, providing perhaps the most striking example of an early form of industrial specialisation in the area but one explained by its close proximity to Dumfries. The inclusion of Gatehouse gave the parish of Girthon a high number in all six trades, though, as with Troqueer, the apprentices were not distinguished. Of the total parish population of 1,150, the village had 24 masons, 24 carpenters, 12 weavers, 17 shoemakers, 17 smiths and 15 tailors.

By the time of the *New Statistical Accounts* the industrial penetration of the south-west had been intensified. Again the greatest industrial concentration was evident in the northern parishes of Ayrshire and in the Irvine valley. In all but three of the sixteen northern parishes the contributors to the *New Statistical Account* wrote of weaving and mostly as a dominating activity. The importance of weavers is evident where the numbers were given: Ardrossan had over 450; Beith, 430; Dalry, 500; Irvine, 400; Kilbirnie, 160; Largs, 246; Loudoun, 878; Stewarton, 300; West Kilbride, 100; and in Kilmarnock, though the numbers seem excessive, 1,200 weavers and 200 printers were employed manufacturing worsted printed shawls and about 1,200 weavers were in the carpet factories. In most parishes, large numbers of females sewed muslin: in Ardrossan 'many families'; in Dalry 'a large number of the females'; in Irvine, nearly 2,000 females; in Kilwinning 'a great proportion' of the females and in Stevenston, 'almost all'. In these conditions most parishes approached, even if they did not quite reach, the position of the parish of Loudoun in the Irvine Valley, of which it could be reported that 'Almost the whole population residing in Darvel and Newmilns, amounting to upwards of 3,000, depend, directly or indirectly, for their subsistence upon hand-loom weaving'.[18]

Some of the ministers in Carrick were aware of how handloom weaving had been consolidated since their predecessors wrote half a century before. The minister of Girvan pinpointed the contrast: 'Then, there were only about 100 looms employed in the weaving of cotton; now, there are nearly 2,000',[19] at Kirkmichael both handloom weaving and needlework were important, while at Maybole, while admitted economic benefits flowed from the system of working for the Glasgow and Paisley merchants, the minister doubted its social benefits at some length, especially in an area with many Irish immigrants. The lessening impact of the expansion further from its centre of Glasgow and Paisley was clear in the other parishes in Carrick which had fewer links with the centre of the textile trades.

Kirkoswald had a few weavers and needlewomen and Ballantrae had also some weavers. It was at the limits of any general penetration. It may be—certainly the minister of Maybole would probably have assented to the proposition—that the penetration would have faded out so far from Glasgow but for the presence of the Irish, ready to avail themselves of the various opportunities of subsistence which it offered.

By the 1840s the declining fortunes of the handloom weavers were imposing problems on earlier opportunities, so that some ministers showed both optimism and gloom in their reports. In the *Old Statistical Account* the minister of Kilbirnie looked back 50 years to a time when there were only three houses, and how 'the late flourishing silk manufactories have wonderfully increased the population of all the little towns in the west country'. He looked forward to an even greater increase 'if the cotton works go on as they are now promising to do', though at that time, 'There are no bleachfields, nor printfields, nor cotton mills as yet on this river [Garnock], though it is finely situated for them all'.[20] All had come to pass by the time the *New Statistical Account* was written: there was a spinning mill of five stories with 4,000 self-acting mule-spindles, employing 350 persons; a flax spinning mill employing 150; the owners of a bleachfield, which employed about 100, had also built a flax spinning mill which, it was expected, would employ about 70; a ropework employed 20, and 150 females sewed muslin. The optimism and the belief in progress was clouded by the conditions of some 160 handloom weavers, who were commended for their efforts to maintain 'a respectable appearance' and educate their children though suffering from low wages and unemployment.[21] In the neighbouring parish of Dalry, with about 500 weavers working for the Glasgow and Paisley merchants, the same distress was noted because of the introduction of the power loom. There the problem was less the level of wages and more the incidence of unemployment. Only concentration on higher grade work, with which the power loom could not compete, helped to mitigate the depression. As many as 430 weavers in Beith were in a similar predicament. The problems, as well as the opportunities, of industrialisation were only too evident in the north Ayrshire parishes. The distress spread further south into Carrick, where it was worsened by the increasing number of Irish immigrants. They continued to enter the trade even when it was already in decline and so accelerated the slide into depression still further.

To move further south to Wigtownshire and Kirkcudbrightshire is to find an even greater contrast in industrial growth from earlier years. The high hopes of the ministers in some of the parochial accounts of the 1790s, that there was no limit to the possible industrial growth of the south-west, especially if such limitations as the high cost of fuel were removed, had been totally abandoned by the late 1830s. There was general acceptance that the two most south-western counties were being by-passed by the events which were transforming Scotland into an urban and industrial society. The tentacles of the Glasgow and Paisley merchants spread throughout Ayrshire, though fading in parts of Carrick, but even that peripheral effect radiating from the centre of the textile industries was hardly evident in Wigtownshire and was virtually absent in Kirkcudbrightshire.

The sharpest distinction in the half-century between the two accounts was in the collapse, or difficulties, of the attempts to introduce the cotton spinning factories which had been the most distinctive feature of the early successful industrialisation of parts of north Ayrshire, the Cart valley and other parts of west-central Scotland, as well as in the main urban centres of Glasgow and Paisley. The efforts of Sir William Douglas at Newton Stewart were over: the buildings had been sold to Lord Galloway and partly stripped and demolished. Their only lasting legacy, according to the jaundiced comment of the parish minister was to increase the number of paupers. At the other centre of Douglas's activities—Castle Douglas—the collapse was as complete, though it left the more substantial legacy of a town which had so impressed the minister of Kelton, within whose parochial bounds it lay, that he had marvelled at a town, 'the suddenness of whose rise rivals the rapid growth of towns in America' and how it had 'already attained an importance that, in most cases, is the growth of ages'.[22] Gatehouse succeeded by comparison with such failures: its history was chequered when compared with Catrine. There were periods of inactivity and changes of ownership until cotton manufacturing ceased in the middle of the nineteenth century, though one mill was converted to produce bobbins for the textile industry until the 1930s. Since the remote south-west had always been on the periphery of the demand for weavers for the Glasgow and Paisley merchants, it now suffered from the drop in the demand for their services. Some continued to eke out an existence in parts of Wigtownshire but more and more precariously. In Penninghame, the weaving of cotton continued but to a diminishing extent as the cost of carriage to Glasgow became an insupportable charge when the prices paid fell. At Stranraer, where a number were still employed by Glasgow merchants, the 'wages allowed are extremely low, and totally insufficient to support a family in a comfortable manner'.[23] At Glasserton, 'Spinning and knitting, which formerly was the employment of old and infirm women, is no longer practiced. Indeed, that class have been the greatest sufferers from the introduction of machinery, for it has taken from them the only employment which they had strength to perform, and their sole means of subsistence'.[24] The only outwork which still survived in Wigtownshire with a modest degree of success was the sewing of muslin and that only in isolated pockets, as in Portpatrick and Kirkcolm. The collapse of the early efforts to introduce new industry had its effect on the expectations and confidence of the contributors to the two Statistical Accounts of Kirkcudbrightshire and Wigtownshire. Some of those who contributed to the *Old Statistical Account* were preposterously optimistic. They welcomed the possibilities of economic growth, though sometimes with reservations over its consequences. They had little knowledge of the ingredients necessary for success except in their repeated insistence on the need for more and cheaper fuel. By 1840 the high hopes had gone and the pages of the *New Statistical Account* are virtually free from the ludicrous expectations of an earlier generation.

There was every cause for this greater realism in the two most south-western counties as the limited examples of industrialisation make clear in four ways. Firstly, they permit several specific contrasts to be drawn in the experiences of parishes between the two dates, usually indicating a decrease in industrial development. At Kirkmabreck, the tan work, the cotton factory, and the mill for lead shot mentioned in the earlier account, 'have long been given up'.[25] The old shot-mill had been converted to making potato-starch and the cotton factory changed to the making of carpets, though little was doing in that line because of unremunerative prices. At Kirkpatrick-Durham the various partnerships already noted 'have long since died a natural death, and now there are neither artisans nor manufactures within our boundaries, whose services are required beyond the immediate neighbourhood'.[26] Even at Girthon, 'The only drawback to be placed in opposition to this representation [the success of the cotton mill at Gatehouse] is the failure and disappearance of the wine company, tannery, and brewery, forced businesses which could not succeed ... '.[27] At Borgue, where in the *Old Statistical Account* the increase of manufacturing was such that it was 'extremely difficult to find a sufficient number of labourers, for carrying on improvements in agriculture', there were no manufactures apart from the produce of two handloom weavers by the 1840s. Even so, it was still hoped that, 'As there is a sufficiency of water power, it is not improbable that mills may hereafter be erected'.[28] At Sorbie, where in the 1790s it was thought that 'a Leeds or an Halifax would perhaps grow out of one of our small villages',[29] only a damask factory and shipbuilding at Garlieston had achieved any significance by the late 1830s.

Secondly, the limited industrialisation was based mostly on agriculture and some of the more modern ventures had reverted to this form. To take two of many possible examples. In Kirkcudbrightshire, New Abbey had 'a grain-mill, a mill for carding and spinning wool, and a saw-mill, which employed about ten persons'.[30] The timber from the saw-mill went mostly to Liverpool. In Wigtownshire, in the parish of Old Luce, 'No extensive manufactures have yet been established in this parish. There are, however, two corn-mills, two carding-mills, one dye-mill, and one flax-mill; but in none of these establishments are many hands employed, nor is any great amount of work executed'.[31]

Thirdly, exceptional but directly linked to the course of industrialisation elsewhere, were various attempts to exploit the natural resources of the region. Suitable natural resources were critical to the success of the north Ayrshire parishes and further afield in west-central Scotland. The remoter south-west had no such plentiful resources, above all it had no coal, and most of the many ventures to exploit natural resources were trivial. Even the two companies which worked the lead seams at Blackcraig from 1764—the Blackcraig and Craigtown Companies—were small concerns compared with what industrialisation brought to other parts of Scotland. At Woodhead, near Carsphairn one of the most dramatic and long-lived ventures had only an important local impact. That was also the case even when the mining activities of Wanlockhead and Leadhills on the edge of the area are being considered. One successful though isolated case of exploitation of natural resources in the early nineteenth century was at Kirkmabreck, where the trustees of the Liverpool Docks developed the granite quarries and employed numbers which fluctuated to as high as 450 in the 1830s.

Fourthly, the lack of industrial growth generally was confirmed by the only parish in the remote south-west with widespread activities being Troqueer, which gained from its proximity to the markets of Dumfries and from the erection of Maxwelltown as a burgh of barony in 1810. It had two foundries, a waulkmill, a dye-house, two roperies, a brewhouse, two tanneries and four nurseries.

The conclusion of the minister of Glencairn in Nithsdale applied not only to his own parish, not only to Nithsdale—apart from Kirkconnel and Sanquhar—but to most of the remoter south-west: 'The distance from coal and water carriage will for ever prevent the possibility of this parish becoming a manufacturing district of any importance'.[32]

The differences in the experiences of the parishes of north Ayrshire from those further south, and particularly from those in Kirkcudbrightshire and Wigtownshire, were soon evident after the first expectations of the 1790s had come to nothing in the far south-west. The difference was to become still more marked between most of Ayrshire and the rest from the mid nineteenth century, when the growth of the heavy industries, particularly of ironmaking with coal-mining in its wake, spread from Lanarkshire, where it had first become established in its modern form. In those parishes which had plentiful supplies of coal and iron ore, the old dependence on textiles was soon overshadowed and in some cases eliminated by the new enterprises. Where there were no appropriate natural resources, which was the case throughout the entire remote south-west, there was no such change and the differences between the parishes of the northern half of Ayrshire and the remainder of the south-west became greater than ever. Though a sharper distinction may be drawn between the experiences of the different parts of the south-west in the nineteenth century, the distinction must not be exaggerated. The northern parishes of Ayrshire registered substantial increases in population but much of it was in communities scattered over a wide area to be near the coalmines. Though industrialised, they were never so urbanised as some comparable parishes in north Lanarkshire. Even the larger towns in Ayrshire, even Kilmarnock, did not lose a strong agricultural basis. The industrial developments in much of Ayrshire were on the periphery of the industrial belt and were a link between the more heavily industrialised district further north and east and the rural area further south.

Industrialisation still had its effects on the economic and social structure of the entire south-west. First, it gave a new demand for agricultural products, especially for the perishable, or semi-perishable dairy produce, which linked the agricultural enterprises of the south-west directly to the needs and prosperity of the heavy industries of central Scotland and to fluctuations in their prosperity. It was a link which helped maintain the prosperity of the agriculture of the south-west and retain the population in the area. The second effect of industrialisation worked in the reverse direction, as it provided opportunities for those in the south-west to move, and to do so easily because of the proximity of the industrial areas, especially when improved communications linked the life of the south-west to central Scotland more easily than it had once been. The two effects pulled in opposite directions and their relative influences varied over time. The condition of agriculture in the south-west was then such that it could support the population, but not necessarily one which was rising sharply, though the lack of industrial opportunities in the area was likely to keep many from moving in to the area from other parts of Scotland. In this way it was self-contained. There was one exception. Those who moved into the area were often Irish. They came less because of the opportunities the far south-west offered, but more simply because it was the first place they reached easily and cheaply on their way out of Ireland.

Chapter 3

The Changing Inhabitants

Demographic changes varied throughout the south-west. At a minor, local level some were already giving rise to comment, not always well-informed, by the end of the eighteenth century. Most commonly noted was the depopulation which seemed to follow the amalgamation of farms for grazing, especially in the upland areas. While some were certainly losing population, the minister of Tongland expressed a judicious view when he remarked that there were 'only arguments for a local, not a general depopulation in this corner; as the additional population in towns and villages, compensate for any local deficiency in a particular part of the country'.[1]

Such differential changes in population became more marked in the nineteenth century when the population of Cunninghame and Kyle increased rapidly, especially after 1841, when opportunities in their heavy industries encouraged migrants to move into them. In the decade before 1851[2] the population of Kyle and Cunninghame rose by 16.7 per cent, and in the second half of the century by 46.3 per cent. The sharpest increases were in the coal and ironworking districts. In Dalry, where some of the earliest expansion took place, the population grew from 2,321 in 1801 to 11,156 in 1861. With the exhaustion of some of its mineral reserves and the closure of its ironworks in 1871, it fell to 7,418 in 1911. By then the centre of mineral working in Ayrshire had moved to Auchinleck, where the population rose from 1,659 in 1841 to 6,174 in 1911. Similar sharp rises were evident all over the Ayrshire coalfield, especially in those parishes which added an ironworks to their coalmining. Kilwinning had 2,700 in 1801 and 7,375 in 1871; Dreghorn had 762 in 1801 and 3,241 in 1871; Dalmellington had 758 in 1801 and 6,125 in 1871. The demographic history of the parishes in Cunninghame and Kyle is similar to what took place wherever there was a greater degree of industrialisation. The more distinctive demographic experience of the south-west was to be found in its remoter parts of Carrick, Kirkcudbrightshire and Wigtownshire.

In each of these three areas the population increased from Webster's census of 1755[3] until the middle of the nineteenth century. In the first decade of the nineteenth century their growth was above the Scottish figure. Thereafter they fell behind the national increase one by one: Kirkcudbrightshire by 1821; Wigtownshire by 1831 (though it had a slightly higher increase again in the 1840s); and Carrick by 1851. Decline finally set in after 1851. Decreases were registered in 1861 and in every census thereafter, with the exception of 1881. Though Carrick and Wigtownshire recorded declines of around 25 per cent in the second half of the nineteenth century, the declines were still sufficiently limited that all three had more people living in them than in 1801.

In the early nineteenth century the greatest transformation was in Carrick, where the increase was concentrated in the parishes of Girvan, Kirkmichael and Maybole, all noted for the growth of weaving and related Irish immigration. Their population increased steadily throughout the period 1755 to 1801 and then rapidly between 1801 to 1831—by 32.0, 38.1 and 29.7 per cent in each of the first three decades of the nineteenth century. The population of these three parishes came to represent a larger proportion of Carrick's total— 36.6 per cent in 1755, 47.6 per cent in 1801 and 62.2 per cent in 1851. Growth was less in other parishes in Carrick but was at its peak in all nine in the decade of 1811 to 1821.

In the second half of the eighteenth century the growth of population in Kirkcudbrightshire was greater than in Carrick but fell far behind in the nineteenth. The growth was also concentrated. In the eighteenth century it exceeded the Scottish figure of 27.1 per cent in half of Kirkcudbrightshire's 28 parishes but was greatest in five: in Crossmichael, Girthon, Kelton, Kirkcudbright and Troqueer the increases between 1755 and 1801 exceeded the natural rate of growth of 10 per cent per decade which modern demographers apply to these years before reliable vital statistics became available. Their share of the Stewartry's population increased from 22.1 per cent in 1755, to 33.8 per cent in 1801, to 34.4 per cent in 1851. Six parishes which registered decreases were in the remote hill country, particularly the three of Carsphairn, Dalry and Kells, while adjoining Balmaclellan recorded an increase of merely 3.7 per cent. Their experience was similar to the hill parishes in Carrick.

The lower overall increase of the first half of the nineteenth century reflected a reversal of parochial experience in Kirkcudbrightshire. The five which had led in the later eighteenth century hardly increased their share of the total population. Unlike the three leading parishes of Carrick, their increase was arrested. Between 1801 and 1851 Crossmichael and Girthon were below the Stewartry's increase; indeed Girthon's growth was the smallest of any parish in Kirkcudbrightshire. Kelton, Kirkcudbright, and Troqueer were above the Stewartry but not the Scottish figure. By contrast, in the early nineteenth century Balmaclellan, Kirkmabreck, and Urr alone exceeded the Scottish figure and Carsphairn and Parton were not far behind. No parish recorded a loss.

Troqueer's continuing importance among the five leading parishes in Kirkcudbrightshire in the eighteenth century is explained by its proximity to the town of Dumfries, from which it experienced an industrial overspill. This ensured that the total for the five parishes, with one-third of the Stewartry's population in 1801, had slightly more in 1851. The failure of the other four to sustain their rate of expansion after the eighteenth century followed lack of consolidation of developments which had been planned and encouraged earlier, notably the decline of the cotton mill at Gatehouse in the parish of Girthon, and the less rapid growth of Castle Douglas in the parish of Kelton. Some of the more rapid expansion in the nineteenth century elsewhere was because of some minor if unexpected industrial growth, as in quarrying at Creetown in the parish of Kirkmabreck or, even more strikingly, in lead-mining at Carsphairn. The temporary nature of much of the incipient industrial development in Kirkcudbrightshire meant that, with the exceptions of Troqueer, gaining from its proximity to Dumfries, and Kirkcudbright, gaining from its status as the country town, there was no permanent base to maintain a rising population. The Stewartry had nothing to compare with the expansion of weaving in Carrick.

Wigtownshire's experience provides a contrast with the others. Its population grew by 39.2 per cent from 1755 to 1801 and by 89.3 per cent from 1801 to 1851, but, because of Carrick's exceptionally high growth in the early nineteenth century, Wigtownshire's growth of 163.5 per cent over the century from 1755 to 1851 did not reach Carrick's 189.5 per cent. It was however of a steadier nature. In addition, growth in Wigtownshire was spread widely over the county. From 1755 to 1801 eleven of its 17 parishes were above the Scottish increase of 27.1 per cent, ten above the south-west's 34.5 per cent and six were above an assumed natural growth for the period of 54 per cent. Three of the six parishes which failed to achieve the Scottish rate of increase recorded a decrease. The broad basis of Wigtownshire's expansion was even more striking between 1801 and 1851. Whithorn's 57.6 per cent was the lowest rate of growth recorded between 1801 and 1851, while only seven of 28 parishes in Kirkcudbrightshire and five of nine in Carrick were higher. Two factors may be used to explain Wigtownshire's experience: new settlements were more widespread, and migration was important. As in Carrick, Wigtownshire had a high proportion of Irish migrants in 1851.

The experience of all three parts of the remoter south-west changed in the later nineteenth century. While the population of Scotland increased from 1851 to 1911 by 64.8 per cent, that of the remoter south-west fell by -21.9 per cent and each part recorded a loss: Carrick of -28.6 per cent; Kirkcudbrightshire of -9.0 per cent; Wigtownshire of -26.3 per cent. The decline was interrupted only slightly in Carrick, Kirkcudbrightshire and Wigtownshire between 1871 and 1881. The most significant change to be explained is the fall in the population of Carrick and Wigtownshire.

The increase in the population of Carrick in the early nineteenth century was arrested sharply in the two decades after 1851, when the population of the district fell by -25.6 per cent. The fall was sharpest in Girvan and Kirkmichael with Maybole also suffering a substantial drop. It was these three parishes which had held the greatest concentrations of weavers who had helped to sustain the growth of population in the early nineteenth century. However, the fall between 1851 and 1871 was spread over all nine parishes. The share of the three parishes in Carrick's population fell slightly from 62.2 per cent in 1851 to 59.4 per cent in 1871. Thereafter the population of Carrick fell by only 816 from 1871 to 1901 and was accompanied by a further internal change. In 1901 Girvan, Kirkmichael and Maybole had 64.7 per cent of Carrick's 22,486, but the slightly increased share was largely because of the position of Maybole, which alone registered an increase from 1871, taking its own share of Carricks's population from 25.3 per cent in 1871 to 35.1 per cent in 1901. Its population fell sharply (by -12.5 per cent) in the first decade of the twentieth century reflecting migration from the parish, particularly to Canada.

Wigtownshire's population followed the same trend downwards as Carrick's and fell by -24.7 per cent between 1851 and the end of the century. The fall was general. Inch alone recorded an increase of 754, which merely reflected Stranraer's expansion into it, and did not offset Stranraer's own loss of 1,021.

Migration and probable high rates of natural increase, encouraged by the opportunities for handloom weaving in Carrick, led to the rapid growth of population in Carrick and Wigtownshire in the early nineteenth century. Kirkcudbrightshire did not experience the same rapid increase and the emergence of some limited industrial developments helped moderate the fall in the later nineteenth century. Kelton and Troqueer continued to account for a substantial share of the population and were joined in the later nineteenth century by the parish of Urr, which had Dalbeattie and Springholm within its bounds. The three had 26.6 per cent of the Stewartry's population in 1851 and 38.3 per cent in 1901.

However buoyant the population in some parts of the south-west in the early nineteenth century, it is possible to show that much of the area was self-contained demographically by a detailed examination of the places of birth of those living in it, and of the places of residence of its natives, though the material is available only on a county basis. In each of the three census years of 1851, 1871 and 1891[4] the native-born still living in the four counties, expressed as a percentage of the total born in each who were still living in Scotland, were as follows:

Year	Ayr %	Dumfries %	Kirkcudbright %	Wigtown %	South-west %
1851	80.2	81.0	79.6	79.8	85.9
1871	73.4	76.8	79.4	72.3	79.8
1891	70.8	69.3	69.2	68.5	76.0

In 1851 each of the four counties had a higher proportion of their natives still in Scotland living in the county of their birth than in 1891. Some of those who left the county of their birth went to the other counties of the south-west, but even the south-west's share of its native-born still living in it fell. Since the natives were leaving, it is not surprising that there was no great movement of others from elsewhere in Scotland to the south-west. There was therefore a high proportion of natives in the total population:

Year	Ayr %	Dumfries %	Kirkcudbright %	Wigtown %	South-west %
1851	75.3	82.5	74.2	73.4	81.8
1871	77.3	81.5	79.0	77.6	83.8
1891	77.2	74.0	70.0	79.8	82.4

Higher proportions in Scotland were to be found generally only in the northern counties. Of those in and south of the Forth-Clyde basin only Berwickshire had as high a proportion as the south-western counties in 1851 and 1891. If the native-born are expressed as a percentage of the Scottish-born population only, the high proportion in the south-western counties is even more striking. Again Berwick was the only comparable southern county. The percentages in the south-west were:

Year	Ayr %	Dumfries %	Kirkcudbright %	Wigtown %	South-west %
1851	85.7	88.2	81.2	89.2	92.1
1871	85.3	86.0	81.8	87.0	91.1
1891	83.3	79.5	74.5	85.8	88.6

Irish immigration explains the rise when the native-born is expressed as a percentage of the Scottish-born population only, especially in Ayrshire and Wigtownshire. In 1851 11.0 per cent of Ayrshire's population and 16.2 per cent of Wigtownshire's had been born in Ireland, compared with only 2.8 and 6.0 per cent in Dumfriesshire and Kirkcudbrightshire, respectively. Except in Ayrshire the percentage of the total population who had been born in parts of Scotland other than the south-west was small.

Year	Ayr %	Dumfries %	Kirkcudbright %	Wigtown %	South-west %
1851	9.8	4.8	3.3	2.3	7.0
1871	10.4	6.6	4.5	3.7	8.2
1891	12.8	9.3	6.0	5.1	10.6

Though the natives of the south-west moved to other parts of Scotland, the south-west was still an area in which the natives were a large part of the total population and particularly so of the Scottish-born population. It was not an area into which a large number of emigrant Scots moved.

When movement did occur from the native county in the south-west to other parts of Scotland it was restricted in its spread. Many moved only within the south-west, though the proportion of those who had moved from their county of birth at each census year to another county in the south-west declined in the nineteenth century, from 28.4 per cent in 1851, to 20.4 per cent in 1871, and to 19.5 per cent in 1891. In all three census years considered Ayrshire had a net gain from the three others and Wigtownshire lost to all three. Kirkcudbrightshire gained from Dumfriesshire in 1851 but lost to it in 1871 and 1891.

Most of those who left the south-west went to the main conurbations in the central belt of Scotland. Only a negligible number penetrated to Aberdeenshire and Angus, the counties with the other major cities. Two distinct flows may be distinguished. The first was the movement from Kirkcudbrightshire to Dumfriesshire, largely accounted for by the close proximity of the town of Dumfries to the county boundary, and thence to Edinburgh. The proportion of the natives who had left Dumfriesshire and Kirkcudbrightshire for other parts of Scotland and were living in Midlothian ranged from 7.6 per cent from Kirkcudbrightshire in 1851 to 12.5 per cent from Dumfriesshire in 1871. In contrast, from Ayrshire and Wigtownshire the proportion ranged only from 4.3 per cent in 1871 to 6.3 per cent in 1851, both from Ayrshire. The second line of movement was from Wigtownshire to Ayrshire and so to the industrial heart of Scotland in Lanarkshire. This was the route taken by Irish migrants as well as by the natives. For the south-west, as for the rest of Scotland, Lanarkshire was the magnet which determined the main movements of population. The four counties supplied Lanarkshire with 21.2 per cent of its inhabitants who had been born in parts of Scotland beyond its own county boundary in 1891, though the four had only 12.6 per cent of the population of Scotland other than in Lanarkshire, or 17.4 per cent of the population born in Scotland other than in Lanarkshire.

The south-west had little to attract Scots to it, especially when the central belt had so much to offer; nor had it much more to offer the Irish, who came chiefly because of the shortness of the passage across the North Channel. In these circumstances the movement of the Irish was an exogenous factor likely to prove unusually disruptive in a traditional rural society. The precise nature of the influence of the Irish is difficult to judge. It is too simple to point out that the numbers of Irish-born in each census year are a higher proportion of the total population than in other parts of Scotland. Even Wigtownshire's 16.2 per cent Irish-born of the total population in 1851 could not be a dominating group in the community by any numerical standard. In any case the proportion of Irish-born in the total population has its own numerical defects. The census may not give a comprehensive record of such an elusive group as many Irish immigrants proved to be. Their high mobility, particularly in an area such as the south-west, through which many passed on their way to other, and, they hoped, better things, meant that many came and went through the south-west between the census years. They were not seasonal migrants but permanent migrants, but not permanently located in the south-west. The south-west fulfilled its traditional role of being a staging post even though some never went further. Inevitably too, the birth-rate among the migrants soon increased the number of Scottish-born but Irish-descended in the population. Finally, concentration on numerical tests detracts attention from less clearly defined but powerful consequences produced by the nature of the Irish immigrants. They were abjectly poor: had they not been so they might never have left Ireland, certainly not permanently, nor would they have come to the south-west but gone to a more attractive destination, especially in the United States. In many ways the south-west was the least attractive of all possible destinations; its advantage was that it was near.

The movement of the Irish to the south-west was not new and by the late eighteenth century they had spread through much of Wigtownshire and Carrick. The comments in the *Old Statistical Account* show marked contrasts between the various districts. These were to be perpetuated. In the 1790s Nithsdale had few Irish: two families were reported in Durisdeer and one person from Ireland in Holywood, but their presence was not something which worried the parish minister. With the potential of the ministers to become greatly concerned about the presence of would-be paupers and sometimes Roman Catholics to boot, it is reasonable to assume that silence indicates absence. References to them were almost as sparse in Kirkcudbrightshire. Troqueer was an exception. Its proximity to Dumfries gave it many beggars at the Brigend and, hardly surprisingly, it was to such a poverty-stricken area that the Irish tended to gravitate. It had a resident Roman Catholic priest, ministering to an estimated 200 of the parish's 2,600 inhabitants. Matters were different in Carrick and Wigtownshire. Unlike Nithsdale and Kirkcudbrightshire, the Irish were recognised as part of the life of Carrick in the late eighteenth century. The report from Dailly, that 'Almost the whole [inhabitants] are Scotch, with exception of a few Irish ...'[5] was a fair representation of how ministers perceived the state of their parishes, but the Irish migrants were well enough known and recognised for there to be an expectation, often a fear, that before long they would be present in large numbers. In Wigtownshire, these expectations and fears had been realised by the late eighteenth century and there the complaints were much more vigorous. They centred on Stranraer and spread into the adjacent parishes of Inch and Leswalt, where the minister reported that they were oppressed by Irish vagrants, 'poor emancipated persons, whose very aspect excites compassion'.[6]

Vagrancy gave way to settlement in ways which made any distinction between who was and who was not a seasonal immigrant difficult, and, even more so, between who was and who was not planning to remain in the south-west. Probably few had any clearly conceived plan when their main intention was merely to survive and so destinations were determined by any chance of employment. Handloom weaving was often the only tolerably permanent occupation available except on the periphery of the south-west in parts of north Ayrshire. Even better prospects were in Lanarkshire, which diminished the likelihood of permanent residence in the south-west.

The resulting characteristic mobility of the Irish in the south-west was evident in the precarious position of the Roman Catholic church, the one social institution which had most direct and distinct influence on them. Since many of the Irish who came to the south-west were from Ulster, they were not all Roman Catholics and so it would be misleading to conclude that the lack of a Roman Catholic presence implied a lack of Irish settlers. Conversely, however, any evidence of it indicated an Irish presence since pockets of native support for Roman Catholicism in the south-west were few and isolated. Even those most intimately involved could not easily assess the strength of Roman Catholicism because of the mobility of the Irish. The Roman Catholic congregation at Newton Stewart was established in 1819 and served the whole of Wigtownshire, with the priest conducting services at Whithorn, Stranraer and Kirkmaiden as well as at Newton Stewart. His flock, 'almost all Irish labourers' was officially placed at 2,670, but the numbers attending mass were only from 200 to 300 from April to June and about 100 to 200 from August to October, leaving the priest in Newton Stewart highly dubious about the total number. An account in the 1830s shows the difficulty even he had in knowing who they were:

> The Catholics of the district are not a fixed population: and, in particular, in regard to this parish and Stranraer, which are upon the route to Ireland, he considered the result to vary greatly from the reality. Especially in this parish, where he resides, and where poor strangers frequently remain till a child is born, in order that it may be baptised, he was certain that the number they indicated was a great exaggeration.[7]

In Ayr the position was similar. The resident clergyman had about 500 in his flock, all Irish and mostly weavers and agricultural labourers, and once again all were noted for their movement.

Such peripatetic Irish labourers were alleged to keep the price of labour low in Wigtownshire, where they were most numerous, but those to whom that was a commendation were likely to consider it more than offset by their fear of the probable burden the Irish immigrants were always likely to impose on the limited social provision available. The nature of the problem of the poor and transient Irish was clear in various official investigations around 1840. The complaints were directed frequently against the issue of passes by parishes to paupers to enable them to travel to their place of residence. Those parishes which lay on the route had to help them on their way. It was obviously advantageous to a parish to try to help paupers by this means in order to be rid of them, but those parishes on the main routes to and from Ireland were liable to suffer. Portpatrick was the Scottish origin or destination of most of the vagrants. Complaints fade more rapidly to the east of Portpatrick than to the north. The minister of Old Luce to the east complained in 1843 that 'Lying upon the road to Port-Patrick they are very much troubled with vagrants, both going and returning; there is scarcely a month they have not to forward some with carts, and they are put to some considerable expense by their falling sick in the parish. Many of them come with passes; most of them from Stranraer'.[8] In the investigations into the poor law in the early 1840s the problem was hardly mentioned to the east of Wigtownshire. Matters were different to the north. The parish of Ballantrae on the route to Glasgow suffered acutely from the general movement and particularly from the passes issued by neighbouring parishes where attempts were made to prevent the Irish trying to settle.

The frequent movement of the Irish in and out of the south-west means that any examination of the numbers in any part at a particular time can underestimate their influence, above all in Wigtownshire and to a lesser extent in those parts of Ayrshire on the way to the industrial opportunities of the central belt. Their penetration of the social fabric of those areas was imprecise but intense. Having left the customs and restraints of one traditional rural society, the Irish were unlikely to be ready to accept, or even understand, those of another. The result was that the Irish were more likely to come into collision with the conventions of the life of the south-west. Even if it is thought in retrospect that prejudice against an immigrant group led to the influence of the Irish being emphasised excessively, it must still be accepted that contemporaries were concerned that the social fabric was changing. They thought so from the early nineteenth century, well before the mass exodus from Ireland in the wake of the famine, which affected the south-west less than many other areas to which the Irish went. Opportunities were greater elsewhere and, if Scotland was the chosen destination of the migrant, a passage by steamboat direct to Glasgow was available by then.

In any case migration from Ireland to Wigtownshire and Ayrshire was established before the famine. The long-standing link was evident in the investigation of the Irish poor in Great Britain in the 1830s.[9] Witnesses from Wigtownshire recollected the Irish migrants who had come for harvest in the eighteenth century, many of whom remained, so that even before 1790 'a large portion of the stationary population was Irish'. The same witness concluded that 'The inhabitants of the district have for more than half a century depended on a supply of Irish immigrants for the performance of all their most servile work, and, until a supply of natives could be produced, the Irish labourers would be indispensable'.[10] Only the hired ploughmen were generally still Scots. Particularly after the rebellion of 1798, the increase in migration spread northwards to the industrial openings available there. The attraction was handloom weaving. In Stranraer and district there were some 150 weavers from Down, Armagh, Antrim and Derry, though they did not stay long but moved on northwards. In Girvan the minister thought half the population was Irish, and that about half of them were Catholics, and most were weavers. In Maybole about one-third of the population was thought to be Irish and again they were mostly weavers; in Maybole it was also noted that 'There are few strange Scotch ..., either from the Lowlands or Highlands'.[11] In both places the witnesses were quite dogmatic that their manufactures and trade would never have reached the extent they had but for the Irish migrants. Further north in Ayrshire occupations were more varied, though weaving still retained the allegiance of many. The Duke of Portland's agent reported their usefulness as labourers, in surface work at the coal mines, in agricultural operations and in nurseries, and did not think that the manufactures of Kilmarnock would have progressed with the same rapidity had there not been an influx of Irish into the town. The same comment was made of Ayr, where the Irish were the only immigrant group of note. The alternative immigrant, the Highlander, was not usually preferred in any case. There were 'very few' in the neighbourhood of Kilmarnock, according to the Duke of Portland's agent: 'The highlanders are a more stubborn race. An Irishman will do any thing he can do; but he is not so steady; so much dependence cannot be placed on him as on a Highlander'.[12] A builder in Kilmarnock had fewer qualifications: 'we prefer Irish as labourers; they are more obedient and serviceable, and they are equally hardworking ... We are not fond of the High-landers'.[13] They had also the attraction, especially to farmers seeking casual labour, that, even though they did not work for lower wages, they prevented an increase in wages which would have followed the migration of native workers to the new industrial openings. It was only in Wigtownshire that the number of Irish was so great relative to the opportunities that they were thought to have lowered wages, and it was there that the penetration of society was most complete. One estimate suggested that nine-tenths of the labouring population was of Irish extraction and it was difficult to determine clearly between the natives and the immigrants, particularly through inter-marriage, which was generally of an Irishman to a Scotswoman and rarely the reverse.

In the *New Statistical Account* references to the Irish are rare in Kirkcudbrightshire. In Carrick they are concentrated in Maybole and Girvan, where the Irish were attracted to weaving; Ballantrae, as always, registered complaints about the annoyance and expenses of having to forward returning Irish paupers southwards along the long stretch of the Glasgow to Portpatrick road which ran through the parish. But in Wigtownshire practically every parish complained about the problem, with the usual wails about their poverty, dirty habits, lack of education, their burden on the poor rates, and all with a greater vehemence than in the *Old Statistical Account*. In Sorbie, '... within the last forty of fifty years, a considerable number of Irish families have settled in the parish'; in Old Luce there was '... a continual influx of Irish immigrants'; in Penninghame, 'Many families from Ireland, travelling in quest of work, on getting temporary employment, frequently settle here'; in Whithorn the number of Irish paupers taking up residence was 'almost incredible'; in Kirkcolm one-third of the labour population was held to be Irish by birth or descent.[14] The ministers in Wigtownshire were only too well aware of the lack of any provision for poor relief in Ireland and advocated it as the only means of relieving the problem. And they expressed the old fear in Wigtownshire that a ready supply of Irish labour would depress the wages of the natives, because the subsistence needs of the Irish were so low.

The views of contemporaries on the position in Wigtownshire and in Carrick—whatever a narrow interpretation of the statistical evidence of the censuses provides—were well portrayed by the factors to the Earl of Stair and to the Duchesse de Coigny when they maintained in 1844 that 80 per cent of the population were Irish or of Irish extraction. The former believed that 'by working at less wages than the natives, they have, in point of fact, driven them away to other places, and have supplied the want of labour so caused', an interpretation he applied to all the extensive Stair estates, except to those around Wigtown, where, however, the parish minister did not allow that exception. Vans Agnew of Barnbarroch agreed, and the minister of Kirkinner summed up for all: 'In a very short time the whole of the labouring population of this parish will be Irish'.[15]

In spite of the many and vigorous complaints about the Irish migrants, they were gradually absorbed into the community, both migrants and the community changing in the process. The numbers arriving from Ireland fell in the later nineteenth century, but they still provided the labour needed for specialised work. First, a tradition of casual agricultural work grew among wives and daughters of Irish settlers, even when born in Scotland, so that where the Irish population 'predominated' female day labourers were 'abundant'.[16] Second was the provision of labour from Ireland for seasonal tasks, often by prior arrangement. On this supply of labour the agriculture of the south-west could rely. In 1836, even in the years of the most rapid increase of the population, one Ayrshire farmer explained that 'we could not get on without them', and that, whatever other problems they created, if they did not come, 'we should have to pay higher wages and perhaps not get the work done so regularly'.[17] Because of the nature of its agricultural enterprises the south-west's demand for labour differed from some other regions. Before turnips were grown, there was comparatively little outside work for women after the limited crop of potatoes was lifted, though women and boys were employed extensively thereafter. In the later nineteenth century the need for such casual labour was numerically significant, mostly in those areas which were not devoted to dairying and above all in the highly localised potato fields of Ayrshire. Generally a strong Irish influence, whether by descent, or by seasonal movement, ensured that labour was available and wages kept down. Sometimes competition from industry restricted the supply of day labourers, but the most general form of industrialisation in the south-west was mining in Ayrshire and in Nithsdale, which provided its own useful reserve of miners' wives.

The casual Irish labourer became associated in the nineteenth and twentieth centuries most of all with the lifting of potatoes, especially the early potatoes, when they became an important part of the agricultural output of the area. In assisting in this development a redoubtable Roman Catholic priest of Girvan alleged that the Irish 'built up great fortunes for the farmers and buyers'.[18] The lifting was organised in an unusual fashion and gave rise to its own social problems reminiscent of an earlier age. Potato merchants bought the potatoes from the farmers at so much an acre. The merchant was responsible for providing the labour to lift the crop, which he did through squads recruited by his foremen often from the west of Ireland. They left Ireland in May or June in time for the lifting in Ayrshire and then moved to Perth and the Lothians, working on as many as twelve farms before returning to Ireland in

November. They still lived in appalling conditions; whether they did so willingly is of little importance since no better conditions were provided. These conditions raised some public interest in the early twentieth century. Complaints about the migratory Irish workers in the south-west became as common as they had been fifty years and more earlier because of fear over public health: the Irish were accused of presenting itinerant potential sources of infection. As before, the Irish were blamed for faults which were not specifically theirs. In 1911, however, the Chief Constable of Ayrshire distinguished the Irish from the 'slum-dwellers and vagrants', the Irish being

> strikingly well-conducted, quiet, reserved and gentle; temperate, moral, and frugal in their habits. Are provided with changes of raiment, and are cleanly ... There is an absence of anything like loose conduct among them ... The slum-dwellers and vagrants that engage for potato gathering are in their best behaviour and habits the very reverse of the description I have given of the Irish squads. They are a low type, many of them the very lowest, debauched and filthy in their habits, coarse and foul in their language, and quarrelsome.[19]

The Chief Constable's warning, though from more modern times, is a reminder that the Irish were not innately vicious, as many of their bitter critics alleged. But they brought the conventions of a different rural society to the south-west of Scotland. In the difficult process of integrating strange conventions, or none at all, with those already existing, the south-west acquired some characteristics which marked it out from rural society generally in Scotland. Its social attitudes, and its social cohesion, were different, most of all in Wigtownshire and to a lesser extent in those parts of Carrick to which the Irish filtered but where there was little industrialisation apart from handloom weaving. Further north in Ayrshire the social change was common to the advent of industrialisation. To the east, in Kirkcudbrightshire and Dumfriesshire, the Irish were less numerous and imposed fewer strains on the social fabric.

To demonstrate these social distinctions is not easy and none can be proved conclusively. One possible illustration is in the educational experiences of the different parts of the south-west. It is not surprising that the provision of education facilities or the use made of them, or both, were more limited in industrial areas, but some educational statistics show that even in the rural districts of the south-west most frequented by the Irish school attendance was as poor as in the industrial areas of north Ayrshire or elsewhere.

It is not surprising that Ayrshire's industrialisation ensured that its educational experience differed from the three other counties.[20] Its proportions of both males and females under 15 attending school in 1871 were less than in Scotland as a whole, whereas the proportions in Dumfries, Kirkcudbright and Wigtown were higher. The parishes with the lowest rates of attendance were the most heavily industrialised: Dalry, Kilwinning and Loudoun never rose above the county average in even one age group; Galston and Kilbirnie did so in one age group only. Mining and weaving were their dominating activities and the educational interests and achievements of these occupations had long been poor. All the parishes of Ayrshire, even those which experienced some form of industrialisation, still retained part of their old agricultural base, but it was in the more traditionally rural parishes of Carrick that educational attendance remained above the county average. Carrick's achievement was good, however, only by comparison with the rest of Ayrshire, which was a poor standard. Its attendances of 44.8 per cent for males and 43.2 per cent for females were better than the county's but were both worse than the Scottish average. Wigtownshire's attendances of 47.7 per cent for males and 46.2 per cent for females were above the Scottish rates, which were heavily weighted by the large population of the central belt, where industrialisation led to a lower level of attendance. When Wigtownshire's attendance is compared with the whole range of Scottish counties, it does not stand out favourably, particularly when compared with rural counties. Male attendance in Wigtownshire did not reach the levels of the rural north-east or of the Highland counties. Female attendance was similar. Wigtownshire's rates were twelfth from the bottom among Scottish counties in each case.

Dumfriesshire and Kirkcudbrightshire provide a striking contrast with Wigtownshire. First, a higher proportion started school earlier in them; second, between ages 7 and 10 they recorded higher proportions attending; third, and, this was generally the greatest difference between industrial and rural areas, their attendance record was maintained from age 10, when those in the industrial areas fell sharply as many children began work. Fourth, both, but especially Kirkcudbrightshire, achieved their success by relying much more heavily than Ayrshire and Wigtownshire on the parochial schools. This fourth contrast was particularly evident in Kirkcudbrightshire where relatively little use was made of private schools which in the three other counties provided the education for between one-quarter and one-third of the total in 1851. By these various tests it is clear that Wigtownshire did less well than Dumfriesshire or Kirkcudbrightshire. In addition, apart from the higher attendance of the five-year-old age group in Wigtownshire than in Ayrshire,

Wigtownshire never had as high a proportion attending schools in any age group as Ayrshire had until the eleven-year-old group, when the proportion of the population attending in Ayrshire experienced the rapid fall common to all industrial areas.

The parochial statistics for Wigtownshire show that the highest attendances were in the parishes with small towns, giving easy access to the schools: in Whithorn, Wigtown, Penninghame and Stranraer. In this Wigtownshire was unlike Carrick, where the towns did not have a better record, but where a large part of their population were Irish-descended handloom weavers. Remoteness by itself was not the explanation of low attendance. Ballantrae in Carrick and New Luce in Wigtownshire had high records, and in Kirkcudbrightshire some parishes had attendance of 100 per cent. Whatever the excuses which may be advanced there is no escape from the conclusion that Wigtownshire had a poor attendance record.

It is not possible to suggest conclusively that the Irish were responsible for some of the distinctive social characteristics of the south-west, of which the level of educational attendance is one. They certainly affected the quality of its social life. Like any other immigrant group they tended to be criticised and blamed for faults which were often not their own, simply because they were an immigrant group. Difficulties arose when they had to be integrated as their social customs clashed so often with those of the Scots, and social restraints had sometimes been lost in migration. In Ayrshire the mine owners segregated the migrants in different miners' rows; in Wigtownshire they permeated the entire community and extended their influence much more generally. It was that influence which could well lead to the loss of the general cohesion of a rural community typical of the rest of Scotland. The south-west was self-contained but it had an additional and disruptive influence in the presence of the Irish.

Part II

AGRICULTURAL ENTERPRISE

Chapter 4

Rival Specialisations

Livestock husbandry has long been central to the agriculture of the south-west. The activities of Sir David Dunbar on the low ground at Baldoon are well-known. Others followed his example on the more extensive high ground. Patrick Heron of Heron, being noted both as 'very capable of business and of a religious presbyterian principle', not only managed the parks at Baldoon but also stocked the bleak, high hills north of Minnigaff with cattle which went to markets in the south.[1] Galloway was also the location of some vigorous but ephemeral opposition to the new enterprises.

Behind this expansion was the growing demand for cattle in English markets, which ensured that the early efforts bore fruit and that the cattle trade became the agricultural specialisation for which the south-west was best known in the eighteenth century, so much so that its defects may be neglected and other lines of specialisation ignored. Once again the *Old Statistical Account* gives parochial confirmation. 'The greater part [of the high ground] is indeed capable of being used in no other way',[2] was the perceptive report from Girvan, while the minister of Kelton looked beyond his parish and asserted that 'the staple commodity of Galloway ... is black cattle and sheep'.[3] The sale of cattle had one very important benefit. It gave a cash income which helped to pay the rent. In Kirkcudbright and New Luce it was the chief source of cash income; in more arable Kirkmaiden, which 'abounds in corn and cattle ... The farmers lay their account with paying one half of their rent by the sale of cattle, and the other half by corn'.[4] Even in Stoneykirk, one of the most arable parishes in Wigtown, it was estimated that about £2,000 was earned annually from black cattle.

Successful and well-established though it was, the cattle trade still gave rise to problems. The first was of marketing, for the simple reason that the greatest demand for cattle was in the south of England. The major market for the cattle from Galloway was at St Faith's near Norwich, but it was one of a cycle in the south-eastern counties of England. Bungay came first in the spring, followed by

Halesworth. The great sales at St Faith's were in September, followed by those at Hempton, near Fakenham, in October. The cattle which remained were sold off gradually at Enfield thereafter.

Sending the animals to such distant markets was obviously difficult. Fattening for home consumption was not an easy alternative because no large local market was available. Bringing them to good condition for the English market at about four years strained local grazing but made a substantial difference to the price. Some breeders who did not have the financial resources to support such a long wait sold their cattle to graziers or jobbers who then fattened them off. The higher prices gained for the more mature animals made their further fattening attractive for those who could finance the wait until the later sale. At Barr it was reckoned that those taken off the hill and sold at the age of three to three and a half years brought in from £4.10s. to £5.5s. each, while those which had been put on enclosed low ground for another year, and were then ready for the English market, realised up to £8 each, though that was probably a good price. Prices were rising at the end of the eighteenth century, but details of the Earl of Galloway's droves in 1782 show that most cattle did not realise the top price.[5] His two spring droves brought him an average of £5.3s. for the first one of 90 cattle and £4.16s. for the 60 of the second. As was to be expected, he did better at St Faith's: one drove of 248 animals brought in £7.9s. a head while another of 281 brought in £8.2s. a head. The returns had fallen at the later Hampton sales, where the average paid for 257 animals was £5.16s. An account of his purchases of cattle and of their subsequent sale in 1782 shows even less successful operations. He purchased 347 animals at a total cost of £2,255.15s.—comprising 140 from the Earl of Selkirk, 104 from Physgill, 93 from Castlewigg, and 10 from others. A total of 32 were kept or killed for Galloway's own use, 9 were sold locally, 53 at Hempton and 253 at St Faith's. The total realised was £2,046.18s. on a cost of £1,939.4s.3d.

Whatever the age at sale there was no escaping the loss which followed the deterioration in condition which was an inevitable consequence of the 28 days or so taken up by the journey to Norfolk. The general belief was that the expense of sending a bullock to St Faith's was about 16s. to 17s., and that the fatigue of the journey led to the loss of weight equivalent to another 17s. More precise confirmation of the common view is in the Earl of Galloway's spring droves of 1782, where the charges on each animal sent south came to almost 14s. Better markets were recognised as desirable throughout the *Old Statistical Account*, though the form could vary. At Glasserton it was thought that 'For both sheep and black cattle

... the establishment, and extension of manufactures has begun to afford a partial market in the 3 counties of Ayr, Renfrew, and Lanark, which is little less convenient than the markets of England'.[6] 'But the English wool-merchants have lately found their way hither.' From Sorbie came a different thought: 'the vast herds of cattle produced by this truly fertile country might be slaughtered and salted at home for the use of his Majesty's navy, trading vessels, etc.'.[7]

The second qualification to the success of the cattle trade was the highly speculative nature of the marketing it entailed. Some proprietors took their own cattle to England in the early days but responsibility for marketing soon fell into the hands of drovers. The owners of the cattle they were taking south were given bills of exchange, which were often discounted at banks. The credit of the drover was therefore of critical importance, but it was often poor. It was estimated that a drover failed once in ten years and paid only 10s. in the £, but by taking and discounting bills the seller of the cattle was effectively guaranteeing the credit of the drover to the bank. The result, as one of the agricultural reporters pointed out at the height of the trade at the end of the eighteenth century was that '... the whole risk, not only of the state of the markets and of the sickness or death of the cattle, but also of the skill, activity, and honesty of the drovers lies upon the farmers'.[8] A remedy was to sell for ready cash or at least never to discount the bills used and so become liable to meet any deficiencies on the part of the drovers, but that was not a feasible remedy for many breeders with limited financial resources.

The third qualification was perhaps the most fundamental of all. It was the general influence which the specialisation in rearing cattle had over the whole region. Everyone believed the trade held out the possibility of ready gains, so time and effort were directed into buying and selling cattle, to the detriment of other agricultural improvements which had the possibility of more lasting success.

> ... it possesses all the fascinations of the gaming table. The fluctua-
> tion and uncertainty of markets, the sudden gains and losses which
> follow, the idea of skill and dexterity requisite, and even the very risk
> connected with the business, are all calculated to excite the strong
> passions of the mind, and to attach the cattle-dealer, like the gambler,
> to his profession.

The author was aware of the implications of this addiction:

> ... if the Galloway farmers in general, who are unquestionably
> an active and intelligent set of men, have not made the same

improvements in agriculture with those of some other districts, it
must be ascribed chiefly to their incorrigible propensity to dealing
in cattle.[9]

Smith's views, while strongly stated, were perceptive. The success
of the cattle trade had its own defects but whatever it achieved must
not be allowed to overshadow the way in which a large part of the
agriculture of the south-west continued in its old ways unaffected
by the expansion of the cattle trade. Both Andrew Wight, when he
toured the area in the 1770s, and the Gallovidian, Robert Heron,
when he did so in 1792, agreed. Wight was particularly scathing:
Wigtown was 'inhabited by a drowsy people, who make no figure
in trade or manufactures, nor are they more eminent in husbandry
...' and on the Lochnaw estate he saw 'excellent soil, execrably
managed. The tenants are poor and torpid, Andrew McCarlie
excepted ... He will deserve to have a monument raised to his
memory, if he can raise any spirit among his neighbours'.[10] When
Robert Heron traversed the same area twenty years later, he was
as critical: 'The general attention to the management of cattle has
rendered the inhabitants of these parts more negligent than they
might have otherwise been, of agricultural improvements ... They
are obstinately attached to the old modes of agriculture'.[11]

The south-west was never entirely geared to the cattle trade and
undue concentration on the dramatic effects of its expansion and
some of the features which accompanied it detracts from the
continuing importance of subsistence agriculture. For many the
possibility of selling some arable crops remained as pressing a
requirement as ever. Even when the cattle trade was at its zenith
there was much traditional agriculture in the region.

The importance of the cultivation of grain, and especially of oats, in
the agriculture of the south-west, was recognised in the *Old Statistical
Account* as much as the cattle trade. It dominated the primitive
rotations which were then being followed. Two or three successive
crops of oats were often taken, to be followed by a green crop of
potatoes, turnips, or peas—sometimes after a summer fallow—then
a barley crop, undersown with ryegrass and clover, from which
hay would be taken before being pastured for several years. Some
new agricultural methods encouraged even greater reliance on the
cultivation of grain. The use of lime did so, especially in the more
arable parts of Wigtownshire, and most of all in those parishes
which had fallen under the influence of an improving landowner.
Paradoxically, these activities sometimes confirmed defects in agricultural practice and did not remove them. The writer of the account

of Sorbie expressed some justifiable apprehension. Though marl in the parish, lime from Cumberland, and an 'inexhaustible' supply of sea shells in the neighbourhood, were used,

> if the present treatment of a most generous soil be persisted in, there is reason to believe that it will be much injured. Three, and sometimes four crops of oats, or barley, succeed each other; and with the last of these crops grass seeds are sown, which are cut for hay in the following year. Thus four, and sometimes five, white crops follow one another; for a crop of rye grass is as severe as a crop of oats, and therefore may be called a white crop.[12]

It is not surprising that the agricultural reporters at the end of the eighteenth century, with their sometimes excessive zeal for improvement as they saw it, were round in their condemnations of this obsession with the cultivation of oats. Fullarton did not mince his words about Ayrshire: Oats, 'the great staple of provision in the county', 'being extremely impoverishing, farmers ought to learn that two crops of it should never be taken successively from any field'.[13] But that was exactly what happened. In Galloway the oat crop had been the basis of agricultural operations 'so long as the ground would carry any'. Even by the late eighteenth century the rotation prescribed by the landlords allowed '2 or 3, and even 4, corn crops running, which are followed by a green crop with dung, and sown out with the next corn crop, to remain for 5 or 6 years in grass'.[14] Some even left out the green crop so that five or six corn crops followed each other and the land was then allowed to return to natural grass. Samuel Smith, the reporter on Galloway in 1810 was one of those who thought that the use of marl, sea-shells and lime as fertilisers had encouraged concentration on the cultivation of grain, but the incentive provided by the higher prices of wartime was probably as important. Whatever the explanation, Smith deplored the concentration. 'The disposition to overcrop was not extinguished' and landlords had difficulty in keeping tenants to proper rotations: '... the barbarous practice of taking three crops of oats on land broken up from grass still prevails in many parts of the country'.[15] In Dumfriesshire in 1794 Johnstone, the reporter, asserted that 'with some bad farmers, the only rotation seems to be to crop their lands as long as they can bear a crop at all'.[16] In the early nineteenth century the comments on Dumfriesshire were so similar to those on Galloway that they could almost be transposed. 'In general corn is too often introduced; and, in many instances, it is done to a ruinous degree ... in the system of cropping, few of them [the farmers] are willing to be convinced of the loss occasioned by running out the land with corn ...' 'Instances are too numerous of three consecutive crops of oats, and, in some cases, even four, but this never occurs in the practice of any good farmer'. For any extensive cropping of this nature the grain had to be oats for no other was cultivated 'so extensively', though, as in Galloway, wheat was cultivated in wartime, usually instead of barley.[17]

The south-west was obviously not well-suited to any intensive arable cultivation, especially of grain, because of its climate; that was the converse of its climatic suitability for livestock. Because of the strong incentive to devote effort and attention to breeding livestock and to dealing in them, the continued attention to producing grain had to have good reasons behind it. The explanation is that it provided subsistence and the surplus could be exported, increasingly so as markets were buoyant, and without running the risks of any association with drovers. Andrew Wight perceived the prospects in the 1770s when he dismissed the possibility that the backwardness of agriculture might be attributed to an insufficiency of demand: 'There is always a brisk demand, either from Whitehaven, Liverpool, Greenock, or Glasgow, and frequently from all of them at the same time'.[18] As the cattle trade provided the rent for some, the trade in arable products did so for others, especially for the parishes of the Stewartry which were able to export extensively because of their good communications by sea. From Anwoth, grain went to Liverpool, Whitehaven and the Clyde ports. From Buittle, barley and oats went to 'England and Glasgow'. From Colvend, barley was sent to Whitehaven, Lancaster, and Liverpool; oatmeal to the manufacturing towns in the west of Scotland, which also took oatmeal from Kirkgunzeon, while Liverpool and Whitehaven provided 'a ready market for barley'. More generally from Borgue, where the principal crops were oats and barley, 'Twice as much of both is produced as to serve the inhabitants of the parish. The surplus is exported to England and the west of Scotland'. At Kelton the vagueness was reduced only slightly by citing the north of England and the west of Scotland as markets for grain. From Lochrutton barley went to England, oats, when made into meal, was sold in Dumfries for the miners at Leadhills and Wanlockhead 'or transported to the west country'. From New Abbey, wheat, oats, barley and potatoes went to England. Even more specifically, 'the greatest part exported' of potatoes went to Bristol, Liverpool and Dublin, while wheat and oatmeal went to Greenock. From Kirkbean: 'A considerable quantity of barley, oats, and potatoes, is exported to the Whitehaven, Lancaster, and Liverpool markets, and frequently to the ports of Clyde'. Even Crossmichael, which had a ready market on its doorstep in the Glenkens and sent barley, oats and oatmeal as far as Dalmellington, shipped more still from the estuaries of the Urr and the Dee to Liverpool and Whitehaven and to the manufacturing districts of Lanarkshire and Renfrewshire. The position of the Stewartry was summed up well at Kirkmabreck, though the direction of its exports was not recorded:

> Thirty years ago there was no kind of grain exported from this parish, but, on the contrary, importations were some times necessary for the support of the inhabitants. Since that period there is an increase of population of about 400 souls, and now there is a considerable quantity of oats, bear, barley, and potatoes, exported annually.[19]

Conditions were similar in Wigtownshire. Grain was exported from Sorbie to London, Liverpool, Dublin, the Isle of Man, and the West of Scotland; from Glasserton to Liverpool and Whitehaven, from Mochrum to Liverpool and Whitehaven, and sometimes to Greenock; from Wigtown, the bulk of the grain sold went to Whitehaven or Liverpool, to Ayr, Irvine or Greenock.[20]

The concentration on the cultivation of grain, especially in Wigtownshire, shows that for many the needs of livestock husbandry long remained peripheral to their activities. Two consequences were particularly important: the relative neglect of a green crop, most of all of turnips, and the neglect of the cultivation of suitable grasses. Those early improvers who had encouraged the expansion of the cattle trade had also propagated the need for both but their methods did not gain widespread acceptance. The attraction of potatoes as a green crop was that it provided subsistence and was also a cash crop for those who had a surplus. They were exported from the Stewartry parishes of Kelton, Buittle, Colvend, Kirkmabreck, Kirkbean and New Abbey, and everywhere they were used for local consumption. Given that interest in the cultivation of grain dominated, this attraction of potatoes as a green crop pushed turnips into the background. Even when the desire for grain crops was reduced, and the needs of livestock met by the extension of the periods under grass in the rotations, potatoes remained an attractive choice of a green crop until their failure in the 1840s. Turnips as the main choice for the green crop came only thereafter—a late choice, when potatoes were relegated to specialist cultivators in a few favoured locations.

The relative unimportance of the green crop in a rotation, and the choice of potatoes and not of turnips where there was one, is notable even in Wigtownshire and Carrick, which were later to grow turnips more extensively than elsewhere in the south-west. The most favourable comment on the cultivation of turnips in the *Old Statistical Account* came from Glasserton, where, following the example and success of some landowners, turnips were more and more being accepted generally, yet even there turnips were considered a green crop 'still too rare'. More common were reports which indicated that turnips were grown only by isolated individuals: in Wigtown by only one farmer; in Kirkinner by 'very few'; in Whithorn they were 'seldom used' and in Kirkcolm, not at all. In Carrick it was the same. Potatoes were raised extensively for domestic consumption and were the chief means of subsistence for many for three-quarters of the year, but as far as turnips were concerned, the most encouraging comment came from Kirkoswald where Lord Cassillis's farm at Culzean had grown them so successfully that others were thinking of following his example. Elsewhere, one farm at Girvan grew them successfully, but at Kirkmichael doing so had not proved successful, 'the soil being too wet, and the servants have an aversion to them, as they are thereby exposed to much cold dirty work'.[21]

In the light of such reports it is no surprise that the agricultural reporters hammered home with their usual vehemence that the green crop was neglected, turnips in particular. In Ayrshire, Fullarton reported that 'not yet above a score of common farmers in the county' raised turnips though potatoes for domestic consumption were 'universally established'.[22] Webster, reporting on Galloway in 1794, drew attention to how 'The green crop, excepting a few acres of potatoes, is always left out'; turnips did not make 'a conspicuous appearance in Galloway; and although the advantage of them is universally allowed, few of the farmers attempt to raise any'.[23] When Smith reported in 1810, conditions had changed very little; in some ways they had deteriorated. He recognised that the pioneering contribution of Craik of Arbigland was limited: it did not spread greatly beyond Dumfries and it did not last. Consequently, 'the disposition to overcrop was not extinguished ...' and landlords had difficulty in keeping tenants to proper rotations. Similarly, the turnip husbandry had almost entirely disappeared, and fallows were either disused, or were executed in so slovenly a manner as to be 'worse than useless'.[24] In Dumfriesshire a similar comment was made. The system of overcropping with corn was held to be most unfavourable to turnip husbandry, which took place 'on a large and respectable scale' only by 'farmers of the first style',[25] though in general cultivation was neither large nor respectable.

The second consequence of the concentration on grain was the lack of interest in grassland husbandry, though, as with turnips, it would have contributed to fattening cattle locally. The only provision for pasturage was often merely to leave the ground uncultivated, though increasingly artificial grasses—commonly clover and rye grass—were sown out with the last grain crop of the rotation. The neglect of grassland was more reprehensible in the south-west, where the mild climate gave the possibility of grass for grazing during a large part of the year and so of a more sensible specialisation than growing grain in an area where seedtime and harvest were frequently late. Wight deplored the practice in the Machars of Wigtownshire of ploughing every ploughable patch 'to the top of the hills, between the rocks and round the rocks' to the detriment of the good natural grass. He commended those proprietors—Agnew of Sheuchan and Fergusson of Kilkerran among them—who had improved grassland as a primary objective.[26] The agricultural reports supported his assessment. Fullarton was highly critical of the lack of attention to improved grasses in Ayrshire and commended the activities of Fairlie of Fairlie, especially when applied on the extensive Eglinton estates in the northern part of the county. As farms came out of lease, Fairlie enclosed them into three parts at least, applied lime, etc., then let them, usually for 18 years on condition 'not to plough the same land more than three years successively. With the third crop, the tenant was bound to sow 3 bushels of rye-grass, and 12 lb. of clover. To cut it for hay only one year, and pasture 5, before the same could be ploughed again'.[27] In Galloway, Webster drew attention to how after five or six corn crops the ground was allowed to grass over, few being accustomed to sowing grass seed.

> The great body of the farmers foolishly persist in this practice, affirming as a reason, that the ground acquires a better sward naturally than when sown out; others possessed of discernment, sufficient to enable them to draw a comparison between a real substantial loss and a fancied advantage, consider it as absurd.[28]

Some fifteen years later there was little improvement. Smith in his report considered that the cultivation of artificial grasses properly must remain 'very imperfect' through failure to clear weeds or to manure adequately before sowing out, so long as the old system of taking two or three white crops in succession remained a common practice. As for haymaking: 'Few of the operations of husbandry betray more ignorance or carelessness'.[29]

Early in the nineteenth century there were signs of change which were to transform the pattern of agriculture in the south-west drastically. The mere physical distance from some major markets had impeded the success of the cattle trade and had introduced the peculiar hazards of speculative purchasing and of financially insecure drovers. Steam navigation brought this traditional way of marketing to an end. The effects were evident even in those parts of the south-west furthest from the sea. At Closeburn in Nithsdale:

> Steam navigation has given a great stimulus to this branch of agriculture … Fat stock can now be conveyed in sixteen or eighteen hours to Liverpool, where there is always a ready market. Before this cheap and easy mode of conveyance was practiced, Edinburgh and Glasgow were the only markets of which the farmer could avail himself, and these were attended with many obvious disadvantages.[30]

In areas nearer to the sea the advantages were even more obvious. The old links across the Solway and the importance of Whitehaven and even more so of Liverpool as markets, were strengthened. By the 1840s steam vessels plied regularly to the Mersey: from Kirkcudbright once a week in summer and twice a week in winter; from the new pier at Carsethorn there were two voyages a week in summer and one in winter; from Wigtown the steamboat went regularly to Liverpool every fortnight. There were some unusual consequences. Perishable goods, which could not easily be sent by the old methods of transport, were able to go by the new, notably fish and game to the north-west of England. The price of salmon rose accordingly. The minister of Borgue was less impressed. He did not think the opportunity to send fish to Liverpool once a week was an adequate inducement to expend capital on smacks or trawl-nets, and he did think it was 'the source of grievous injury to the morals of this and several adjoining parishes'[31] by providing a better outlet for poachers. The improved marketing of game, though its effects continued, was of small significance compared with the major effect of steam navigation on the traditional movement of livestock.

  Both corn and cattle had been purchased by dealers and drovers on credit and the speculative activities which followed frequently led to bankruptcy and loss to the consignors. Sale for ready payment was much more attractive and was to become more general with the growth of auction marts later in the century. The old methods did not die out at once. Droves of cattle still went south in the 1840s, though the practice was in decline. At Kelton, cattle were still brought from the Highlands and from Ireland, and even from the north of England, to be grazed for a year with those reared locally before being taken by dealers to the English markets. They also went south from Buittle, Rerrick, Leswalt, Sorbie, Kirkcolm and Kirkcowan. The end of the droves to the south came finally with the railways. By the second half of the nineteenth century the old practices had passed.

For the extension of the fattening of cattle, and even more so of sheep, the old concentration on grain, with its neglect of grassland and of turnips had to go first of all. The move was encouraged by the general fall in grain prices after the Napoleonic Wars, which made the old rotations less attractive, and by two new developments. The first—of general applicability—were the benefits which followed the use of artificial manures, particularly bonemeal, superphosphates and guano. It was estimated that by the 1870s most farms used them to an amount costing about one-third of their rentals, and allowances to encourage the use of bonemeal were commonly granted by landowners to their tenants. The second factor was more directly relevant to the south-west. Conventional wisdom believed that turnips were not so suitable for the fattening of cattle, which required supplementary feeding, but turnips alone fattened sheep successfully. They soon came to occupy such a prominent place in the arable husbandry of the south-west, with the exception of Kyle and Cunninghame, that they were long the backbone of its farming and nowhere more so than in Wigtownshire.

By the time of the *New Statistical Account* it is possible to trace the change in parish after parish. The move to turnip husbandry, though not as extensive as in other parts of Scotland, was noted more generally than any other agricultural change. In Kirkcudbrightshire at Borgue steam navigation and the introduction of bone manure had 'materially affected' the system of husbandry and the turnip crop had 'very much increased'; at Buittle:

> The turnip husbandry is greatly extended ... Feeding of sheep, for the last five or six years, has, with the exception of 1834, been profitable to the farmer; and the facility with which they are conveyed to the Liverpool market, by means of steam vessels, has contributed to produce this result.

Two reports, unusual in their comparative nature, were at Kirkbean where 'The system of turnip husbandry, and conveyance of fat stock, etc. to the Liverpool market by steam' were the 'most striking variations' between the two Statistical Accounts, and at Crossmichael where 'The practice of feeding sheep with turnip on the ground, is becoming very common' and, with a breadth of geographical interest and knowledge unusual in the accounts is added: 'In Galloway the whole of the turnips are generally consumed on the ground, while, in Perthshire and Forfarshire, a-half to two-thirds are given to cattle in the feeding byre'. Similar comments were passed at Balmaghie, Minnigaff, Twynholm and Urr.[32] The same battery of comment on the extension of the cultivation of turnips often to feed sheep came also from Wigtownshire, specifically from Kirkinner, Sorbie, Whithorn, Inch, Penninghame, and from Closeburn, Glencairn, Holywood, Keir, Kirkmahoe and Penpont in Nithsdale.

The experience of Carrick differed in one respect. The cultivation of potatoes lessened the possibility of grazing livestock off turnips in the same way as in Kirkcudbrightshire and Wigtownshire. In Dailly and Straiton, along the banks of the Girvan, potatoes took the place of turnips. In Kirkoswald potatoes held their own as 'immense quantities' were shipped annually from Girvan. Girvan itself was the centre of the potato trade, but turnips were grown there with wheat:

> ... the soil is particularly favourable for turnip husbandry, and for several years past, a considerable quantity of the different kinds of turnips have been sown with marked success; still, however, potatoes seem to be the favourite green crop, owing chiefly to the land being got sooner cleared after them, than after turnips, for the sowing of the wheat.[33]

As turnip cultivation spread, the potato crop became confined to a more limited area.

The need for more turnips to fatten livestock following the advent of steam navigation changed the pattern of rotations from their old concentration on grain. The inclusion of a green crop, usually of turnips, became standard practice. Grain remained important, though less dominating. Oats still led, though barley was often raised as the second grain crop of the six-shift rotation: grain, green-crop, grain, grass for hay or pasture, two years of pasture. Wheat was grown only in a few favoured parishes in Wigtownshire and in Carrick. It was preferred to barley in Stoneykirk and excellent crops were grown on the Baldoon clays, 'the Carse of Gowrie of Galloway' in the parish of Kirkinner, which produced about 10,000 bushels of wheat annually.[34] The absence of a green crop between two grain crops was deplored, as in the Glenkens, where a succession of grain crops remained as the practice faded elsewhere.

The growth of the practice of feeding sheep off turnips on the lower ground led to much greater attention being given to the breeding of sheep than formerly. In the 1770s, as he moved towards Wigtownshire, Wight complained that throughout Galloway 'Sheep are almost totally neglected in a country more fit for them than any other part of Scotland. This is wonderfully bizarre'.[35] The complaint remained common until well into the nineteenth century. When turnips became more common, ewes and wedders were brought by graziers from the Inverness or Falkirk markets and put on turnips, but the practice had faded by the 1870s, and the animals which were then fattened were mostly lambs bought by low-ground farmers from the breeders in the hill country of the south-west itself. In the first decade of the nineteenth century and earlier the trade in sheep had little to offer the hill farmers. Since wedders had to be kept for several years before being marketed—for as many as six years in upland Carsphairn—the return on sheep rearing and fattening was often dismal. It was not possible to walk the sheep as far as the cattle, so ruling out the possibility of tapping many markets in the south. Some of the wedders from Carsphairn went to the north of England in summer but most went to Edinburgh. So long as cattle were a more attractive proposition, the hill ground was turned over to them and they so poached the ground to render the grass unsuitable for sheep.

As the demand for sheep for fattening on low ground grew, the hill country began to exploit its potential for breeding. Improvement followed, as on the enormous area of hill ground at Minnigaff. The objective was to encourage early maturity. To that end the old fault of overstocking was changed and the hogs were commonly wintered on low ground. Quality improved but the numbers fell in hill parishes, such as Kirkcowan and Penninghame, so that at first Galloway could not produce sufficient for the needs of its low-ground farmers, many of whom had to continue buying at the Highland or Falkirk markets. Conditions were similar in Nithsdale, where some parishes had the largest sheep populations of any in the south-west, particularly of the blackface which was gaining increasing acceptance.[36] Prices of lambs rose sharply in mid-century, exceptionally high because of rinderpest in 1866,[37] and, though they fell from the heights of that period, the trend upwards continued and this long neglected branch of the agriculture of the south-west prospered.[38]

Steam navigation opened up the possibilities of fattening cattle and sheep at home and of avoiding the long trek to markets in the south. There was, however, a corresponding disadvantage, which in the long-run, was to lead the south-west to new specialisations. Direct communication from Ireland to Liverpool or Holyhead deprived Portpatrick or Stranraer of much of their traffic, and Galloway of much of the cattle which had formerly traversed it. The defects were soon recognised in the decline of the markets at Kelton Hill and Gatehouse. Rather sadly it was pointed out in the *New Statistical*

Account from Girthon that

> The Irish horses and cattle, which formed the staple articles at
> [the various markets at Gatehouse], instead of being sent through
> Galloway, are almost all transported direct in steam-boats from Belfast
> and the other Irish towns to the leading markets in England ... It is
> owing to this cause alone that the markets of Gatehouse, as also those
> of other towns in Galloway, have declined.[39]

In the longer term other areas, particularly the north-east of Scotland,
built up a successful trade in supplying the London market by sea,
and other competitors, notably from overseas, dislodged the old
cattle trade from the south-west still further.

While the remoter south-west was experiencing such changes, the
agriculture of Kyle and of Cunninghame was already developing
along different lines to produce a specialisation which was to bring
about a transformation throughout the whole south-west later in
the nineteenth century. Apart from Muirkirk, most of the Ayrshire
parishes with extensive sheep walks were in Carrick. Some Highland
cattle were brought to others, among them Coylton and Dalry, but
even in the few parishes where sheep and cattle were raised to be
sold as stores or fattened, they were minor enterprises compared
with what was common practice in Galloway. By contrast, the dairy
was the dominant activity in parish after parish by the end of the
eighteenth century. In Kyle various parishes noted the making and
selling of butter and cheese in the *Old Statistical Account*: Craigie,
New Cumnock, Old Cumnock, Dundonald, Galston and Stair.
Significantly, in Sorn in the previous ten or twelve years the
making of cheese had been perfected through some of the tenants
moving into the parish from Dunlop and neighbouring parishes
in Cunninghame where dairying was firmly established, whence
it spread throughout the south-west. Two-thirds of the parochial
accounts of Cunninghame referred to its importance (in Beith,
Dalry, Dreghorn, Dunlop, Kilmaurs, Kilwinning, Largs, Loudoun,
Stevenston and Stewarton). Most of these parishes gained from
the demand from Glasgow and Paisley for their cheese, while one
or two also tapped the Edinburgh market. Though the making of
cheese had been pioneered in Dunlop, and the parish gave its name
to the cheese made most of all in Scotland initially, the method had
spread, even far from Cunninghame, and the writers of the accounts
of other parishes, while acknowledging the origins of the cheese,
were ready to claim that their natives could make it just as well. By
the late eighteenth century some had large numbers of milk cows for

dairy purposes: Dunlop had 758 and nearby Dalry had 1,100. The size of the farms and their herds were small, about ten to 20 in each herd, apart from the odd cow or two kept chiefly for domestic purposes. Some of the north Ayrshire parishes were noted for their large number of proprietors, so that dairying on a small scale was often the accompaniment of small-scale ownership. Beith had 105 heritors, ignoring proprietors in the village; Dalry had 90, even though one of them, resident in the parish, owned about one-third of it; Stewarton had eight large and about 100 smaller heritors; apart from the Earl of Eglinton, who owned a third of the parish, Kilwinning had eight other large proprietors and 60 small. While in other parts of the south-west store cattle, even potatoes, all contributed to supply the cash the tenants needed, especially to meet their rents, the tenants of Cunninghame and Kyle relied increasingly on the cash received from selling the products of their dairies. In those parishes which had a surplus for sale it was almost always of dairy products and not of the grain which was characteristic of Kirkcudbright and Wigtown.

Fifty years later, at the time of the *New Statistical Account*, the domination of the dairy throughout Ayrshire, except in the upland parishes of the south, was more evident still. Once again the lead was given by Cunninghame. To parish after parish in both Kyle and Cunninghame the comment of the minister of Dundonald could have been applied: 'Ayrshire is "cows and dairy produce" all over'.[40] In many parishes the sale of the produce of the dairy was essential to pay much of the rent, perhaps usually about two-thirds, often calculated as so many cheeses even if it was paid in money. Tabulation of the number of milk cows, which in Ayrshire were practically all kept for their dairy produce and of the output of cheese in a string of parishes in Kyle and Cunninghame provides confirmation of their highly specialised agriculture.

TABLE 4.1

	Cunninghame			Kyle	
	cows	cheese		cows	cheese
Ardrossan	675	10,000 stones	Craigie	759	
Beith	900	18,900	New Cumnock	1,690	
Dalry	1,405	32,125	Old Cumnock	c. 1,000	c. 23,500 stones
Dunlop	910	21,500	Dalrymple		3,600
Irvine	370		Galston		29,500
Kilbirnie	536		Ochiltree	1,043	
Kilmarnock		12,000	Riccarton		22,400
Largs	604		Stair	481	

It is not possible to consider any aspects of agricultural history in the south-west from the early nineteenth century without giving dairy farming a leading position especially since the system spread southwards from these north Ayrshire parishes. Most of the cheese was bought by Glasgow merchants but, already indicative of markets which were to become more important in north Ayrshire, producers in a few parishes near the growing urban industrial districts were able to sell fresh milk or more commonly, butter and buttermilk, the last especially to miners later in the century. Local markets offered an outlet in parts of north Ayrshire as its own industrial activities expanded. In Beith: 'A considerable quantity of milk is also carted in to the adjoining villages, which is found a more profitable mode of disposing of it, when the distance is great, than by making cheese or butter'. At Dreghorn they made butter and sold milk in Irvine. At Largs: 'The farmers at a distance from the town make cheese with all the cream or skim-milk cheese and butter, while those near the town either sell all their milk to the inhabitants, or churn all their milk, make butter, and supply the town with butter-milk'. At Stevenston, less cheese was being made than formerly, 'as it is in general thought more profitable to dispose of the dairy produce in milk and butter'.[41] There is a difference in the parochial accounts of Kyle, which, if they mention the disposal of the dairy produce at all, note that it is being made into cheese, once again usually for the Glasgow merchants, though sometimes for disposal locally, as in Dalrymple where, though most of the 3,600 stones made annually went to dealers, some went direct to customers in Ayr and Maybole.[42] As dairying spread southwards, so the exploitation of the liquid milk and butter markets grew, especially when the concurrent expansion of the railway network enabled produce to be sent fresh to market. As this happened, the parishes concentrating on the manufacture of cheese were to be found increasingly in south Ayrshire and then later in Kirkcudbrightshire and above all in Wigtownshire.

The concentration on dairying placed arable cultivation in a sub-ordinate position more appropriate to the physical conditions of the area.[43] Even by the late eighteenth century grain was cropped less in Ayrshire, least of all in Cunninghame, as the need for more grass grew. The sowing of clover and rye grass was noted specifically in the *Old Statistical Account* in Ayr, Craigie, Loudoun, Stevenston and Tarbolton. In Dunlop, grass was 'always a plentiful crop, and of the finest quality'.[44] In Stair, the minister, also a minor local landowner, praised himself for encouraging the use of artificial grasses which he introduced in 1737. In some parishes where progress was deemed inadequate, there was no doubt of the direction which should be taken. The writer of the account on Dalry commented that the parish

> is better adapted for grass than for corn. What a pity then it is, that better methods were not fallen on to improve the grass? This will not be done, till the ground be properly prepared by fallowing, cleansed well from its old roots, and proper grass-seeds thrown into it. It is by grass that the farmer at present pays his rent; all pains, therefore, should be taken to improve it.[45]

By the time of the *New Statistical Account*, it was generally recognised that better grass was the main contribution the land could make in many parts of Ayrshire to the prosperity of its agricultural interest in general. Again it was in Cunninghame that the largest proportion of the land was in grass: two-thirds in Dalry and two-thirds to three-quarters in Stewarton.[46] Restrictions in leases on the amount of land which could be ploughed at any one time were not resented. In Dunlop, where the tenants were bound to plough only one-quarter of their ground annually. 'This restriction seems to be very unnecessary, as few of them seem inclined to cultivate as much as they have leave to do'.[47] The need for pasture for the milk cows determined the rotations. They varied even within one parish. In Dalrymple, five different rotations were cited, and in Dundonald, 'the system of tillage is by no means uniform', but these comments were exceptional and, as specifically in Dundonald, the variety was in the context of basic similarity.[48] It was a rotation of two grain crops, the second of which was undersown with grass, hay, and then about five years in pasture, though the last varied slightly. The system was practised all over Cunninghame and Kyle: Beith, Dalry, Dreghorn, Kilbirnie, Stewarton, Coylton, Dundonald, Galston, Ochiltree, Riccarton, Sorn and in most of Tarbolton. There were two variants. The first, and much less important, was to take another, that is a third grain crop. The practice was still common in Dunlop and was accompanied by leaving the ground in pasture for up to ten to 12 years, and in Stewarton, where a third crop was accompanied by pasture for from five to eight years.[49] These were survivals of older practices. The second variation accorded more with improved practice and was the introduction of a green crop. If introduced, it came between the two grain crops and led to a reduction in the acreage under pasture. In most parishes recognition of the possibility of following this rotation was often only theoretical, not practical, and limited to a few farms with special qualities. It was extensively followed only in some of the parishes with lighter soils: in Monkton and Prestwick, in St Quivox, in about one-third of Tarbolton, in the lighter soils near the sea in Dreghorn and in parts of Coylton.[50]

Two aspects of this rotation should be noted. The first was the old relative absence of the green crop, and particularly of turnips, much more than in other parts of the south-west, where soil was more suitable and better drained.[51] At Dalry turnips had been introduced only in the year before the *Old Statistical Account* was written; at Dreghorn only 'two farmers in the parish have several times sown a few acres of turnips'; at Stevenston, 'the turnip husbandry is never attempted'. In Kyle at Craigie, no turnips were raised; at Monkton and Prestwick, 'the culture of turnips is only beginning to be introduced'; at Galston, though the soil in part of the parish 'is well adapted for turnips, but little of that root has as yet been raised'; at Symington, though the soil was thought to be suitable, green crops were grown only in small quantities.[52]

The absence of turnips remained a conspicuous feature of the arable cultivations of Kyle and Cunninghame. The *New Statistical Account* showed a perpetuation of the old practice. In Dalry, lack of manure, which was required for potatoes and beans was a limiting factor; in Dunlop, turnips were 'not grown to any extent'; in Coylton, 'till of late' turnip husbandry 'was not much attended to'; in Auchinleck, 'a field of turnips is more rarely to be met with' and their absence was commented on at Stair.[53] As with the possibility of the use of a green crop in general, so the theoretical attractions of turnip husbandry were recognised and they were fed to dairy stock, but only to a limited extent. In Dalry, for example, 'The number of stock fed on turnips is limited, and consuming them on the field with sheep is unknown'.[54] Where turnip husbandry was more common it was to provide for the fattening of animals and that, of course, was not the main objective in most parishes in north Ayrshire. Turnips tended to be grown in districts towards the sea and so with lighter and sandier soils. They were alleged to be grown on every farm in Tarbolton, which was inland, but the quantities were not specified. In Dreghorn the common rotation was followed in the more inland parts of the parish but a green crop was introduced between the grain crops on the lighter soils and 'The turnips raised on the farms here are used for fattening cattle and sheep'. In nearby Dundonald only one proprietor had 'set the example of flaking sheep upon turnips, elsewhere found so beneficial, and for which much of the agricultural land in this parish is particularly adapted'. In Kilmarnock and in the adjacent parishes of Monkton and of St Quivox, both with similar soils, sheep were fed off turnips on the ground in the same

ways. There were some indications that the cultivation of turnips
was spreading in the dairying parishes; that it was doing so was
asserted specifically in Stewarton and Coylton, but that it could lead
to problems in the dairy was evident in the work of a pioneer of their
use in St Quivox, who had to mix a little saltpetre with his butter to
remove 'any unpleasant turnip flavour'.[55]

The second notable aspect of the rotation, particularly marked in
the northern parishes, with their heavier soils, was the practice of
sowing rye grass with the last grain crop of the cycle and then
harvesting it for seed in the following year. The procedure was
explained fully in the account of Dalry:

> The rye grass is allowed to ripen for seed, and after being mown, it
> is tied and stooked in the same manner as corn. When it has stood a
> sufficient time to allow the seed to harden, it is thrashed, and the seed
> sold to dealers, who export it to the English markets, from whence,
> under the name of English seed, it often returns the succeeding spring
> to other parts of the country.[56]

In each of the parishes where the practice was explained, the writer
was aware that it was regarded unfavourably by many and went
on to deplore it himself, and for similar reasons. In Dalry it was
maintained that the hay which resulted was of poorer quality and
left fields bare, as though with corn stubble, which were 'greatly
poached' by the cows being allowed to wander over them in
winter, and that it was sometimes June before the pasture was
in good condition again. In Dunlop the practice was considered
'nearly as scourging to the land as an additional corn crop'. In
West Kilbride '... this is a practice by no means consistent with
good farming, the succeeding pastures being greatly deteriorated by
its scourging effects, so that nothing but the pressing necessities of
the cultivator can excuse such a course'. In Tarbolton, '... the rye
grass is often allowed to stand for seed in land which is not in
a proper state for a crop so very exhausting'. The best that could
be said in defence of the system was at Galston, where, 'however
it may be condemned by the modern school, [it] has at least the
praise of being long established, and highly esteemed by those who
practice it'. The sanctity of conventional use carried little weight
with the writer of the account on Dalry: 'If a more rational system
of laying down grasslands were practiced, and the frequent drain
system fully extended, the dairy produce of the parish might be
doubled'.[57]

The importance of the dairy decreased further south, depending on time and place. In the late eighteenth century some attempts to emulate the more northerly districts of Ayrshire were evident in Carrick, but rarely in Wigtownshire and not at all in Kirkcudbrightshire. Their day was yet to come. In Carrick dairy products were rarely sold for cash beyond the parochial boundary, in marked contrast to conditions in Cunninghame. A rather vague, yet probably accurate assessment from Kirkmichael showed their relative unimportance:

> The chief exports are oats, oatmeal, black-cattle, woolen (sic) cloth, and from one district, some butter and cheese', which is not surprising since it was also held that 'The common breed of cows are not remarkable for the quantity of milk they give, nor is the dairy, as an article of export, much attended to in this part of the country, though good butter for private use is made here. The manufacture of cheese is not understood.[58]

Only in the more generally fertile parish of Kirkoswald was progress more recognised:

> The dairy was in a most neglected state in this parish forty years ago. Good butter and cheese were scarcely to be found. Now the milk cows are changed to the better, are put into parks sowed down with white and yellow clover, and when they live in the house by night or by day, are fed upon cut red clover. Every steading of farm houses has an apartment by itself for a milk house, and every conveniency suited to it. Both butter and cheese are now exported from the parish to the markets of Ayr and Paisley.[59]

In Wigtownshire even less progress towards dairying had been made and the relative backwardness of what was done was recognised. In Glasserton, because much of the milk was fed to calves, the quantity of butter and cheese made annually was smaller in proportion to the number of milk cows than in the parishes of Ayrshire. In Mochrum, where 'no great attention is paid to milk, or manufacturing of it into butter and cheese' some of 'the famous cows of Kyle' had been introduced to improve production but had not succeeded.[60] A ludicrous description of dairying in Galloway by Webster may serve to indicate the difference between its progress in the different parts of the south-west:

> When the maids go to perform this operation [milking], which is

done at stated periods, the cows and calves are brought together; the calf is placed at one side of the cow, and the maid goes with a pail to the other; and thus the operation of milking and sucking goes on at the same time. This, however, is sometimes suddenly interrupted, from the cow's partiality to the calf, announced by a blow with her foot, which often overturns both the maid and the pail.[61]

By the time of the *New Statistical Account* dairying had penetrated into the far south-west, though not nearly on the scale of north Ayrshire. The change was greatest in Carrick and especially in those parishes adjacent to some of the local markets growing through immigration and handloomweaving. At Ballantrae:

> On one farm, there are about seventy cows kept during the whole year,—on each of two others above forty, on several others thirty, and from that downwards; and these same farms raise annually as much farm produce as any others in the parish. About 5000 stones of sweet milk cheese are made annually in Ballantrae.

At Colmonell: 'Of late years, the produce of the dairy has been an object of considerable importance. The Cunningham breed of cattle have in consequence greatly increased, and much attention has been paid to their improvement'. In Girvan, the Galloway breed had been supplanted by the Ayrshire, 'chiefly for the dairy'. In Dailly the cattle were 'chiefly of the dairy or Ayrshire [breed]'. In Maybole the cattle were 'almost exclusively' Ayrshire. At Kirkoswald, where less than fifty years before the greatest progress of any had been noted, there were many dairies of 'first quality', the produce being made principally into cheese for the Glasgow market.[62]

The same penetration was evident in Wigtownshire. Kirkcolm was the centre of pioneering work by James Ralston of Fineview some thirty years before the *New Statistical Account*. By the 1840s his dairy had gone and there were none so large, but the parish had thirteen dairies of Ayrshire cows; the largest had 42, the smallest had 15 and in total these dairies had 357 cows. Away from the major arable and cattle-rearing parishes of Kirkinner, Sorbie and Stoneykirk, dairying was noted generally in the *New Statistical Account*. In Glasserton: 'The dairy system is now beginning to be considered more profitable than breeding ... And we have already in this parish three or four farms stocked with Ayrshire cows'. In Whithorn: 'Of late years, diaries have been introduced, and the Ayrshire breed is threatening to supplant the Galloway'. In the southern, lower and more fertile parts of Old Luce, 'dairies have of late become very general, and upwards of 6,000 stones of cheese are annually produced'. In Penninghame, Ayrshire cows were being introduced, 'when milk is the principal object in keeping them ... In this district, the object formerly was to rear cattle. There is much more attention paid to dairy produce ...'. At Kirkmaiden: 'There are in the parish several large dairies ...' and there it was also noted that the prevalence of the dairy system (where the milk was made into cheese) 'has perhaps been the principal [sic] cause of the too frequent use of tea and its accompaniment *loaf bread*'. The change was stated in some cases to have been due specifically to the low prices being obtained for cattle. So it was in Old Luce, Kirkcolm and Penninghame. The report on Inch summarised the situation for all: 'In consequence of the low price of *Galloways* in the English market, many of our farmers have introduced the Ayrshire cow, and turned their attention to cheese-making'. The Ayrshire was the cow used, though the Galloway bull was often used on the dairy stock, the cows being renewed by introducing queys from Ayrshire. In Glasserton, where it was maintained that the Galloway 'has hitherto been preserved pure and genuine' and 'found in its utmost perfection', that time was felt to be 'approaching, when it shall only be said that such things *were* ...'. The Ayrshire 'will contaminate the Galloway breed, perhaps displace it altogether'. There were some less obvious causes 'which have a tendency to increase the evil, and to accelerate the progress of deterioration. [Some] believe that the very sight of Ayrshire cows in the neighbourhood corrupts the native breed, and that it causes Galloways of the purest breeds and blackest colour, to produce red, speckled, and spotted calves'.[63]

The transformation to dairying was patchy eastwards in Nithsdale and in Kirkcudbrightshire. In the former, Ayrshire cows were to be found throughout, specifically recognised in Closeburn, Holywood, Keir, Kirkconnel, Morton and Tynron, but only in Kirkconnel, which was a parish with coalmining and so a local market for dairy produce, was a major change to dairying and cheesemaking recognised. The parish had about 560 Ayrshire cows and about 160 followers, of which about 113 were reserved each year to replace the dairy stock. Consequently, '... few or none of the west Highlanders or Galloway breed of cattle are grazed or fed in this parish for the English market as formerly'.[64] Such changes had not taken place in Kirkcudbrightshire, but they were recognised as possible. At Tongland the Galloway still dominated, though the Ayrshire had been introduced on three or four farms with a view to dairying. At Balmaclellan, the cows were all Galloways except for a 'few' Ayrshires. In Balmaghie there were 'a number of Ayrshire cows'. At Crossmichael, Ayrshires were kept for dairies. At Kirkbean: 'There are two dairy farms ... which keep about 40 Ayrshire cows each'. At Kirkmabreck the picture was confusing. When the account was first written in 1840, the minister reported: 'pretty extensive dairies, conducted upon the Ayrshire plan' at three farms and that 'Ayrshire cows are increasing very much', but a footnote added in 1844 stated that 'Ayrshire cows are already beginning to decrease'.[65] Decline, if there was one, was not to continue, but the reports indicate the patchy nature of the change to dairying in Kirkcudbrightshire even by the mid nineteenth century. The penetration had made its way from north Ayrshire, through Kyle and Wigtownshire but was yet to move eastwards along the Solway extensively.

Dairying throughout the south-west did not merely emerge passively from Ayrshire, especially from its northern parishes. It was often taken actively to other parts by the 'men from Ayrshire', who were regarded as a plague by those in Wigtownshire whom they were often displacing,[66] a move which was a prelude to a later one to Essex and the eastern counties of England. By the later nineteenth century it was possible to hold that Ayrshire was the breeding ground for dairy farmers as well as for dairy cows—'a veritable congested district, which rears twice as many farmers than there are farms for', pushing up rents in the south-western counties and beyond, and leading John Speir to assert that 'At least 30 per cent of the farmers of Wigtownshire are Ayrshire men, or their descendants, and any farms becoming vacant in the counties of Wigtown, Kirkcudbright, or Dumfries are generally taken by dairymen, most of whom come from Ayrshire, with a few from the counties of Lanark and Renfrew'.[67] This was the form of agricultural production which was to dominate the south-west in the later nineteenth century.

Chapter 5

Domination by Dairying

The move to dairying sheltered much of the agriculture of the south-west from the more damaging effects of the changing pattern of world trade in foodstuffs and raw materials in the latter half of the nineteenth century. Generally Scottish agriculture did not suffer so much as further south. Few areas were primarily arable. Those which were did not grow wheat as extensively as in the arable counties of England and so did not endure the same tribulations in the years from the early 1870s, when the price of wheat was almost halved in two decades. The prices of other crops dropped less, though those of barley, oats and potatoes still fell by about one-third. To some extent all arable husbandry suffered from foreign competition.

Livestock husbandry had few comparable trials until the later nineteenth century. New methods of preservation, especially the introduction of refrigeration from the 1880s almost doubled meat imports in twenty years but consumption of meat was rising. Dairy farmers suffered even less severely, though late in the century they had to meet competition from American cheese and from the dairy products of some European countries, notably Denmark, where the farmers responded to increased competition in grain by specialising in dairy products. The adverse effects were mitigated for the south-west by the demand from the urban areas of central Scotland, where industry remained generally prosperous until 1914. Dairy farmers gained most of all if they were able to exploit the demand for liquid milk.

The south-west took major steps to meet this buoyant demand for dairy products. The most important single change was in the breeding of Ayrshire cattle. Their origin from native cattle, much improved by the introduction of blood from elsewhere, is unclear and a matter of dispute, but the breed became well-established in the nineteenth century. By the 1870s two different types were being bred. One was a small cow suitable for showing and the other an animal with good milking qualities. The characteristics of both types were merged only in the 1920s. The development of the breed owed much to the activities of a few individuals: in the eighteenth century to Bruce Campbell, factor to the Earl of Marchmont at Sornbeg, Galston, and to John Dunlop of Dunlop; and in the nineteenth century to Theophilus Paton of Swinlees, Dalry, and to Parker of Nether Broomlands, Irvine. The Ayrshire Cattle Herd Book was started in 1877 and published its first volume in 1878.

Another major step taken was to improve the manufacture of cheese. Cheddar replaced Dunlop cheese in the 1850s, when the Ayrshire Agricultural Association, first formed in 1835, established a two-way traffic in instruction with Somerset. By the 1880s, helped by grants from the Highland and Agricultural Society, extensive instruction in cheesemaking, and to a lesser extent in buttermaking, was given throughout the south-west. More permanent arrangements became available when the Kilmarnock Dairy School was started in March 1889. Instruction on the farms was necessary to improve techniques because creameries were rare. The most important in the south-west, at Dunragit, was started only in the 1880s. It processed the milk from 1,500 to 2,000 cows and fed the whey to some 300 to 500 pigs. The introduction of the manufacture of Cheddar cheese, particularly in Wigtownshire from the mid-1850s, so changed dairy management and improved profitability so much that the value of farms rose as their leases came to an end, and landlords had to provide better accommodation for the dairy. Milk recording came in the early years of the twentieth century, and the elimination of bovine tuberculosis, carried beyond the work of a few pioneers in Ayrshire in the 1920s, was virtually complete there shortly after 1945.

A more reliable examination of agricultural activities and specialisation at a parochial level can be gained in the later nineteenth century from the agricultural statistics, which are available from the 1860s.[1] They show the increasing grip of dairying on all parts of the south-west in the years before 1914, though with a variety derived from the early specialisations of different districts still lingering on. It was a grip which led to a pattern of arable husbandry different from wider Scottish experience in the years from 1870 to the First World War.

The south-west, and each of its four counties, had a higher percentage of land under cultivation (including permanent pasture) than the whole of Scotland in 1870: over one-third compared with less than one-quarter. The proportions rose very slightly in Scotland and a little more in the south-western counties until the 1890s. Thereafter they were practically stationary until 1914. The south-west had its own way of using the land. (See Table 5.1). In 1870 about half the total acreage returned as being cropped in Scotland was in grass (both temporary and permanent); in the south-west it was about two-thirds. In 1910 Scotland had two-thirds in grass while the south-west had over three-quarters. The domination of grassland husbandry was confirmed further by the increase in the acreage under permanent grass between 1870 and 1910: by 55.9 per cent in Scotland (964,996 to 1,504,296 acres), and by 57.6 per cent in the south-west (272,102 to 428,857).[2]

TABLE 5.1   DISTRIBUTION OF AGRICULTURAL LAND

		Grain	Roots	Grass temporary	permanent	Other
		%	%	%	%	%
Ayr	1870	21.4	6.7	33.7	37.9	0.3
	1910	14.8	5.2	27.3	52.6	0.1
Dumfries	1870	25.3	13.5	27.9	32.9	0.4
	1910	16.6	8.5	27.9	46.9	0.1
Kirkcudbright	1870	21.1	11.1	27.6	40.0	0.1
	1910	13.3	7.2	27.7	51.7	0.1
Wigtown	1870	29.5	14.2	37.7	18.0	0.6
	1910	20.5	10.4	41.5	27.5	0.1
South-west	1870	23.8	10.6	31.6	33.7	0.3
	1910	16.0	7.4	29.9	46.6	0.1
Scotland	1870	32.0	15.7	30.1	21.7	0.5
	1910	25.1	12.5	31.1	31.0	0.3
Aberdeen	1870	36.8	18.2	39.5	5.3	0.2
	1910	33.3	15.3	45.7	5.5	0.2
Berwick	1870	33.7	18.4	29.3	17.7	0.9
	1910	27.7	15.5	29.4	27.3	0.1
Fife	1870	38.2	20.7	23.7	16.7	0.6
	1910	28.6	15.7	24.9	30.5	0.3
Angus	1870	38.7	21.1	31.0	9.0	0.2
	1910	34.6	19.6	34.0	11.5	0.3
East Lothian	1870	41.5	23.9	20.8	13.2	0.6
	1910	34.2	21.9	24.6	18.6	0.7
Kincardine	1870	38.6	19.3	35.3	6.6	0.2
	1910	33.6	17.0	38.9	10.2	0.3

The increase in Ayrshire between 1870 and 1910 was exceptional as it was accompanied by a decline in the acreage under temporary grass which may be taken to indicate a more long-term commitment on the part of its farmers to grassland husbandry. By 1910 Ayrshire, Dumfriesshire and Kirkcudbrightshire had almost identical proportions of over 25 per cent of their land being cropped under temporary grass and comparable proportions of around 50 per cent under permanent grass. As in so many aspects of arable husbandry, Wigtownshire's position was slightly different, with a smaller proportion under all grass than the three others but with a higher one under temporary grass.

The converse was a considerably smaller proportion of the cultivated acreage of the south-west under grain and roots than in Scotland: 277,955 acres or just over one-third of the total cultivated acreage in 1870 and 215,392 or just under one-quarter of the total in 1910. Scotland had 2,120,962 acres under grain and roots or less than half the total cultivated area in 1870 and 1,823,665 acres or over one-third of the total in 1910. Among the four counties of the south-west Wigtownshire had the highest proportion of its cultivated land given over to grain. Nevertheless it never reached 30 per cent and dropped to just over 20 per cent in 1910, lower than the figure for Scotland. In the south-west the acreage under roots was usually less than half of the land under grain. Once again Wigtownshire had the highest proportion of cultivated land under roots. Though Dumfriesshire had nearly the same proportion in 1870, it had fallen by 1910. Ayrshire's proportion was always strikingly low: a mere 5.2 per cent of the cropping land in 1910.

The pattern of land use was markedly different in the eastern counties, even though the move to grassland husbandry was a general response to the changing international conditions. In 1870 none of the six eastern counties in Table 5.1 reached Wigtownshire's 55.7 per cent under grass, far less Ayrshire's 71.6 per cent. The proportions under grass in the eastern counties were higher in 1910 but were still below Wigtownshire's 69.0 per cent. Though the proportion under grain and roots fell in the east, the lowest figures—Berwickshire's 27.7 per cent in grain in 1910 and Aberdeenshire's 15.3 per cent in roots—exceeded even Wigtownshire's leading proportions among the south-western counties of 20.5 per cent in grain land 10.4 per cent in roots.

The sources from which the additional acreage under grass was drawn between 1870 and 1910 also differed between east and west. (See Table 5.2). By 1870 the south-west had so much under grass that significantly more could come only by bringing more land within the classification of being under cultivation. A particularly large part of the increased acreage under grass in Dumfriesshire was provided in that way. Aberdeenshire's experience was similar, and it was joined by Angus as the only other eastern county where the additional land brought in for cropping was the single largest source for the additional grassland. Elsewhere in the east the additional land under grass was gained chiefly from reductions under grain and roots. Nevertheless, in spite of starting from an already low basis, the south-west's acreages under grain and roots fell more sharply than in the six eastern counties between 1875 and 1910. In the six the acreage under grain fell by 8.8 per cent from 547,779 to 499,780 acres and roots by 9.8 per cent from 287,404 to 259,239 acres. In the south-west the acreage under grain fell by 23.5 per cent from 191,957 to 146,919 acres and roots by 20.4 per cent from 85,998 to 68,473 acres.

TABLE 5.2   SOURCE OF CHANGE IN LAND USE. 1870 TO 1910

County	From Additional land %	Grain %	Roots %	Other %	To Grass temporary %	Grass temporary %	permanent %
Ayr	48.7	26.4	4.6	0.8	19.5	–	100.0
Dumfries	70.5	18.1	10.5	0.9	–	19.4	80.6
Kirkcudbright	59.5	26.9	13.2	0.4	–	16.8	83.2
Wigtown	59.2	27.5	11.0	2.3	–	41.5	58.5
South-west	59.8	24.0	9.3	1.0	5.9	16.6	83.4
Scotland	56.6	28.8	13.0	1.6	–	24.1	75.9
Aberdeen	84.7	2.5	12.6	0.2	–	93.9	6.1
Berwick	16.0	52.1	24.5	7.4	–	5.7	94.3
Fife	37.3	40.0	21.6	1.1	–	15.4	84.6
Angus	57.8	33.8	8.4	1.7	–	58.6	39.7
E. Lothian	25.5	61.0	13.5	0.4	–	42.7	56.9
Kincardine	26.1	50.7	23.2	0.9	–	53.8	45.3

Throughout Scotland oats increased its share of the reduced acreage in grain, leading to the virtual elimination of wheat and barley in the south-west. Oats accounted for 97.0 per cent of the acreage under grain in 1910 in the four counties, individual percentages ranging from Ayrshire's 93.5 per cent to Kirkcudbrightshire's 99.6 per cent. Among the six eastern counties East Lothian was the only one with less than half its grain acreage in oats (42.6 per cent). Berwickshire, Fife and Angus all had less than 60 per cent and only Aberdeenshire, with 90.8 per cent, approached the position in the south-west. There was greater variation in the distribution of the root crops. Three of the eastern counties had more than 80 per cent of their roots acreage under turnips, Aberdeenshire's 89.9 per cent being the greatest concentration. Fife and East Lothian had less than 60 per cent. In the south-west Ayrshire was markedly different with only 42.4 per cent of its small roots acreage under turnips. Wigtownshire had 88.1 per cent, Kirkcudbrightshire had 82.0 per cent and Dumfriesshire had 79.4 per cent.

The changes brought about by the new patterns of international trade and the responses to them were to be seen in practically every parish throughout the south-west. Marked changes took place in the two decades between 1875 and 1895. Oats, which had been the main crop, became more dominant between 1875 and 1895. In 1875, even in a parish such as Dalmellington, where only 130 acres were recorded as under any kind of crop (grain or green), 90 were in oats; in other parishes where there was a relatively large acreage under grain or green crop, little was cultivated apart from oats, as in Fenwick, where 1,676 of the total of 1,806 acres under all crops were in oats. In 1895 Dalmellington's pattern was virtually unchanged with 89 of its total cropping of 131 acres under oats; by then Fenwick had 1,214 acres in oats out of a total of 1,334 in all crops. The widespread cultivation of oats is evident in parochial experience, the examination of which is confined in this section to the three most south-western counties and to Nithsdale, the most westerly part of Dumfriesshire where agricultural and other conditions are more comparable with those further west. The distribution of the acreages between the parishes is shown in Table 5.3.

TABLE 5.3

				Number of parishes with acreages under oats of			
		–500	*500– 1000*	*1000– 2000*	*2000– 3000*	*3000– 4000*	*4000+*
Ayrshire	1875	7	14	22	3	–	–
	1895	7	14	22	2	1	–
Nithsdale	1875	3	4	5	–	–	–
	1895	3	4	5	–	–	–
Kirkcudbrightshire	1875	4	9	13	2	–	–
	1895	3	13	11	1	–	–
Wigtownshire	1875	1*	1	6	8	1	–
	1895	1	2	4	9	–	1
TOTAL	1875	15*	28	46	13	1	–
	1895	14	33	42	12	1	1

* Including one parish (Stranraer) with nil return.

The pervasiveness of the oats crop is clear. Every parish grew some in both years, with the unimportant exception of Stranraer, which, as in some ways the most urban of all parishes in the remoter south-west, had only an acre of potatoes under cultivation in 1875, though in

1895, when its acre under roots had been split equally between potatoes and turnips, it managed also an acre of oats. The greater extent of cropping in Wigtownshire was evident by nine of its 17 parishes having over 2,000 acres under oats in 1875 and ten in 1895. In both years the parish of Stoneykirk was far ahead of any other, with 3,958 acres in oats in 1875 and 4,608 acres in 1895. Such large parochial acreages, with over half the parishes in each year having well over 2,000 acres in oats, were unusual elsewhere in the south-west. Only five other parishes (three in Ayrshire and two in Kirkcudbrightshire) had similar acreages.

Maybole had 3,152 acres under oats in 1875 and 3,169 in 1895. The next highest acreages outside Wigtownshire were Urr's 2,479 in 1875 and Tarbolton's 2,155 in 1895, but Wigtownshire had four parishes above Urr's figure for 1875 and eight parishes above Tarbolton's figure for 1895. Wigtownshire's parishes with less than 2,000 acres under oats were the hill parishes or those which had a small total acreage, or were urban: in each year Kirkcowan, New Luce, Portpatrick, Sorbie, Stranraer and Wigtown were in the group, though apart from the exceptional experience of Stranraer, only the two distinctly upland parishes of New Luce in both 1875 and 1895, and Kirkcowan in 1895, fell below 1,000 acres.

TABLE 5.4

			Number of parishes with acreages under wheat of								
		Nil	−50	50+	100+	200+	300+	400+	500+	600+	700+	800+
Ayrshire	1875	3	20	7	6	5	1	3	–	1	–	–
	1895	23	15	7	1	–	–	–	–	–	–	–
Nithsdale	1875	7	4	1	–	–	–	–	–	–	–	–
	1895	12	–	–	–	–	–	–	–	–	–	–
Kirkcudbrightshire	1875	16	8	3	–	1	–	–	–	–	–	–
	1895	23	5	–	–	–	–	–	–	–	–	–
Wigtownshire	1875	2	2	2	4	2	2	1	–	–	–	2
	1895	8	7	1	1	–	–	–	–	–	–	–
TOTAL	1875	28	34	13	10	8	3	4	–	1	–	2
	1895	66	27	8	2	–	–	–	–	–	–	–

The domination of oats meant that few parishes had large acreages of other grain crops. About three-quarters were growing some wheat in 1875, including almost all those in Ayrshire and Wigtownshire, though less than half in Kirkcudbrightshire and Nithsdale, but the amounts grown were generally small. By 1895 wheat was virtually eliminated from the south-west except for a few favoured pockets.

Nearly two-thirds grew no wheat: all 12 parishes in Nithsdale and all except five, accounting for a mere 50 acres between them, in Kirkcudbrightshire. A few parishes in Ayrshire and Wigtownshire had large acreages in 1875 but not by 1895. In 1875 Ayrshire had 16 of its 46 parishes growing over 100 acres of wheat with Maybole's 665 acres the highest; Wigtownshire had 11 of its 17 parishes doing likewise, with Stoneykirk's 832 and Kirkmaiden's 847 much greater than any others. In 1895 23 parishes in Ayrshire grew some wheat but only St Quivox, with 108 acres, was above 100. The reduction in the cultivation of wheat in Wigtownshire was as marked: nine of the 17 parishes grew some but only Kirkmaiden with 224 acres was above 100.

TABLE 5.5

| | | Number of parishes with acreages under barley of | | | | | | | | |
		Nil	–50	50+	100+	200+	300+	400+	500+	600+
Ayrshire	1875	5	32	3	3	1	1	–	–	1
	1895	18	23	1	2	1	–	1	–	–
Nithsdale	1875	1	9	2	–	–	–	–	–	–
	1895	9	3	–	–	–	–	–	–	–
Kirkcudbrightshire	1875	4	21	2	1	–	–	–	–	–
	1895	21	6	1	–	–	–	–	–	–
Wigtownshire	1875	1	10	–	2	2	2	–	–	–
	1895	5	6	3	2	–	1	–	–	–
TOTAL	1875	11	72	7	6	3	3	–	–	1
	1895	53	38	5	4	1	1	1	–	–

Barley was cultivated more widely, even in 1895, but in very small quantities to some extent because of harvesting difficulties. Though only 11 of all 103 parishes grew no barley at all in 1875, only 20 grew more than 50 acres; in 1895 even this limited cultivation had been reduced: 53 parishes, just over half the total, grew none. As with wheat, the larger acreages, though small, were in Ayrshire and Wigtownshire. In both 1875 and 1895 they contained all the parishes in the south-west which grew more than 100 acres, except for Kirkbean's 104 acres in Kirkcudbrightshire in 1875. The highest acreages in both years were in Ayrshire: Kirkoswald's 654 in 1875 and its 415 in 1895.

Every parish in the south-west grew some potatoes in both 1875 and 1895 but only in small quantities. In 1875 eleven parishes in Ayrshire had over 200 acres under potatoes but elsewhere only Stoneykirk in Wigtownshire with 284 acres was in that position. In 1895 it had 237 acres in potatoes but had been joined by Troqueer in

TABLE 5.6

		Nil	–50	50+	100+	200+	300+	400+	500+	600+	700+	800+	900+	1000+
						Number of parishes with acreages under potatoes of								
Ayrshire	1875	–	8	16	11	5	1	2	1	2	–	–	–	–
	1895	–	11	18	5	2	5	–	–	1	1	1	1	1
Nithsdale	1875	–	3	5	4									
	1895	–	–	–	–									
Kirkcudbrightshire	1875	–	10	12	6	–								
	1895	–	19	5	3	1								
Wigtownshire	1875	–	2	5	9	1								
	1895	–	3	8	5	1								
TOTAL	1875	–	23	38	30	6	1	2	1	2	–	–	–	–
	1895	–	42	35	15	4	5	–	–	1	1	1	1	1

TABLE 5·7

		Nil	−50	50+	100+	Number of parishes with acreages under turnips of 200+	300+	400+	500+	600+	700+	800+	900+	1000+	2000+
Ayrshire	1875	–	6	13	15	5	2	1	–	3	–	–	–	1	–
	1895	–	6	15	16	2	3	1	2	–	–	–	1	–	–
Nithsdale	1875	–	–	1	2	2	2	3	–	2	–	–	–	–	–
	1895	–	–	1	2	2	2	1	1	2	1	–	–	–	–
Kirkcudbrightshire	1875	–	1	–	2	2	6	3	6	4	1	1	–	2	–
	1895	–	1	–	2	2	6	4	5	3	3	–	–	2	–
Wigtownshire	1875	1	–	–	1	–	1	1	1	–	–	2	1	8	1
	1895	–	1	–	–	1	1	1	–	1	–	2	2	7	1
TOTAL	1875	1	7	14	20	9	11	8	7	9	1	3	1	11	1
	1895	–	8	16	20	7	12	7	8	6	4	2	3	9	1

Kirkcudbrightshire with 214 acres. Ayrshire was still ahead. It had 12 parishes with over 200 acres, stretching up to Kirkoswald's 1,139.

The turnip crop provided a contrast. Ayrshire grew relatively few, less than 200 acres each in 1875 in 34 of its 46 parishes and more than 500 acres in only four. In Nithsdale three of the 12 parishes grew less than 200 acres and two grew over 500. The greatest contrast was with Kirkcudbrightshire and even more so with Wigtownshire. In the former only three of its 28 parishes had less than 200 acres in 1875 and 14 grew over 500; in the latter only one of the 17 grew less than 200 acres (apart from Stranraer's nil return) and 15 grew more than 200.

The limited cultivation of roots, and especially of turnips, in north Ayrshire was the 'rotation without roots'[3] which had been evident early in the nineteenth century, and which was well established by its second half. The cultivation of turnips was virtually abandoned on the heavier clay soil in the early 1860s as the dairy farmers became more concerned with the state of their grassland. By then the upland farms, especially around Kilmarnock, concentrated on a special seven years rotation: two crops of oats in succession, then two of hay, followed by three years in pasture. A special feature was that the first hay crop was ryegrass, which was allowed to seed and was then threshed, a practice which brought strong condemnation from agricultural writers in the 1860s,[4] and a feeling of superiority from some in neighbouring areas where the practice of seeding was not followed. It was 'happily very little followed in Dumfriesshire'.[5] The practice was merely tolerated by the informed in the 1870s.[6] Later writers modified the condemnation, even while still disapproving,[7] largely because experience in north Ayrshire had shown that the practice was not as harmful there as many thought it should have been. It was notable that those who condemned the practice did not necessarily accompany their criticism by advocating the cultivation of large crops of roots. One was even critical of those landlords who insisted on extensive cultivation of roots when other feedingstuffs were available cheaply.[8] By the late nineteenth century there was an acceptance that the peculiar 'rotation without roots' suited some of the districts most given over to dairying.

The differences apparent within the parochial variety in arable practices spread from north Ayrshire to the south of the county and to Wigtownshire. The most striking difference is the one just mentioned, the difference in the cultivation of turnips. The sixteen parishes in Cunninghame had 1,408 acres in turnips or 15.9 per cent of Ayrshire's total of 8,865 in 1875. West Kilbride grew most—nearly 200 acres—because sheep were fed off turnips on the fields which produced the parish's early potatoes. Nine of the parishes in Cunninghame and ten of the remaining 30 in Ayrshire grew less than 100 acres of turnips in 1875 but only Stranraer in Wigtownshire (growing none because of its peculiar position), Carsphairn in Kirkcudbrightshire and Tynron in Nithsdale were in the same position. The contrast remained in 1895. In Ayrshire 21 parishes had less than 100 acres of turnips, 11 of them in Cunninghame, which had 1,720 or 26.5 per cent of the county's total 6,484 acres, a slightly higher share than in 1875. West Kilbride's 273 acres were again substantially greater than in any other parish in Cunninghame, almost double the next highest at Dreghorn.

The cropping of grain revealed by the agricultural statistics show how the agriculture of Kyle and especially of Carrick contrasted with that of Cunninghame and approximated to the practices of Wigtownshire. Carrick had some of the parishes with the largest acreages of oats in Ayrshire in 1875. Maybole had 3,152 acres and its 666 acres in wheat were also the highest in Ayrshire. Though acreages under barley were generally low, the six parishes which grew more than 100 acres were all in Carrick, Kirkoswald was the highest with 654 acres: the three other parishes in Carrick which grew less were generally in the uplands. By 1895 the arable practices of Carrick were still closer to Wigtownshire's. As in other parts of Ayrshire, the cultivation of wheat had been almost eliminated. Maybole grew only 59 acres. The four Ayrshire parishes which grew more than 100 acres of barley were all in Carrick, and, though once again Maybole had most, it had only 291 acres, and it had the largest acreage—3,169 acres—of the dominant oats crop.

It was, however, in the cultivation of roots that the differences were most conspicuous. Carrick never grew the same quantity of turnips as Wigtownshire, but much more than the rest of Ayrshire. In 1875 six of the seven Ayrshire parishes growing over 300 acres were in Carrick and the other three in Carrick had all high acreages compared with those in Cunninghame. In 1895 five of the seven Ayrshire parishes with over 300 acres of turnips were in Carrick.

If the cultivation of grain and of turnips took the pattern of agriculture in Carrick close to Wigtownshire's, its cultivation of potatoes was its own specialisation, rivalled only in the parishes of West Kilbride and St Quivox further north. In 1875 11 parishes in Ayrshire grew over 200 acres each and 12 in 1895. In 1875 Stoneykirk was the only parish in the south-west to have over 200 acres and in 1895 only Stoneykirk and Troqueer. Within Ayrshire Carrick's leadership was clear in both years. It had five of the 11 parishes with over 200 acres each in 1875 and six of the 12 in 1895. Of the five parishes with over 400 acres in 1875, three were in Carrick; in 1895 the acreages of all three had risen substantially to 2,958 of Ayrshire's total of 9,958 acres.

The key to the differences lies in the extent and nature of the concentration on dairying in the various parts of the south-west. Arable cultivation had often been subordinated to livestock husbandry and increasingly that meant to the needs of the dairy as the nineteenth century reached its close. The significance of dairying is evident in the south-west's high cattle population and, even more so, in its large number of cows/heifers in milk/calf. From the 1870s both increased more rapidly than in Scotland as a whole, so that the south-west's share of both in Scotland grew. The large and rising cattle population complemented the contrast between the arable husbandry of the south-west and other parts of Scotland. The south-eastern counties of Berwick and East Lothian had very small shares of the cattle and the cows/heifers in milk/calf in Scotland.

TABLE 5.8

| | Berwickshire | | East Lothian | |
| | cattle | cows/heifers | cattle | cows/heifers |
	%	%	%	%
1875	1.5	0.9	0.7	0.5
1895	1.4	0.7	0.8	0.4
1910	1.5	0.7	0.8	0.5

Superficially, the eastern counties from Fife to Moray were more comparable to the south-west. These six counties and six in the west (the four in the south-west with Lanark and Renfrew) had similar shares of the total cattle population in 1875, 1895 and 1910, but different shares of the cows/heifers in milk/calf in Scotland.

TABLE 5.9

| | Eastern counties | | Western counties | |
| | cattle | cows/heifers | cattle | cows/heifers |
	%	%	%	%
1875	31.1	23.6	28.3	35.4
1895	30.6	21.7	29.3	39.0
1910	30.2	21.3	31.2	40.5

This high proportion of cows/heifers in milk/calf to the total cattle was a feature of the cattle population of the dairying districts. Low proportions were common in the arable eastern counties and especially in some, notably Aberdeenshire, where there was a concentration of cattle. Counties with higher proportions, but small cattle populations, were in the far north and west where subsistence, or near-subsistence agriculture meant that a relatively high proportion of the total cattle stock was kept to meet domestic dairy needs. Others with high proportions of cows/heifers in milk/calf to total cattle stock also had large cattle populations in general. They were the specialists dairy producers. The six counties with the highest proportions in three years were:

TABLE 5.10

	1875 %		1895 %		1910 %
Renfrew	57.7	Renfrew	64.3	Renfrew	66.3
Lanark	50.9	Midlothian	57.0	Midlothian	62.1
Ayr	50.7	Dunbarton	55.9	Dunbarton	59.2
Midlothian	50.6	Lanark	53.6	Lanark	54.6
Dunbarton	47.3	Ayr	51.0	Ayr	52.2
Wigtown	47.2	Wigtown	49.8	Wigtown	49.7

The displacement of Ayrshire to join Wigtownshire in fifth and sixth places respectively was significant. The sharp increases in the proportions of cows/heifers in milk/calf to total cattle, which took Midlothian to second place, and was notable also in Renfrewshire and Dunbartonshire, were in counties which had, or were near to, large urban centres. Though they had high proportions of cows/heifers in milk/calf to total cattle, their total numbers of cows/heifers in milk/calf were much less than in the other three counties. In 1895 the counties of Renfrew, Midlothian and Dunbarton had 36,107 or 8.5 per cent of the total cows/heifers in milk/calf in Scotland, compared with 112,602 or 26.6 per cent of the Scottish total in Lanark, Ayr and Wigtown. The concentration of cows/heifers in milk/calf in Ayrshire and Wigtownshire was more remarkable as they did not have the same ready access as Lanarkshire to a large urban market for milk. It is an indicator of how the south-western counties, and especially Ayr and Wigtown, were the dairying specialists of Scotland by the end of the nineteenth century.

There were differences as the number of cows/heifers in milk/calf grew throughout the south-west in the later nineteenth century. In the pioneering districts of Cunninghame and Kyle the numbers continued to rise, by 12.6 per cent from 36,284 to 40,862 between 1875 and 1895. Twenty of the 37 parishes in Cunninghame and Kyle had over 1,000 cows/heifers in milk/calf each in 1875 and one more by 1895; Carrick had only three in both years. The absolute numbers in the north remained high but the rate of increase was not so rapid as further south, so that the share of Cunninghame and Kyle in the south-west's total fell slightly from 39.5 per cent in 1875 to 37.1 per cent in 1895. The greatest increase in the later nineteenth century was away from the pioneering dairying districts. The greatest, of 30 per cent, was in Kirkcudbrightshire, but its total numbers were still the smallest of the four counties. In 1875 none of its parishes had over 1,000 cows/heifers in milk/calf and only four in 1895. The high ground over much of the Stewartry was physically unsuitable for dairying and the attractions of sheep-rearing gave the upland areas an economically attractive alternative in any case. The four parishes which had over 1,000 cows/heifers in milk/calf in 1895, and which had also the highest numbers in 1875, were Borgue, Kirkcudbright, Kelton and Rerrick—all in the south away from the major areas of hill country. It was in Wigtownshire, however, that the spread of dairying produced a density of dairy cattle rivalling and in some ways exceeding, that of Cunninghame. Its overall increase in cows/heifers in milk/calf of 27.8 per cent was almost as great as Kirkcudbrightshire's and its absolute number was greater. In 1875 six of its 17 parishes had over 1,000 cows/heifers in milk/calf; in 1895, 13 had over 1,000. In 1875 four (Inch, Kirkcolm, Kirkmaiden and Stoneykirk) had each over 2,000; Stoneykirk had over 3,000. In 1895 Old Luce had joined them with over 2,000 and by then Stoneykirk had almost 4,000. Taken together the five parishes had 11,656 cows/heifers in milk/calf in 1875 and 13,650 in 1895, or 61.9 per cent and 56.7 per cent of the total in Wigtownshire in the two years. Even Cunninghame did not approach the concentration of dairying in parts of the Rhins of Galloway by the end of the nineteenth century.

Chapter 6

Working the Dairy

The need to milk a dairy herd regularly in a limited period of time proved a technical impediment to increasing the size of the farming unit. The optimum size of herd was small and suited the wide distribution of holdings in the south-west in small, but not the smallest units. In Ayrshire in 1836 one of 150 acres was considered large and 'generally speaking they are from 50 to 100 acres or 150 acres'.[1] That pattern was confirmed in the rest of the nineteenth century. When the continuous series of agricultural statistics started in the mid 1870s, about two-thirds of the holdings in the south-west were less than 100 acres and not quite ten per cent above 500 acres. The large units, notably in Ayrshire, were the sheep farms in the hill areas. The south-west did not have the high proportion of very small holdings common in some parts of Scotland, but had a higher proportion in the range of from 50 to 300 acres (50.2 per cent in Ayrshire; 41.8 per cent in Dumfriesshire; 42.9 per cent in Kirkcudbrightshire; 46.7 per cent in Wigtownshire; compared with 26.8 per cent in Scotland). This 'moderate size'—defined as from 100 to 300 acres—was considered most profitable in the late nineteenth century.[2]

In the twentieth century a convenient source for a wider examination of the scale of landholding is in an analysis of the distribution of gross rentals shown in the valuation rolls for 1906, and which may be taken as representative of conditions prior to 1914.[3] The south-west had 10,065 or 11.3 per cent of the total number of 89,065 holdings in Scotland in 1906. Ayrshire had 3,212 (3.6 per cent of those in Scotland); Dumfriesshire, 3,415 (3.8 per cent); Kirkcudbrightshire, 1,956 (2.2 per cent); and Wigtownshire, 1,482 (1.7 per cent). The south-west's characteristic distribution of holdings is evident by comparison with conditions in Scotland generally. It fell between two extremes. The first extreme was represented by those counties which had very high proportions of their total holdings with small gross annual rentals of under £50, generally in the Highlands and Islands. Caithness, Orkney, Inverness, Ross, Sutherland, Shetland each had over 90 per cent in that category which ensured that Scotland as a whole had 69.9 per cent of its holdings below £50 annual rental. The south-western counties had relatively small proportions in this low-rented group. Ayrshire's was exceptionally low at 26.3 per cent. Dumfriesshire's 57.9 per cent was the highest; Nithsdale's alone was 51.2 per cent, Kirkcudbrightshire's was 50.1 per cent and Wigtownshire's was 48.4 per cent. Only six counties in Scotland away from the south-west had proportions lower than Nithsdale's 51.2 per cent: West Lothian, 48.4 per cent; Lanark, 46.4 per cent; Berwick, 45.8 per cent; Peebles, 37.4 per cent; Renfrew, 33.0 per cent; Midlothian, 5.6 per cent. The south-west was not then an area where holdings with very small gross rentals prevailed, which distinguishes its structure most sharply and obviously from the Highlands and Islands, and also from the counties of the north-east, which were near the overall Scottish percentage of 69.9: Banff was above it with 74.9 per cent; Moray and Aberdeen were almost identical at 69.2 and 69.1 per cent respectively.

The second extreme was represented by counties which had substantial proportions of their holdings in the high rental group, those with gross annual rentals in excess of £300. Two groups of counties with different patterns of agriculture fell into that category: those which had the best arable stretches in Scotland and those with large sheep farms. These were Midlothian, East Lothian and Berwick on the one hand and Peebles, Selkirk and Roxburgh on the other. The proportion in the high-rented category reached double figures in no other county and led to a low Scottish figure of only 3.6 per cent. All four counties of the south-west had similar proportions of rentals of £300 and over: Kirkcudbright was the highest at 8.2 per cent and Wigtown was the lowest at 6.6 per cent.

In contrast to the extremes, the south-west had more in the middle-rented category. Ayrshire led, with 66.9 per cent of its holdings with rentals of between £50 and £300 and 39.7 per cent between £50 and £150. Because it had so many holdings in the low-rented category, Dumfriesshire naturally had less in the middle-rented group. Yet its 35.1 per cent was still above the Scottish percentage of 26.5 per cent. The figure for Nithsdale alone was 41.2 per cent, bringing it near to those for Kirkcudbrightshire (41.7 per cent) and Wigtownshire (45.0 per cent).

Counties other than those in the south-west which had more than 40 per cent of the holdings with gross rentals of £50 to £300 had large urban conurbations within their bounds or were immediately adjacent to them. That they were also dairying districts is confirmed by their number of cows/heifers in milk/calf in 1906.

TABLE 6.1

| County | Cows/heifers in milk/calf | Holdings of £50–300 rentals | |
		number	% age of total holdings
Renfrew	17,451	1,108	61.5
Lanark	39,710	1,751	49.1
Midlothian	11,894	338	46.3

Together these three had 15.9 per cent of Scotland's cows/heifers in milk/calf in 1906 and 13.7 per cent of Scotland's holdings of £50 to £300 rentals. A similar concentration is evident in the four counties of the south-west.

TABLE 6.2

| County | Cows/heifers in milk/calf | Holdings of £50–300 rentals | |
		number	% age of total holdings
Ayr	51,414	2,145	66.9
Dumfries	21,503	1,198	35.1
Kirkcudbright	16,819	815	41.7
Wigtown	24,708	669	45.0

The four counties had 26.3 per cent of Scotland's cows/heifers in milk/calf and 20.8 per cent of Scotland's holdings of £50 to £300 rental. Together these seven counties had 42.2 per cent of the cows/heifers in milk/calf and 34.5 per cent of the middle-rented holdings.

The parochial statistics show how most in the south-west conformed to the general pattern. The few parishes which had more holdings than usual in the small rental category of under £50 a year generally embraced the burghs or their landward parts, where the land tended to be split into much smaller holdings than was usual. Dumfriesshire had the only six parishes in the four counties of the south-west which had more than the Scottish proportions of 69.9 per cent, and all were near the urban settlements which encouraged the growth of the small holdings. They were, Dumfries (landward), 72.0 per cent; Langholm, 87.7 per cent; Lochmaben (landward), 70.6 per cent; Moffat, 77.5 per cent; Morton, 82.2 per cent; Torthorwald, 72.6 per cent. Annan (landward) followed at 68.2 per cent, but there was then a gap to the more strictly agricultural parishes, led by Wamphray at 63.7 per cent. The three other counties were not comparable. Kirkcudbrightshire had two over 60 per cent: Crossmichael at 63.9 per cent and Kirkcudbright (landward) at

63.0 per cent. Wigtownshire also had only two over 60 per cent and both were close to settlements: Leswalt at 60.8 per cent and Wigtown (landward) at 60.0 per cent. Ayrshire was different yet again. Dalmellington had 64.7 per cent in the low rental category and Monkton and Prestwick had 64.6 per cent, but the former had only 34 holdings and was a mining parish; the latter was near some urban settlement, some of them mining communities, and was affected by the ancient rights of Prestwick's freemen.

Parishes with a larger number of farms in the highest rented category of over £300 a year were those with some of the south-west's rare arable stretches or with sheep walks. Ayrshire had 223 such farms; Dumfriesshire had 238; Kirkcudbrightshire, 160; Wigtownshire, 95. The whole of Scotland had 3,510. Twelve parishes in Ayrshire had more than eight farms each in the category; ten in Dumfriesshire, nine in Kirkcudbrightshire, and eight in Wigtownshire. The parish with the farms with the highest rent in the whole south-west—in the range of £2,500 to £3,00—was Borgue, but it had only seven farms in the higher range. The importance of good arable land, especially particularly favoured ground such as the early potato fields of Ayrshire, gave rise to a large number of its higher rented farms. The parish of Maybole had 20, followed by 16 in Ayr (landward). A few highly-rented sheep farms were found in Carsphairn and in Dalry in Kirkcudbrightshire, which had nine each, and in the Nithsdale parishes of Closeburn, Durisdeer, Kirkconnel and Sanquhar.

The detailed distribution of holdings in parishes with large numbers of cows/heifers in milk/calf in north Ayrshire and in the Rhins of Galloway shows their characteristic pattern of landholding. All had a large number of holdings in the range of £50 to £300 gross annual rentals in 1906. Though some had good arable stretches, as in Kirkmaiden and in Stoneykirk, farms with high rentals were few, especially in north Ayrshire. There was one significant difference between the two districts. The Wigtownshire parishes had higher proportions of farms at the lowest rentals. Their very small farms helped provide a larger labour force for the areas of greater arable cultivation, especially for its root crops. In contrast, north Ayrshire was supremely the area of the family dairy farm.

Small holdings were effective economic units for dairying when the physical difficulties of milking large numbers of dairy cows limited the advantages of larger herds. In the main concentrations in Ayrshire and Wigtownshire the typical size of herds varied. Ignoring holdings of under 40 acres, the typical dairy farm in Cunninghame and Kyle was described in the 1860s as being between 100 and 120 acres, and larger by perhaps about 50 acres or more in Carrick, with a milking stock of 18 to 22 cows, and turning out one cheese daily during the season. The successful manufacture of Cheddar cheese was considered to require a larger herd of about 30 cows or more, and so in Wigtownshire, where more cheese was made, the size of herd was more dispersed. It was estimated in the 1870s variously at 20 or 40 to 100 and in the 1880s at 20 to 140, though commonly 60 to 80.[4] Even in Wigtownshire, near towns and villages, where the milk was sold fresh or made into butter, as it was more often in Ayrshire, herds were as low as 20. At the other extreme were some farms with up to 200 cows, but maintained in different dairies as 100 were thought the maximum which it was expedient to herd together.

In the smaller units, especially those of Cunninghame and Kyle, the family provided most of the labour, often only one unmarried servant living in,[5] the traditional 'boy for byres' of later newspaper advertisements. Their dairies were too small to offer suitable employment to skilled persons and responsibility for them devolved entirely on the wives and daughters of the farmers.[6] The dairy farmers 'themselves, wives, sons, and daughters ...' were 'all the year round, being worked like slaves'.[7] For them there was no rest, even after six days labour:

> Dairying entails a seven day week, and the scene at Kilmarnock on a Sabbath morning when the milk is being shipped awakens considerable misgivings on the part of the onlooker. He can imagine the excess of labour undergone by all hands on the farm before the milk has been brought so far, then the labour in shipping and the labour in distribution.[8]

Some regular labour was employed except on the smallest units. The highly knowledgeable John Speir, whose origins were in the dairying districts of Cunninghame, suggested 'generally about two or three or four on each farm' in 1895. He also held that '... every family in most of them ... are by far too hard working ... The farmers in most cases do a great proportion of the work; even the wives in many cases do the bulk of the cheese-making ... They work, and work very hard'.[9] A decade later the editor of *The Scottish Farmer* Andrew MacNeilage, again with roots in the south-west, explained the conditions more fully. On a farm of 140 acres, which was one of average size, the typical labour force was 'one ploughman, one odd man ("orra" man in the north), who assists in the byre and delivers the milk, one harvester (in season), four women workers—i.e. two girls, one for house, and the other for dairy and byre, and these, along with other two milkers, constitute the female staff'.[10]

The heavy dependence on family labour was clearly feasible only in the small dairy farms, especially those in Ayrshire which were more dependent on exploiting the market for liquid milk and less on the manufacture of cheese. In the larger dairies family labour remained important but inadequate. The result was the growth of the system of bowing, which persisted in a modified form in a few cases until after the Second World War. The general principle behind bowing was that the farmer, who may well have been a tenant himself, supplied practically all the capital, working as well as fixed. The dairy herd was supplied with pasture in summer and feeding stuffs in winter, one writer of 1876 suggesting 'the usual allowance being five or six tons of swede and common turnips per cow, with 2 $1/2$ cwt. of beanmeal, and hay and straw'.[11] The allowance of grass and feeding stuffs varied to compensate for any deficiencies in the quality of the farm on the assumption that the critical point in dairying was not in the field, or to quote one of the most skilled cheesemakers in the later nineteenth century: 'Cheese is not made in the field, or in the byre, or even in the cow, *it is made in the dairy*'.[12] The bowers' agreements ran usually for a year from Martinmas, but they were frequently renewed. Payment was in money or kind. If in money the rate was based on each cow, ranging from about £8 to £15 in the 1870s to £12 to £18 before 1914. Part-payment in cheese was common in the larger Wigtownshire dairies, and in the 1870s was from 17 to 20 Ayrshire stones of 24 lbs. each. The latter was an attractive arrangement when bowers were often unknown to the farmers and had no capital.

As with many of the tenant farmers who spread dairying throughout the south-west, many bowers came from the small family farms of Ayrshire in which many of the dairying skills had first been developed. The tenure provided the larger farmers with access to the skills of the bowers and gave the bowers, with skills and with a reputation with their families of being 'hard-working, industrious people',[13] but with little or no capital, a way of acquiring some capital and an independent reputation, which enabled them to take full tenancies of farms later. It was a striking method of social mobility, 'the first step towards his becoming a farmer'.[14]

Extensive bowing emerged in the dairying areas after the Napoleonic Wars, and by the later nineteenth century was described as 'pretty

common'[15] in Ayrshire and 'the almost universal custom'[16] in Kirkcudbrightshire and Wigtownshire. It remained common until the First
World War but was gradually abandoned as farmers took dairies
under their own control and employed a full-time dairyman or
dairymaid, relatively highly paid, sometimes on the basis of sharing
the proceeds above a certain sum. There were good reasons for the
change. The successful operation of a bowing required harmonious
relations between both parties, but relations were so close that there
could easily be friction. Bowers were deemed 'sharp fellows'[17]—they
had to be to survive—and payment in kind was sometimes thought to
be advisable to ensure that they would not depart with the proceeds
of their sales, though this rarely happened.[18] Friction was more
common over details of the operation of the dairy herd. The agreement often specified the amount of cheese a bower had to supply
and on the other hand prescribed detailed feeding and grazing
arrangements. Difficulties could then easily arise from any attempt
to change the provisions, perhaps necessary to exploit changing
opportunities in the markets for dairy products. As creameries
became more widely available, the need for the skills of the bower
declined.

When a dairyman was employed directly by the farmer instead
of a bower the result was often to pass the entire responsibility for
the dairy to another family, and so to perpetuate, not to change, the
family structure of agricultural work in the south-west. A full-time
dairyman also provided the labour, especially of milkers, from his
own family. Dairying was then very much an extended system of
family labour.

Whether the dairies were conducted chiefly by family labour,
bowers or employed dairymen, female labour played an essential
part. In Ayrshire 'every process connected with the milk, the
butter, or the cheese, is conducted by women'.[19] Not surprisingly,
the inadequacy of female labour was noted in the late nineteenth
century and could not be met by employing much of the casual
labour available for seasonal fieldwork. Though employment in the
dairy was often part-time, it was permanent, apart from seasonal
fluctuations in milk production. The milkers, each of whom could
deal with about ten cows in one and a half hours, were the leading
part-timers. Married men were expected to provide workers, especially milkers. Though such provisions were often not enforced, the
main objective in an engagement could be to obtain the milker rather
than the ploughman, and the milkers could be the determinants of
mobility.

The great cause of removing in a dairy district is the milkers, every cotman being bound to supply a milker; This in many cases necessitates a second class man to be taken, on account of his supplying one or two good milkers, when it is found he is unfit for the work required of him, and has to be parted with. The milkers themselves too are often the cause of removal, as when so many women meet twice a day in a byre very often they quarrel amongst themselves, and some of them have to be removed in order to have quiet restored.[20]

Apart from the milkers, dairies necessitated skilled dairymaids, especially when cheesemaking on any scale was carried out. As early as 1802 Sir John Sinclair had suggested, as the second of three requirements for extending a dairy farm: 'To procure an attentive and skilful dairy-maid, as the whole success of the undertaking must depend upon her good conduct'.[21] In the 1890s, 'A good chief dairymaid, especially in a cheese-making district, is difficult to obtain, and the remuneration required is said to be constantly rising',[22] and John Speir was suggesting that this difficulty was leading to the use of milking machines,[23] though his faith in the march of scientific progress was not always realised.

TABLE 6.3   DISTRIBUTION OF EMPLOYMENT IN AGRICULTURE, FORESTRY AND FISHING BETWEEN MALES AND FEMALES

	Ayr		Dumfries		Kirkcudbright		Wigtown		Scotland	
	M	F	M	F	M	F	M	F	M	F
1841	96.1	3.9	75.0	25.0	90.4	9.6	93.4	6.6	90.7	9.3
1851	80.1	19.9	81.0	19.0	80.8	19.2	89.1	10.9	80.8	19.2
1861	82.5	17.5	78.2	21.8	80.8	19.2	85.1	14.5	83.5	16.5
1871	83.0	17.0	77.7	22.3	84.0	16.0	85.8	14.2	84.3	15.7
1881	76.2	23.8	80.0	20.0	83.4	16.3	0.9	19.1	79.3	20.7
1891	84.8	15.2	86.7	13.3	90.2	9.8	84.0	16.0	87.7	12.3
1901	80.1	19.9	87.6	12.4	90.7	9.3	82.1	17.9	87.5	12.5
1911	83.2	16.8	90.7	9.3	91.7	8.3	84.7	15.3	89.6	10.4

Source: C H Lee, *British regional employment statistics, 1841–1871* (Cambridge, 1979).[24] (Much of the information on female employment in the censuses, especially for 1841, must be treated with care as it is not always reliable.)

It is instructive to examine in detail the demand for female labour in the agriculture of the south-west in the nineteenth century. Male and female participation in employment was similar throughout the area and comparable to Scottish experience, but the ratios of male to female in the agricultural labour force of the four counties differed. In 1851 the proportions were similar, except in Wigtownshire, which had a lower proportion of females. Thereafter the proportion of females in Kirkcudbrightshire declined steadily; in Dumfriesshire it fell after 1871 and by 1911 the proportions for the two counties were almost the same. Employment in the agriculture of both was male-dominated. The experiences of Ayrshire and Wigtownshire provided a contrast. In the latter the proportion of females in the labour force rose from its low level in 1841 until 1881, though always below the Scottish figures, while in the former the proportion, though always above the Scottish figure, fell and rose again to its highest value of 23.8 per cent in 1881. The experiences of the two dairy counties converged from 1881. Ayrshire and Wigtownshire were then counties which offered relatively greater opportunities to females than to males in agriculture in the later nineteenth and early twentieth centuries.

The same conclusion emerges from a consideration of the absolute numbers employed. While male employment in the four counties fell more heavily than in Scotland as a whole between 1851 and 1911, and more heavily in Ayrshire and Wigtownshire than in Dumfriesshire and Kirkcudbrightshire, the number of females employed in agriculture fell only slightly more extensively in Dumfriesshire and Kirkcudbrightshire than in Scotland as a whole. In Ayrshire it fell less and hardly at all in Wigtownshire. In the latter the increase in the employment of females in 1881 compensated for much of the decline of males. Where agriculture was strongest in the local economy, female labour was in demand.

The labour requirements of the dairying districts of the south-west were then very different from many other parts of Scotland. The small farms being dependent on family labour, and the larger units being let out to bowers or worked by hired dairymen, meant that an important source of labour was an extended family system. The social mobility afforded by bowing and the opportunities for females as skilled and well-paid dairymaids in addition to a wider demand for female labour in the byres were characteristics of the social structure of the south-west. The additional demand for milkers was not for casual, but for permanent, though part-time labour, which provided a stable demand for long periods and was not simply the extraordinarily heavy demand for short periods required by activities confined to a much shorter season. To meet such contingencies Irish labour was present. In these conditions comparisons between the experience of the south-west and other parts of Scotland break down. The Irish migrant and the strength of dairying in the nineteenth century gave the area too many distinct characteristics.

Part III

LANDOWNERSHIP

Chapter 7

Who Owned the Land?

The owner occupier, who was to become increasingly common after the First, and more so after the Second World War, was virtually unknown in much of the south-west before 1914. There were some, notably in north Ayrshire, but their holdings were small and insignificant in total. The changes in agricultural practice which led to the introduction of dairying and to the emergence of a new race of farmers took place on the basis of an apparently firm pattern of ownership of land by a few proprietors.

The basis of the stability was less secure than it appeared to the casual observer. The social and political power of the landowners lingered from the past, but it was a wasting asset as its economic and political foundations crumbled. Agriculture no longer provided a secure economic base for the landlord's prestige, partly because of its own declining fortunes, partly because its contribution to national prosperity was being swamped by industrial and commercial achievement. Changing political power removed some of the landowners' prestige nationally, but it continued locally in the south-west until 1914 because, apart from parts of north Ayrshire, there was little challenge to the landlords' domination by a new race of industrialists. The social structure of the south-west changed less radically because it did not have the industrial capabilities of other regions. Few of its leading proprietors had much landed property elsewhere, and, though once again Ayrshire was an exception, the affluent industrialists and merchants who joined the landed proprietors in the south-west did so to share their prestige and did not spread their holdings into the area so extensively that they challenged those already established. Though the landowners' prestige persisted locally, it was no more secure in the long run. The Return of landholding published in the 1870s[1] shows its distribution before the disintegration started. It does much more. It shows the declining importance of the agricultural rent roll in the economic fortunes of the landowners and the way in which their prosperity was more likely to increase if derived from non-agricultural sources.

The Return was based on information in valuation rolls. Comparisons with the rentals of estates where it is possible to make them show that the valuation rolls are generally reliable records of the rents charged though not always of those paid. The reliability of the Return itself, especially its coverage, was questioned when it was first published and was subjected to a thorough investigation by John Bateman shortly afterwards.[2] His work provides greater confirmation of its reliability for the south-west than for other areas. 'The Scotch and Irish returns, as regards workmanship, compare most favourable with the English—the Scotch returns being, however, undoubtedly the best ... Even Scottish counties, like English ones, vary in degrees of goodness and badness; Kirkcudbrightshire being *facile princeps* in excellence ...'.[3]

There is no reason why the Return should not be used as a guide to the pattern of landholding in the south-west in the early 1870s at the start of the years of agricultural depression. A comparison of the information given in the Return with that given by Bateman shows some differences between the two. Many of them follow inevitably from the passage of time between the two and from the inclusion of additional material.[4] Such changes were likely to be greater in Scotland, which Bateman first tackled in the edition of his work in 1878, and which he continued to revise until the fourth and most reliable edition in 1883. The major differences were caused because new owners had entered into possession between the dates of the two compilations, sometimes leading to major changes in landholdings. In the south-west the Macadam-Cathcart estate was split on the succession of Frederick Macadam in 1878 and the Portland estate on the death of the fourth Duke in 1879.

The Return permits three tests to be applied in assessing the importance of landownership—acreage, the annual value of the land, and the gross annual valuation, which includes rental from industrial possessions, such as minerals. A striking example of how different tests change the relative standing of the landowners is in the position of the Duke of Portland. If ranked by acreage held in the south-west alone, he was twelfth; his 25,369 acres were far below the Duke of Buccleuch's 254,514, and even considerably below the next four from the top, from Mrs Macadam-Cathcart's 75,849 acres to the Earl of Stair's 83,158. The Duke of Portland, however, held some of the best agricultural land in Ayrshire, so, when judged by annual land values, he moved up to fourth place, his value of £35,125 being exceeded only by the Duke of Buccleuch's £94,618, the Earl of Stair's £44,002 and the Marquess of Ailsa's £38,825. Portland also had mineral and harbour rights, with an annual rental of £26,807, so that when judged by gross annual value of all kinds, he moved into second place with £62,732, second only to the Duke of Buccleuch's £97,630. The Earl of Eglinton, with holdings in Ayrshire similar to Portland's, moved into third place by gross annual value with £46,552, while the Earl of Stair and the Marquess of Ailsa went down to fourth and fifth places.

Landowners who had only poor quality land with limited non-agricultural potential moved downwards, sometimes dramatically. Mrs Macadam-Cathcart's 75,849 acres, split evenly on the hill country between Ayrshire and Kirkcudbrightshire, placed her fifth in order of landowners by the acreage held. The poor quality of the land gave it a rental of only £15,101, placing her fourteenth in rank by annual land value, though the possession of minerals of value of £8,734 in Ayrshire raised her to tenth place in the order given by gross annual value. William Forbes of Callendar, with 43,464 acres, mostly in Kirkcudbrightshire, and Edward Stopford-Blair of Penninghame, with 37,268 acres in Wigtownshire, had no such advantages and so moved from ninth and tenth places by acreage, to twenty-third and twenty-fifth places by annual land value and to twenty-fifth and twenty-eighth places by gross annual value respectively.

A more general demonstration of how ranking changed with the application of different tests follows from an examination of the alterations in the position of the top ten by acreage when the two other tests are applied, and demonstrates the misleading nature of many assessments of ranking by the popular test of acreage. (See Table 7.1). When ranking is determined by annual land values, instead of by acreage, four proprietors are eliminated from the list of the top ten and the position of three others lowered. All, especially the four who were eliminated, owned large tracts of poor quality hill land or moss. The four new-comers to the list held better quality land: Portland and Eglinton in Ayrshire; Selkirk in Kirkcudbrightshire; Oswald in both. When the ranking is determined by total gross annual values, Portland and Eglinton continue to rise and displace Stair and Ailsa from second and third place: Oswald and Bute each rise one place, transferring positions with Galloway and Johnstone respectively. The possession of land in the industrialising districts of Ayrshire was the key to the higher ranking of all these proprietors. Buccleuch's position as leader remained unchanged, whatever the test. When ranking is determined, not by acreage, but by annual land value or gross annual value, Portland and Eglinton emerged as leaders while Galloway and those whose land was in the less fertile parts declined in importance. The south-west was an area where the location of land led to considerable differences in the wealth and prospects of individual proprietors.

TABLE 7.1   TEN LARGEST LANDOWNERS IN THE SOUTH-WEST

By acreage	By annual land value	By annual gross values
Duke of Buccleuch	Duke of Buccleuch	Duke of Buccleuch
Earl of Stair	Earl of Stair	Duke of Portland
Earl of Galloway	Marquess of Ailsa	Earl of Eglinton
Marquess of Ailsa	Duke of Portland	Earl of Stair
Mrs Macadam-Cathcart	Earl of Eglinton	Marquess of Ailsa
J Johnstone of Annandale	Earl of Galloway	R A Oswald of Auchincruive
Marquess of Bute	R A Oswald of Auchincruive	Earl of Galloway
H Murray-Stewart of Broughton	J Johnstone of Annandale	Marquess of Bute
W Forbes of Callendar	Marquess of Bute	J Johnstone of Annandale
E S Blair of Penninghame	Earl of Selkirk	Earl of Selkirk

The appropriate ranking of landowners to be adopted depends on the problem being investigated. If it is the social and economic importance of the landowners in agricultural and rural life, then it is possible to exclude from consideration the information in the Return on the land and mineral holdings of industrial undertakings and of railway companies and to pay less attention to industrial valuations which were chiefly of minerals. Those whose land had a high gross annual value because of its industrial capabilities had the advantage of being able to draw support from other sources to bolster their rural activities, but the benefits of industrial values revealed in the gross annual value of land in the Return affected only a few and is better left for separate and more specific discussion. The best test to apply, initially at any rate, is that of land value. The possession of more valuable land gave rise to a degree of influence in the social and economic life of what was still chiefly a rural society beyond what was open to those with more extensive but less valuable land.

The Return listed 17,759 owners of land of one acre and above in the south-west: Ayrshire had 9,376, including 1,006 in the burgh of Kilmarnock; Dumfriesshire, 4,177; Kirkcudbrightshire, 2,386; Wigtownshire, 1,820. Most owned very little. Ownership was concentrated in a few hands. At the top a mere four proprietors had each over £35,000 of annual land values (Buccleuch—by far the largest proprietor, Stair, Ailsa and Portland). Together their holdings accounted for 11.1 per cent of the total annual land value of the south-west. Seven had acreages in excess of 50,000—Buccleuch, Stair, Galloway, Ailsa, Macadam-Cathcart, Johnstone of Annandale, and Bute—and they held 30.5 per cent of the land area. They were the largest proprietors by far and show how the test of acreage can present evidence of more concentrated ownership than the test of land values.

When the number of owners is increased the proportion of land held by them rose much less steeply, by whatever test is applied. To show the distribution it is useful to classify the owners of much of the land in two groups: the major landholders, who had annual land values of over £2,000 in the four counties of the south-west, and lesser proprietors, whose holdings were valued at between £1,000 and £2,000 annually. The first group had 121 owners and the second had 127, a total of 248. The 121 major landowners had 50.6 per cent of the land value, and 73.3 per cent of the acreage. The addition of the second group of 127 landowners, those with holdings of annual land value of £1,000 to £2,000, did not alter the position dramatically. When combined, the total of 248 landowners had 60.1 per cent of the annual land value and 82.8 per cent of the acreage. So much was owned by so few. With such a large proportion of the total acreage of the south-west owned by only 1.4 per cent of the proprietors of land of over one acre, the dominant economic and social position of the few is evident.

The position in the four counties varied sharply in some ways. Of the 121 who had holdings of over £2,000 annual land value in the four counties taken together, 17 had land in two counties and two in three, so that, when the holdings of the 121 are split between the four counties, the number rises from 121 to 142: 56 in Ayrshire, 32 in Dumfriesshire, 36 in Kirkcudbrightshire, 18 in Wigtownshire. The reduction in the size of holdings which followed this distribution between the four counties lowered the number of proprietors with holdings of over £2,000 annual land value in each county to: 52 in Ayrshire; 28 in Dumfriesshire; 29 in Kirkcudbrightshire; 17 in Wigtownshire.

The larger areas of infertile hill country in the south-west ensured a similar contrast in each county between the more concentrated ownership when judged by acreage than when judged by annual land value. The contrast was most evident in Ayrshire, where the land had the greatest diversity in agricultural potential. The top 16 owners held 53.6 per cent of the county's acreage, but even the 52 who each held land in Ayrshire valued at £2,000 and over had only 42.3 per cent of the annual land value of the county. Individual holdings demonstrate the same conditions: Ailsa's 76,015 acres were valued at £35,825 annually and Mrs Macadam-Cathcart's 35,960 acres were valued at £9,427. At the other extreme possession of a much smaller acreage of fertile land led to a higher annual value, such as Oswald of Auchincruive's 11,004 acres valued at £14,297. Smaller properties in the more fertile areas explain the high ratio of annual land values to acreage among those with £1,000 to £2,000 rentals. Fifty-five such proprietors had 10.9 per cent of the acreage and 9.5 per cent of the land value of the county. Similar contrasts can be drawn in Dumfriesshire and Kirkcudbrightshire but in Wigtownshire more land of relatively good fertility, and with the hill areas more narrowly confined, ensured less marked contrasts. Four landowners had 52.8 per cent of its acreage and four had 43.0 per cent of its annual land value.

A distinction of social as well as of economic significance can be drawn between Ayrshire and Kirkcudbrightshire on the one hand and Dumfriesshire and Wigtownshire on the other. The latter pair had each one major landowner—Buccleuch in Dumfriesshire and Stair in Wigtownshire—with holdings on a scale not matched by any proprietor in the other two counties. The result was that in Ayrshire the top two had 8.3 per cent of the annual land value and 16.6 per cent of the acreage; in Kirkcudbrightshire the figures were 10.9 and 17.8 per cent; but in Dumfriesshire they were 24.9 and 46.9 per cent; and in Wigtownshire, 30.8 and 38.8 per cent. The percentages for the top ten were: Ayrshire 24.0 per cent of land value and 42.9 per cent of acreage: Kirkcudbrightshire, 29.5 and 49.8 per cent; Dumfriesshire, 40.1 and 61.7 per cent; Wigtownshire, 63.7 and 74.9 per cent. The more restricted spread of ownership in Dumfriesshire and Wigtownshire meant that half the acreage was owned by four proprietors in each and 21 and six proprietors respectively had half the annual land values; in Ayrshire and Kirkcudbrightshire the comparable figures were 14 and ten proprietors with half the acreage and 46 and 39 with half the land value respectively.

Most landowners in the south-west had the bulk of their land in one county only. Of the 19 proprietors of total land with an annual value of £2,000 or more in the south-west who also held land in more than one county, 11 had land in the south-west valued at £1,000 or more other than in the county of their main holding, and one had holdings of that amount in two other counties. Only six had annual land value of £2,000 and more in one other county.[5]

Landowners with such widespread holdings were found in all four counties. The 11 with holdings valued annually at £1,000 and more in a south-western county other than that of their main holding were Galloway, Macadam-Cathcart, Bute, Murray-Stewart, Forbes, Oswald, McDouall of Logan, Moore of Corsewall, Mackenzie of Newbie, Ferguson of Craigdarroch and Maxwell of Orchardton. Two of this group had their main holding by annual land value in Ayrshire: Bute and Macadam-Cathcart. The former had 20,157 acres in Wigtownshire and 43,734 in Ayrshire. The value of the Ayrshire property, of £22,757 annual land value and £25,263 gross value, greatly exceeded the value of £2,937 in Wigtownshire which was on distinctly poor ground. His interests in the south-west were chiefly fixed in Ayrshire. Mrs Macadam-Cathcart's property stretched out over the county boundary between Ayrshire and Kirkcudbrightshire and was not split in any other significant way. Her interests, as with those of Lord Bute, were chiefly in Ayrshire, where her residence and her especially valuable mineral rights were. The difference in value on her estate in the two counties was marked. Her greater holding of 39,889 acres in Kirkcudbrightshire had an annual land value of £5,674 and the lesser 35,960 acres in Ayrshire a land value of £9,427 and a gross value of £18,161 annually.

In Dumfriesshire the county's large landowners held little land elsewhere in the south-west and what was held was compara- tively insignificant. For example, the greatest of them all, the Duke of Buccleuch, had 1,000 acres valued annually at £100 in Kirkcudbrightshire, a truly insignificant holding by his standard.

Similarly in Kirkcudbrightshire two of the largest landowners had interests in some of the other counties but not sufficient to affect their main concentration in one only. Murray-Stewart of Broughton and Cally had 1,584 acres in Wigtownshire. Though much less than the 45,867 acres in Kirkcudbrightshire, its relative annual land value of £1,707 was greater though absolutely small compared with the value of £14,616 of his holding in Kirkcudbrightshire. William Forbes' 40,445 acres of annual value of £7,640 in Kirkcudbrightshire swamped his 603 acres of £1,236 value in Ayrshire and his 2,416 of £732 value in Dumfriesshire. Two other landowners in the Stewartry had their properties more evenly distributed. Only one was a major proprietor. R A Oswald had 24,160 acres in Kirkcudbrightshire at Cavens and 11,004 acres in Ayrshire at Auchincruive; the former's annual land value was £16,185 and the latter £14,297 but increased by industrial interests to £17,827 gross annual value.

In Wigtownshire the interests of two landowners spread into Kirkcudbrightshire. McDouall of Logan had 2,600 acres there of annual value of £1,346 but 16,290 acres of £11,786 annual value in Wigtownshire. The Earl of Galloway had major holdings in both counties and is a rare example of a major landowner in both. Wigtownshire was also the county with the largest holding by annual land value of Carrick-Moore of Corsewall, whose total of £6,780 included 3,515 acres at £2,133 in Kirkcudbrightshire and 2,079 acres at £1,727 in Ayrshire, as well as 3,362 acres at £2,920 in Wigtownshire.

Two holdings of land in Ayrshire and Wigtownshire could be discussed conjointly. In the early 1870s they were held by closely related members of the same family, though their possessions were to move apart later. The Earl of Stair's interests extended significantly from Wigtownshire to Ayrshire through the Countess's possession of 19,266 acres of the Bargany estate, of annual land value of £12,764, and gross annual value of £13,616. Hunter-Blair had 12,610 acres at Blairquhan in Ayrshire of annual land value of £7,135 and his eldest son David, had 8,255 acres at Dunskey in Wigtownshire, of annual value of £4,948.

The large landowners therefore tended to have their south-western land holding concentrated in one county. The most notable exceptions were the Earl of Galloway, with extensive interests in both Wigtownshire and Kirkcudbrightshire, and, of lesser importance, R A Oswald, with interests in both Ayrshire and Kirkcudbrightshire. Taken together, the Earl and Countess of Stair had major interests in both Wigtownshire and Ayrshire. Mrs Macadam-Cathcart's spread of interests into Kirkcudbrightshire came from a border property with its basis in Ayrshire. Few other landowners had interests in more than one county and when their interests did spread, they were usually of limited importance. So it was with even the major landowners of Buccleuch, Ailsa, Portland, Eglinton and Johnstone of Annandale.

Each landowner could therefore be identified closely with a particular area, a concentrated interest which was not diluted by extensive holdings beyond the south-west. The further geographical concentration can be illustrated in two ways. The first is by examining the holdings beyond the south-west of the area's largest and most influential proprietors. Eighteen had 20,000 acres or £15,000 annual land value or both in the south-west. According to Bateman, seven of them had no holdings beyond its borders. The holdings in the south-west of the remaining eleven were mostly a large part of the total land holding by the crucial test of annual land value.[6] (See Table 7.2).

TABLE 7.2

Landowner	Annual land values (from Bateman) SW	Total	SW of Total %
Johnstone of Annandale	£27,884	£28,236	98.8
Selkirk	19,749	21,273	92.0
Eglinton	37,029	41,310	89.6
Murray-Stewart	16,323	22,822	71.5
Stair	43,452	67,905	64.1
Glasgow	13,856	34,588	45.6
Buccleuch	95,339	217,163	43.9
Forbes	11,100	25,442	43.6
Loudoun	15,286	39,977	38.2
Portland	19,671	88,350	22.3
Bute	25,692	151,135	17.0

A notable feature of all these landowners is that each played a leading role in the life of the south-west, the second means of viewing their geographical dominance. These leading roles were played partly because their holdings there, though sometimes only a small part of the total, were large and especially so in those counties in which they were located. So it was with Bute in Ayrshire and Wigtownshire, where he had 2.7 and 1.3 per cent of the total annual land values respectively; with Portland and Loudoun in Ayrshire, where they had 4.1 and 1.8 per cent of the annual land values; and above all with Buccleuch in Dumfriesshire, where he held 11.2 per cent of the annual land value. Forbes, was least influential, partly because, apart from his small property in Ayrshire, his holding in the south-west was of low-value hill ground, and partly because it was peripheral to his main concentration in Stirlingshire. An additional reason for his lack of influence may have been because he was a relative newcomer to the south-west.[7] The large landowners, whatever the size of their holdings elsewhere, were well-established in the south-west. Frequently they may not have lived on their properties in the south-west, or did so only occasionally, but their resident factors ensured a direct and personal interest.

By extending the analysis down the scale to include landowners with 10,000 acres and/or £5,000 in annual land value in the south-west, 45 more landowners are included and of those 11 held some land out of the south-west. (See Table 7.3). Of this second group of the lesser proprietors, two (Carrick Moore of Corsewall and Brown of Lanfine) had only trivial holdings elsewhere. Two aspects of the remainder of the group are worthy of comment. First, the land held by seven of them in the south-west was in Dumfriesshire, and second, three of the seven—Mansfield, Jardine of Lanrick and Herries—had sufficiently large holdings elsewhere that the balance of their interests was out of the south-west. When their widespread interests are combined with those of Buccleuch, Dumfriesshire was more noted than any other county of the south-west for landowners whose interests elsewhere were significant.

TABLE 7.3

Landowner	Annual land values (from Bateman) SW	Total	SW of Total %
Brown, Lanfine	£6,378	£6,523	97.8
Carrick-Moore, Corsewall	6,778	7,003	96.8
McDouall, Logan	13,132	14,441	90.9
Jardine, Castlemilk	11,232	13,382	83.9
Beattie, Crieve	3,105	4,020	77.2
Jardine, Lanrick	8,239	11,118	74.1
Johnstone, Westerhall	6,834	9,550	71.6
Johnstone-Stewart, Physgill	8,166	11,976	68.2
Walker, Crawfordton	3,542	6,883	51.1
Lord Herries	7,143	19,152	37.3
Earl of Mansfield	13,389	42,968	31.2

Lastly, it is then possible to suggest that the concentration of landholding in the hands of proprietors whose interests were mainly in the south-west was not offset by the presence in the area of large landowners whose interests were chiefly in other parts of the country. A rough test is to determine the relative importance of the holdings in the south-west of all those proprietors in the Return and also given by Bateman as possessing in total 10,000 acres and/or annual land values of £5,000 or over and who also had land in the south-west of 500 acres and/or annual land values of £250 per annum.[8] Only seven proprietors were in this category. (See Table 7.4).

In a few cases the proportion of their total holdings to be found in a south-western county was substantial, and was over 25 per cent of both the acreage they held and of the gross annual value it yielded in three cases: two in Ayrshire and one in Dumfriesshire, but in none of these three cases was the main interest of the landowner in the south-western county in which he held land. Of the two in Ayrshire, the base of the interests of William Mure was at Caldwell, just beyond the northern boundary of the county; the other case arose through the attribution of the Ayrshire property of Lady Oranmore and Browne to her husband's in County Mayo. In Dumfriesshire Lord Rollo's property did not counterbalance his main interests in Perthshire. Three of the others were large landowners—of the standing of possessing 50,000 acres and/or £25,000 annual land value in total—James Farquharson of Invercauld (though he held jointly with the Hon J Manners Yorke both of whom had married daughters of Oswald), the Earl of Home, and the Earl of Hopetoun, but their holdings were not great. The first and second held 1,760 and 2,271 acres respectively in Ayrshire and the third held 2,549 acres in Dumfriesshire.

TABLE 7.4

Landowner	Acres in the south-west of total %	Annual land value %
Sir R Abercromby (Kirkcudbrightshire)	11.4	15.0
J R Farquharson (Ayrshire)	1.6	14.6
Earl of Home (Ayrshire)	2.1	1.0
Earl of Hopetoun (Dumfriesshire)	6.0	4.3
W Mure (Ayrshire)	27.9	29.8
Lord Oranmore (Ayrshire)	39.6	42.5
Lord Rollo (Dumfriesshire)	41.6	26.6

In general then the south-western counties were not ones in which large landowners in other parts of the country had major holdings. The pattern of landownership in the south-west was one where most of the proprietors had a large part of their property in the south-west and indeed often in one county. Dumfriesshire tended to be more exceptional, though its domination by Buccleuch almost guaranteed it a category of its own. Such concentrated ownership, not only of a geographical area, but of the total holding of a proprietor, led some to hold dominating roles in the south-west and particularly in some parts of it. Examples were Selkirk and Galloway in different parts of Kirkcudbrightshire; Stair and Galloway again in Wigtownshire; Buccleuch and Johnstone of Annandale in Dumfriesshire; and Ailsa, Eglinton and Portland in Ayrshire.

The landowners of the south-west seemed firmly established in the 1870s. A century later some of the greatest and most influential had sold all, or virtually all of their landholding and the new race of owner-occupiers had come to dominate rural society. It is a social change of immense significance, which could hardly have been conceived by contemporaries before 1914.

Chapter 8

Attacking the Landowners

The landowners were easily identified and in the isolated self-contained communities typical of many of the more remote areas before 1914 an individual in possession of most of the land had such power and authority that it was easy to attribute all faults to him. The criticism was of long-standing, rooted in old contentions, but given additional virulence by the conditions of the later nineteenth century. The old contentions were often linked to the legal framework of the estate and the privileged position of the landlord in its operation, especially his powers over his tenantry. They gave rise to a festering resentment which continued after the issues had evaporated or had ceased to be onerous. Critical generalisations were often easier to sustain than detailed objections. That they failed to recognise regional variations is evident in the investigations made into two topics which affected the relations of landlord and tenant.

The entailing of land was one bone of contention. Its central features were the three cardinal prohibitions: an entailed estate could not be alienated from specified heirs; debts affecting the estate could not be contracted; the succession could not be altered. The adherence to such prohibitions was supported by clauses which nullified any contraventions of them and by others which ensured that any heir of entail became merely a pensioner for life of the estate, with little freedom to apply new and improved methods. Provision for entail was in a statute of 1685[1] and over 500 deeds were recorded in the Register of Tailizies (Entails) in Scotland by the later 1760s.[2] About twice as many deeds were recorded in the next 70 years, about 25 annually in the early nineteenth century. Not all deeds were separate entails by different landowners. Larger properties were entailed in stages: some deeds were amendments to earlier ones, and not all proved to be completely valid, though they were offset by others which were not registered, or the registration of which was delayed, but which were treated in practice as though they were. Various estimates have been made of the extent of land entailed, but any accuracy is impossible.

Almost as soon as the system was established it was subjected to criticism from the leading figures in the intellectual life of Scotland. Their criticism drew attention to a paradox. The statute of 1685 which provided for entails was passed at the same time as a series of others aimed at the improvement of agricultural practice, but it was suggested that improvement was more difficult to achieve on entailed estates. The only justification the critics could find for entailing land was to ensure the security of landed property when large estates were virtually independent principalities which had to rely on their own defensive capabilities. Almost as soon as the statutory provision was available, this justification was gone as the law could guarantee adequate security and entailed estates were considered a social and economic liability through impeding change in the ownership and use of landed property. Adam Smith was one who stated the criticism against their rigidity: 'They are founded upon the most absurd of all suppositions ... that the property of the present generation should be restrained and regulated according to the fancy of those who died perhaps five hundred years ago'.[3]

Attempts to limit entail were resented because of the attraction of ensuring a succession. The social desire to do so overrode economic objections to the procedure until the consequential economic difficulties became insuperable. From the later eighteenth century a series of acts modified the provisions. Some of the amending legislation was directly relevant to agricultural improvement. A start was made in the provision in an Act of 1770 (Montgomery Act) for the heir in possession to charge a certain proportion of expenditure against the estate as a means of encouraging improvements. The opportunities to do so were carefully restricted. The amount which could be borrowed was limited by the total rental of the estate and by the heir being able to borrow only a certain proportion of the total expenditure incurred: the borrowing could take place only after the expenditure had taken place and had been recorded in the register of improvements in the sheriff court, and since the security which could be offered was only the rents of the estate and not the property itself, the attractiveness of the security to the borrower was lessened. The Act was not wholly effective and trammelled the working of estates with complex legal restrictions and inhibitions. Subsequently, provisions for burdening entailed estates with family obligations and limited powers to sell parts of the estate paved the way for major legislation in 1848 (Rutherford Act), which gave the heir in possession restricted powers to disentail. Fresh entails were prohibited in 1914.[4]

The attack on entails which came in the nineteenth century was more practical than the intellectual case advanced against them in the previous century. It often took the form of criticism of the landowners, who were themselves confused in their attitudes to entails. The old desire to perpetuate the succession to the estate continued, giving rise to complicated provisions, as in the Stair and Selkirk successions. On the other hand restrictions often became intolerable in the effective conduct of the estates. Recognition of disadvantages as well as of advantages was clear in the evidence given to the Select Committee on Scotch Entails in 1828 by Patrick Irvine, WS and landowner in Aberdeenshire. The security an entail offered to the landowner remained the advantage which seemed attractive to those to whom the perpetuation of succession was of overriding importance: '... Scotch Entail ... by which the heirs of Entail can keep possession of the property so long as they do not disobey the terms of the Entail. The creditors cannot attack that property or estate in any matter or way; they may attack the rents but not the estate'. The disadvantage was the old one: 'the proprietors subjected to all the inconveniences arising from their restricted rights of property, and the hazard and expenses attending judicial discussion for the purpose of rendering effectual or of defeating the settlements of their predecessors'. Heirs of entail are 'deprived of the credit which the possession of property in land confers on all other classes of men'. In short, '... the restrictions imposed by Entails tend very strongly to prevent improvements'.[5]

The evidence given to the Committee on Scotch Entails was so consistent that in its second report of 1828 the Committee felt 'justified in reporting the prevalence of an universal opinion, that the law of Entail in Scotland demands immediate alteration and amendment'.[6] The only witness who offered more modified criticism was James Loch, a member of the Committee, who suggested that the law was not so unfavourable but who still recognised the difficulties in practice when he accepted that the effective running of an entailed estate required rents to be rising and resources for improvement to be more readily available than was generally to be found.[7] The witnesses from the south-west, of whom there was an unusually high proportion, agreed in their condemnation, though their interests were diverse. R A Oswald, a major landowner in Ayrshire and in Kirkcudbrightshire, highlighted the difficulty of improving encountered by an heir of entail:

... Without he has funds from some other quarter, he has not the means of commencing anything like improvement except through the intervention of tenantry, or some other indirect method; he cannot do it directly from the funds of the estate, from the circumstances of his not being able to give any valid security upon the estate.[8]

Archibald Bell, sheriff-depute of Ayrshire for 13 years, agreed that the law of entail was inexpedient for much the same reason. It prevented the improvement of land and was often 'inconsistent with the rights and interests of creditors'. He also thought the dignity of landed families could be preserved without such a strict law, though close questioning by the committee showed the importance still attached to the issue.[9] From Wigtownshire, Alexander McNeil, agent for the British Linen Bank, explained that the general opinion there was that 'the Entail law is hurtful to society'. He was not impressed by the provisions of the Montgomery Act of 1770 which allowed borrowing.

I have never found that any men of capital would advance money upon such a security. There is one hardship in the very threshold of it, that the money must be laid out upon the estate in the first place, before you can make a credit. Now where is the heir of entail to get the money: the money must be expended and the vouchers recorded before any security could be given.[10]

McNeil drew attention to a problem raised generally by others but which was given force by the case he cited and that was the difficulty which arose from the frequent litigation to which entailed estates gave rise. He referred in particular to the notorious case of the Sheuchan estate, which had been sold to meet debts for which it had been held liable in 1784. Twenty-eight years later the House of Lords held the sale to have been invalid. The property was restored to the then heir of entail, the purchasers losing the land and any improvements on it, leading to an immense and tangled litigation.[11]

The conclusion from the evidence of 1828 was that the improvements which the Montgomery Act of 1770 were supposed to make possible were still difficult to achieve and that investment in land was inhibited for the same reason. Until 1848, and the provisions of the Rutherford Act, the impossibility of significant disentailing meant that even those who were opposed to the entailing of land were enmeshed in the practice and could do little about it, even after the Rosebery Act of 1836 gave power to sell parts of an estate to meet debts. Private acts of parliament had to be obtained to deal with critical problems of indebtedness. As the Faculty of Advocates had complained as early as the 1760s, the procedure of entailing—the proliferation of the fetters as it was so often portrayed—meant that 'the bulk of the land of Scotland [was withdrawn] from being the subject of commerce'.[12]

The effects on the tenants of fetters on an entailed estate are less obvious. To them the difference in being on an entailed or on a non-entailed estate were slight but three are worth noting. The first was that the legal complexities of running an entailed estate delivered it easily into the control of the legal profession, especially the Edinburgh agents, who were also in a position to obtain the funds from insurance companies from which much borrowing to support estates took place. The local factor's freedom to take decisions was correspondingly circumscribed. His complaints were matched by those from the tenants. The second was that a way of improving an entailed estate was to place the responsibility for doing so on the tenant in his lease and to give him favourable terms in consequence. This change was liable to lead to objections and misunderstandings. In such circumstances the tenant was usually more aware of the burdens imposed on him and less of the beneficial clauses of the lease. The third difference was more general, and less likely to disturb or worry the tenant in the short run, and that was the way in which it was easy for an heir of entail to adopt a policy of drift on his estate, one of inaction, which for a time allowed him and his tenants to continue without change in their traditional ways. The attraction of such inaction was obvious in the short run, but in the long run it led to an accumulation of problems. If external circumstances were favourable, and in particular if prices were rising, a policy of inaction may have been able to continue to the apparent advantage of all, but not if economic conditions were adverse. Such was the conclusion to be drawn from some of James Loch's evidence to the Committee on Scotch Entails of 1828. In the later nineteenth century his view was even more to the point. Accumulated problems then made the need for action more pressing still. Entailed estates had not made adaptation any easier.

The same difficulty in reaching a definitive conclusion was obvious in another legal matter, another bone of contention, and one of more direct concern to the tenants. It was the Scottish legal right of hypothec, which gave a landlord a general right over a tenant's moveable property as security for payment of the rent, the general right being converted by a legal process into a real right over certain goods, which could then be realised to meet the rent. In less exact but more practical terms, the produce of the land could be hypothecated for the rent of the year of which it was the crop, though not for any previous or subsequent years. Livestock on the farm was similarly available to be appropriated for the rent of the current year until three months after the usual term for payment for the rent. That was not all. The landlord had the power, which was obviously of great concern to grain merchants, to recover the crop from third parties to whom it may have been sold and to bring it back to the tenant's granary as security for the rent if the term for payment had not yet arrived, or to appropriate it for payment if the term was past. Later decisions gave the purchaser of such produce some slight security in that produce sold by bulk in the open market could not be hypothecated unless the purchaser had been warned that the rent had not been paid. In these ways the landlord was in the position of a preferred creditor for the payment of his rent. Before the drastic revision of the law of hypothec in 1867[13] only four claims were preferable to those of the landlord: those of the crown, feu duties, current wages due to servants, and funeral expenses.

The law of hypothec was the Scottish equivalent of the English law of distress, but there were significant differences. Comparison was not wholly to Scotland's disadvantage. Seizure could take place in England without legal process and extended to all goods on the premises, even to those which did not belong to the tenant. However, the disadvantages in the Scottish procedure were potentially more controversial, particularly hypothecation before rent was due, whereas in England distress could be enforced only after the rent was due, and in England no action could be taken over goods already sold.

The practice of hypothec is difficult to unravel. Its complexities were well summed up by a landowner in the south-west to Disraeli as a practice 'which no Englishman can pronounce and few Scotsmen defend'.[14] Behind the growth of the agitation in the nineteenth century—from around 1830 to the full investigation of the procedure and subsequent legislation in the 1860s—was the growing interest in hypothec of 'the manure merchant and the mechanical engineer' in agriculture, as the Royal Commission which investigated the matter put it.[15] Thomas Biggar, a merchant and a farmer at King's Grange, Urr, put their view: 'So far as I have been engaged in trade, I have found the law very disadvantageous, because the landlord has generally been paid in full, while the manure merchant and other dealers have had to come in for a very small dividend'.[16] The position of the merchants was obvious; more complicated issues surround the use of hypothec for the prime purpose of ensuring payment of the rent.

The discussion of the influence of hypothec over rent in Scotland should be combined with a related issue which, though distinct, greatly influenced the practice and the case both for and against its use. This was the question of when rent should be paid: whether on the due date, or earlier—known as fore-renting, or later—known as back-renting. The general practice in Scotland was a form of back-renting, or payment of the rent some time after it might have been expected to be due. There were local variations but generally when entry was at Martinmas, which was common on arable farms, the first half year's rent was payable at the following Martinmas and when entry was at Whitsun, common on a stock farm, at the subsequent Martinmas, though sometimes by convention the rent was collected only at the Lammas or Candlemas following. The attraction of some form of back-renting is obvious. It gave the tenant an opportunity to realise some of his produce before he had to meet the cash require-ments of the rent. Where entry was at Martinmas, the incoming tenant paid the outgoing for any winter wheat or had access to carry out the cultivation himself, and had no rent to pay until his first harvest. Where entry was at Whitsun, the tenant was apparently less favoured, since the outgoing tenant had the year's crop and the incoming tenant had to pay his first half year's rent at Martinmas. The disadvantage was less in practice. The Whitsun entry was mainly on pastoral farms, where the incoming tenant was given the full grass and hay of the year for entry, and so in a dairying district was able to gain from the summer flush of milk. The extent to which his interests were protected is obvious in the leases. On the Dunragit estate, for example, the standard form held that if a lease began at Whitsunday, a tenant was enti-tled to enter the land due to be in green crop in the year of entry and to have accommodation for men and horses to work the ground; the outgoing tenant had not to pasture meadows from 15 March in the year of removal, nor the sown-out grass from the removal of the crop but had to pass them over to the incoming tenant on payment of the seed sown in the previous year.[17]

One consequence of the variety of practice was that a cava-lier attitude often developed towards the payment of the rent, especially when the formal payments were further avoided by various allowances.[18] One able Ayrshire farmer was quite specific: 'There is perfect confidence among the tenants that they will not be called upon to pay at the terms mentioned in their leases. They never take it into account at all. I did not take it into account myself', not surprising perhaps because in his case entry to the farm was at Martinmas and, though the first half-year's rent was due at Whitsunday, it was not paid until the following November.[19]

The practice of back-renting was used to support their case by those who defended hypothec. It was averred that hypothec enabled tenants of limited means and of uncertain creditworthiness to lease farms which no landlord would have been willing to let to them without its security. Hypothec could be defended as giving the security for one year's rent. The supporters also predicted that its abolition would lead to the end of back-renting, probably even to the adoption of some form of fore-renting, and would place a further barrier in the way of prospective tenants with few resources having a chance to lease a farm.

The opponents of hypothec replied that it encouraged landlords to act recklessly, to lease farms to whoever offered the highest rent, irrespective of competence, secure in the knowledge that their position as preferred creditors guaranteed they would incur no loss whatever happened to other creditors. In any case, it was argued, though hardly reliably, that any prospective tenant who was reasonably creditworthy could receive help from the banks. If they were not sufficiently creditworthy, then they were better out of farming altogether. Just as the arguments of the grain and manure merchants, while often couched in other language, represented an assertion of their direct interests, so the views of the farmers were usually those of well-established tenant farmers, who, whatever may have been the case in the past, faced few of the financial problems of obtaining ready cash which dominated much of the life of a new and struggling tenant. The advantages of hypothec to the tenant, especially when linked to back-renting, were of no interest to the established farmers and it was their voices which were heard. In the nineteenth century everyone with any knowledge of the situation admitted that the problem of the small tenant was most acute in Ayrshire. One major farmer in the county commented that:

> If the result of the abolition of the law of hypothec was to make farms fore-rented, I am afraid many of the small tenants would go to the wall altogether, but at present they are not in a flourishing condition ... The smaller farmers must either become ploughmen, or go to the colonies. But ploughmen are in quite as good a condition as these small tenants, and bring up their families quite as respectably.[20]

The doubtful validity of many of the allegations that hypothec harmed the tenant is evident by the way in which it is possible to reproduce arguments almost identical to those of the 1860s from the evidence to the Royal Commission on Agriculture of the 1890s, by which time the main effects of hypothec had been removed. It was still alleged by the established tenant farmers that the landlords were anxious only to accept the highest rent and so they were condemned for encouraging the entry of those who were incapable of making good commercial or experienced agricultural judgements. The landowners were still belaboured as in the 1860s by the established tenant farmers.

Even at the height of the complaints and opposition to hypothec in the 1860s, the problems to which it gave rise were not rife in the south-west. Hope-Johnston's factor in Annandale pointed out that 'For the last twenty years, out of 150 farms I have not twice had occasion to exercise the right of hypothec'.[21] Two comments from different quarters confirm that it was not a live issue, but a third shows that, whatever its prevalence or usefulness, it was felt that hypothec had to go. William Sproat held:

> We have very little experience of it. I have only known a rare case or two of sequestration in my district in all my experience. These were not extensive farmers; but I don't know so much about Wigtownshire; but in Kirkcudbright I have known scarcely any cases. The farmers in my district see the examination of witnesses before this Commission, but we know very little about the hypothec otherwise.

He admitted there was no agitation for repeal, though—hardly a surprising situation—those who spoke of it disapproved. 'We don't think it would affect either the landlord or tenant at all'.[22] Another witness, James McLean, confirmed the drift of these sentiments: 'I have not heard the subject of the law of hypothec discussed among the agricultural community, and there is no excitement about it among the tenantry in our county [Wigtown]'.[23]

The third comment, the most balanced of all to the Commission, came from David Campbell, agent for the Royal Bank in Ayr, and recently factor for R A Oswald, as his father had been before him:

> The wealth, intelligence, and influence of the farming and merchant and mechanic capitalists have increased so much, that the abolition of this singular preference, as concerns landed property, can, I think, only be a question of time. A tenant, whose rent requires to be secured or recovered by hypothec, is not an advantageous tenant; and to maintain him in possession, which the hypothec does and professes

to do, is an object unworthy of public solicitude. The law has created now more than ever an uncomfortable and injurious feeling, that the landlords, as a class, are disposed to be selfish, and jealous of those with whom their tenants require to have pecuniary transactions, and all for an object which is not worth its odium.[24]

Campbell's assessment of the situation was accurate. There were some arguments in favour of hypothec, especially when associated with the practice of back-renting, but they were not conclusive, and contradictory interpretations could also be based on the same facts. Were rents high in Ayrshire because of the high demand from the country's many small and aspiring farmers or because hypothec encouraged the landlords to lease them farms against normal commercial and agricultural judgements? Would these small farmers have been better off elsewhere or working on the land in other capacities? Would fore-renting follow the abolition of hypothec and did it matter anyway? No confident answer to these questions could be given.

The case against hypothec was strongest when it concentrated on the position of the landlord as preferred creditor. The general view was that he secured his rent while others suffered. John Kennedy, a major grazier, used to dispose of sheep in the south-west and 'found very great inconvenience and suffered considerable loss' from the landlord's preference. In 50 cases of sequestration in Nithsdale in the last 35 years, he lost in 25; 30 were on the Buccleuch estates and he lost in 16 of those. 'In almost every case the landlord got full payment; the other creditors generally got a very small dividend, and frequently nothing. My experience entitles me to say that, in most cases, the landlord's rights were asserted inconsiderately, and injuriously to the ordinary creditors'.[25] The case against hypothec advanced by the merchants was much stronger and Campbell was right to make their opposition the key to abolishing the provision whatever other advantages it may be deemed to possess. The agent for the Commercial Bank in Ayr, Hugh Cowan Gray, pointed out that a tenant was 'very seldom' sequestrated without the commercial community losing. 'So far as I know, the landlords have got their rent. It is very seldom that there is not enough on the land to pay the rent.'[26] Even if the land came back to the landlord in worse condition, such preferential treatment of the landlord was no longer acceptable in the 1860s, especially against the increasingly influential merchants.

To be sure of exactly what happened in the south-west is not easy because of inadequate information. Neither the roll books of

Wigtown Sheriff Court (taken as an example) nor the records of actions which survive reveal many cases of landlords exercising their right of hypothec to the extent of initiating a process of sequestration for rent. With the introduction of a separate register of sequestrations for rent after 1867 it is possible to be sure of the number of cases until the abolition of hypothec in rural subjects over two acres after 1880. The total number of cases in Wigtownshire from 1867 to 1880 was 438 (245 in Stranraer Sheriff Court after 1871 and the remainder at Wigtown).[27] Not all were cases of sequestration for the rent of farms, but an examination of those taken by the main proprietors show that sequestration in those years was not a general policy but was adopted only in special cases, usually against tenants who habitually failed to pay the rent or in even rarer cases where the sequestration for rent was associated with a general sequestration in bankruptcy. The misleading effect of taking the number of actions, relatively small as it was, as a guide to the general policy followed is evident from those of the main proprietors in Wigtownshire. The Earl of Stair took 50 actions in Stranraer Sheriff Court from 1871 to 1893, but they were against only 33 tenants. The Earl of Galloway took 28 actions in Wigtown Sheriff Court against only ten tenants, one of whom was sequestrated for rent every year from 1873 to 1877 and another from Martinmas 1878 to Martinmas 1882 and again in 1886 and 1887. On the Park and Dunragit estates, though the owner changed in 1875, neither the number of petitions for sequestration for rent nor even the tenants at whom the actions were directed changed markedly: between 1872 and 1890 there were 14 actions against nine tenants, one tenant being responsible for four of them. The Lochnaw estate had 15 actions between 1868 and 1882 against nine tenants, one being responsible for three and being also subject to a general sequestration in bankruptcy at the time of the last in 1882. A specific example from the Galloway estates shows how ineffective many of these actions must have been. A tenant was sequestrated for rent in 1888 and 1891 to try to recover the annual rent of £350 for four years, but his arrears at the end of 1887 were £1,710; in 1890 they were £1,784; a year later they had climbed to £1,945. At the end of March 1893 he paid £702 for two years rent and the balance of arrears outstanding—£1,419—was written off as he was then bankrupt and the tenancy came to an end in 1892.[28] Sequestration for rent was often used when the case was already hopeless.

An indication of how the landowners allowed their position as preferred creditors to be lost is shown in the few cases where sequestration for rent was accompanied by a general sequestration in bankruptcy. Of those tenants on the Stair and Lochnaw estates who were sequestrated for rent after 1867 in the sheriff courts of Stranraer and Wigtown a mere handful—about a dozen – proceeded to general sequestration. In these cases the preferred creditors were due only a small proportion of the total debts, though that could still lead to greater resentment when they took whatever few disposable assets remained; and among the ordinary, non-preferred creditors, arrears of rent due to the landlord was sometimes a substantial item. Consequently, the suggestion that the landlords gained at the expense of other creditors was less likely to be the case than their strict legal position would imply. Moreover, the landlords were not responsible for initiating many of the processes which led to the general sequestration in bankruptcy. That was usually done by a grain or manure merchant, those who complained so vehemently about the preferred position of the landowner and whose action may well be explained by their fear that the landowner would absorb any assets which remained if they did not act first of all. As a rule the preferred creditors were a small part of the total liabilities, usually swamped by debts due to those who had financed the speculative activities which almost always presaged bankruptcy, debts due to the banks and to livestock dealers.

It is perhaps symptomatic of the time that much of the agitation over such complex and chiefly legal matters as entailed estates and hypothec attracted less attention from the general run of tenant farmers. Whenever their views were asked they objected to such privileges as the landowners retained but almost as part of a ritual. Matters were different when tenants considered their lease. The centrality of its terms in the relation of landlord and tenant is obvious in the two Royal Commissions on Agriculture in the later nineteenth century. As some of the old problems—as of entails or hypothec—were lessening or had gone, controversy over the lease remained. A leading witness from the south-west in 1881, George Cowan of Glenluce, showed the relative lack of concern over the traditional issues which soured relations between landlord and tenant. Differences between entailed and unentailed estates could not be determined; they depended instead partly on the individual cultivator and partly 'upon the want of getting improvements'; nor was there much difference in the rents charged on the entailed and on the unentailed estates. Though 'in some cases' he thought the law of hypothec 'operates rather severely against the creditors of a farmer other than the landlord', he admitted there were 'not so very many' cases in his district. While complaining about the depredation of game, and especially of rabbits and pigeons, he agreed that 'As a rule, we do not suffer much from game in Wigtownshire'.

Such interests, or lack of them, and even the emphasis, was not unrepresentative of the area. When the questioning passed to the terms of his lease as they affected compensation for unexhausted improvements, Cowan's views became more definite and critical: ' ... it would be a great benefit to agriculture generally, if there was such compensation'.[29]

The acceptance of a lease which turned out to be unattractive agriculturally or economically reflected adversely on the commercial competence of the tenants. Too often they accepted obligations without the consideration and foresight required and then expected to be relieved of the obligations when conditions proved contrary to their expectations. Few were willing to approach their leases in the way that George Kynoch, woollen manufacturer, manure manufacturer and merchant, from Keith, who, with a wealth of wider commercial experience, held that '... when a man takes a lease of a farm for 19 years, I think he should look at it as a mercantile transaction, as we do in business ... I have never gone along with the people who look at it otherwise than as a business transaction'.[30] It was easy for Thomas Biggar to suggest that 'the landlord should be left to manage his own business, in the same way as a mercantileman is left to manage his ...'; the same doctrine could also be extended to the tenant.[31]

Much of the criticism assumed not only that the lease was enforceable but that it was strictly enforced. In many cases it was not. Obviously there was little incentive to do so if the farm was well managed, even if not in strict accord with the terms of the lease, and there was even less if enforcement might have precipitated the bankruptcy of the tenant. Objections were raised notably to three aspects of the leases: two restricted the freedom of the tenant's actions and the third, perhaps the most controversial of all, dealt with the provisions for compensation for improvements, especially at its end. The first restrictive condition was the requirement to follow certain rotations of cropping, the second was the compulsion to consume the produce of the farm on it; the third was the question of who was to provide compensation for improvements and who defined what they were. The objective of the first restriction was to ensure good husbandry and that arable cultivation on the farms gave a generally acceptable distribution between grain, green crops and pasture at the end of a lease. The objective of the second was to ensure the maintenance of fertility. Witnesses before both Royal Commissions gave plenty of examples of both. Their comments also show the difficulty of maintaining a good case against the provisions: first, because the terms of the leases were often unexceptionable and in common form, derived generally from legal books of styles, and second, because variations were permitted if they could be justified in terms of good husbandry and were so common that permission to adopt them was frequently not sought.

The first can be illustrated from the terms of the leases on the Dunragit estate, on which George Cowan was a tenant, terms which were similar to those on other properties. The Dunragit leases were on printed forms which continued to be used with only minor alterations even when the estate was sold in 1874 by its old, traditional proprietor to the trustees of J C Cunninghame, of old family but new ironmaking wealth. Paragraphs 9 and 10 remained unchanged between the two proprietors and were such that any competent farmer could not easily raise objections to them. The former prescribed in detail the rotations to be followed and the manuring by both dung and artificials; the latter required the consumption of all the straw, chaff, natural hay and turnips by stock and the dung to be used on the farm.[32]

Variations in the implementation of such leases were common. Even the critical witnesses before the Royal Commissions admitted that a great deal of freedom was usually left to tenants in their choice of rotations, apart from the admittedly reasonable requirement that the farm should be in a normal rotation at the end of the lease. Effectively this was the only stipulation made on the Galloway estate. Even James Hope, who was usually critical of the landowners in 1881, did not object to such provisions,[33] and more general evidence in the same investigations showed that tenants did not observe the restrictions rigidly and that they were inserted only as an ultimate sanction against bad tenants. The case against the detailed terms of the lease must be qualified in practice, but they were a potential if not always realised deterrent to tenants in the improving leases for which landowners have often been commended. Prescribing detailed agricultural practice sometimes failed to take account of the need for local conditions. It inhibited experimentation and, in more modern times, the application of scientific methods. The restrictions on the sale of produce off the farm is a case in point. It became more onerous and was certainly more irrelevant as the increasing use of artificial fertilisers rendered the need for the provision otiose. John Speir attacked the detailed provisions in leases on both grounds: 'Factors say these restrictive clauses are not intended to be acted up to, and to their credit they seldom are. Indeed in many cases they could not be acted up to ...'. Worse still,

... technical education ... is entirely ignored in their leases. These as a rule not only tell the farmers how to farm, but prevent them making any changes, unless by the consent in writing of the landlord or his agent, who in many instances makes no pretence of knowing anything of farming. While landlords and factors encourage technical education with the one hand and restrict the application of it with the other, they need not wonder if the average farmer treats with cold contempt their endeavours to further it.

Speir was an untypical critic; his technical knowledge and his willing-ness and ability to apply it far exceeded that of any ordinary farmer. In one respect he was very perceptive: 'If landlords and factors only half gauged the antipathy against these restrictions, they would do away with all not really necessary to safeguard the interest of the landlord'.[34] A basic source of dissatisfaction was that the tenants signed, or were cajoled by factors into signing, leases they had hardly read, did not digest if they did read them, and in any case soon forgot them, which could easily lead to resentment when they were brought to heel by a factor over some long-forgotten provision. That even the able and far-sighted objected to the provisions shows that there was a deep-seated resentment at the provisions, however they may be justified.

Resentment was most acute over the major issues of how the tenant was to be compensated for improvements, whether manurial residues or any other, at the end of a lease. Who was responsible for improvements was a thorny question. No reliable, objective answer is possible but an examination of the claims and counter-claims before the two Royal Commissions shows that proprietors and tenants both felt they had done their share. It is immaterial who was right; the suspicion of each other inhibited reaching a solution on compensation for improvements acceptable to both sides.

The methods adopted by the proprietors to encourage improve-ments varied. Those which they undertook on their own responsibil-ity did not give rise to the same dispute. Difficulties arose when there was co-operation between landlord and tenant, some forms of which differed little from straightforward allowances towards a reduction of rent. Three methods can be distinguished. The first was for the landlord to provide some of the materials needed for improvements, particularly those which required cash outlay, leaving to the tenant the use or application of them. Instances were the provision of tiles for the many drainage schemes being undertaken early in the nineteenth century and, later, the provision of bone meal to use as a fertiliser. A second method, used extensively on some estates such as Lochnaw but not on others, was to give the tenant a cash payment, sometimes direct but more often in the form of a reduction of rent, to meet the cost of an improvement, usually in the construction of new buildings. The dwelling houses on the Lochnaw estates were substantially reconstructed in this way in the mid-nineteenth century. The third, and most common way was for the proprietor to advance whatever sum of money was needed for an improvement to the tenant, who was then charged interest on the sum advanced, though often the amount was only what was required for the purchase of materials or of special services, as the labour required was normally undertaken by the tenant.

The objections came much to the fore at the end of a lease. The tenants held that they had made the improvements—though the different methods of financing them show that the extent to which it was possible to maintain their view varied—and that when the farm came up for reletting the landlord reaped the benefits. Objections were raised most vociferously when the tenant wanted to renew the lease. Then he felt he was doubly exploited; having paid for improvement as he saw it, he felt he was having to pay again as he took a further lease at a higher rental. The problem was not merely one of determining the value of the unexhausted improvements, or manurial residues, it was one of determining if the improvements had permanently moved the farm into a higher rental category. It is easy to be sympathetic to the tenant, but the landlord was aware of his own contribution and felt entitled to some recognition of it. Sometimes he contributed directly; sometimes he provided a loan, when much of the evidence indicates that finance was not readily available to the tenant farmer from other sources.

The question of compensation for improvements—as with most complaints against the landlord—has to be considered in the context of the system of landownership and letting. The existence of the long lease in Scotland meant that many of the improvements, whoever was responsible for them, had yielded their benefits before the end of the lease. Tenants, however, rarely shared the expectation of the landowner that at the end of a lease the farm should be available for reletting in good condition generally through a reasonable expenditure on improvements during the currency of the previous lease. The landlord assumed, in other words, that no responsible tenant would offer a rent for a farm which did not take account of his obligation to improve the farm during the currency of the lease to maintain it at the same comparative standard as when he leased it in the first instance. What the tenant called improvements, therefore, the landlord viewed merely as maintenance so payment in one form or another was demanded by both. Criticism of the landowner is valid only if it is accepted that the tenant should not have been expected to assume such long-term responsibility for improvement. If the tenant felt otherwise, then he could be accused, if not of general irresponsibility, of commercial incompetence or of short-sightedness at least. It was, or course, difficult for the average tenant to see as far ahead as was demanded by a nineteen-year lease, though the hazards of a long-term agreement were as likely to affect the landlord as the tenant. When prices were rising or stable, tension was unlikely to become acute as the loser, if there was one, was likely to be the owner. If prices were falling, as they did in the later nineteenth century, then the difficulties were likely to fall on the occupier with more limited resources.

One major witness from Wigtownshire to the Royal Commission of the 1890s may be taken to represent the approach of an influential tenant. William McConnell maintained that the rent should be distinguished from improvements. Rent, he thought, was determined by different factors, though he did not make clear what they were; he implied only some relationship with the level of prices. As for improvements, he asserted that they were made or not by the tenants and that their value should be determined by what they were worth to the outgoing tenant, with the incoming tenant responsible for paying accordingly. It would seem that McConnell had in mind the adoption of the highly controversial method of dealing with the payments for bound sheep stocks. When McConnell came to discuss restrictions on consumption of produce on the land, he argued that the tenant should not be compelled to ensure the consumption of any extra produce which appeared through the application of fertilisers, specifically bone meal. Very simply, he held that, since all improvements came from the tenants, all benefits from them should be reaped by the tenants. The rent was regarded as payment for the use of land and should be altered only because of general price changes.[35]

Some of these long-standing sources of discontent between landlord and tenant—such as the strictness of the fetters of entail, and hypothec—began to be modified in the middle of the century, but, as the evidence to the Royal Commissions makes clear, the landowners were not regarded any more favourably in consequence. The issue of compensation for improvements became more dominating than ever. A comparison of the evidence between the two Commissions, though only some fifteen years separated them, shows, if anything, increased antipathy from the tenants, even though those giving evidence, and showing the antipathy, were often highly successful.

Two explanations of the heightened criticism may be offered. The first was simply that, for all their continued social and political prestige, the power of the landlords was steadily declining. The basis of landownership remained largely untouched before 1914 in the formal sense that landholdings were still concentrated and, when there was a change—often forced reluctantly on the proprietor because of an increasing burden of indebtedness which could not be easily serviced—any sale of the property which resulted did not break up the estate as it was rarely a sale to tenants or others to become owner occupiers but to another landlord. The difficulties of selling some properties demonstrated that landownership was not so attractive as it had once been but, if a property was bought, it was still leased in the traditional way.

The major cause of the proprietors' difficulties was, however, that they were under increasing political pressure. Even as their economic resources declined, so they faced increased taxation and increased expectations of expenditure on behalf of their tenants. Death duties from 1894 were symptomatic of their problems, though, for all the complaints of the onerous nature of growing public burdens they were not as heavy as they were claimed to be. In Ireland, and in parts of Scotland, it was easy to portray the landowner in an unfavourable light. Some may have justified the criticism but it was reflected on all. Those who criticised landowners before royal commissions and on other public occasions were not necessarily playing directly and deliberately to the gallery but they caught the mood of the moment and so it became increasingly probable that tenant farmers would attribute many more of their problems to the landowners than was reasonable on any objective criterion. Even where they did not suggest that the landowner was directly responsible for whatever troubles they faced, tenants had been so used to assuming that the landlord could assist in difficult times, often in ways requested by the tenant rather than desired by the landowner, that they continued to expect assistance. The relation of landlord to tenant was one where help was expected and little consideration was given to the extent of help needed, or to whether it was likely to be perpetual and so, perhaps most vital of all, beyond the resources of the landowner.

As the economic conditions of the tenants deteriorated in the later nineteenth century, their sense of grievance against the landowners grew. The landlords could not easily be held responsible for most of the causes commonly thought to be behind the adverse economic conditions—increasing imports of foreign produce, disease, the weather—but it was very easy to move to suggestions that the landlords had remedies under their control. Conditions in the south-west were, however, less onerous than in many other parts of the country, though economic conditions worsened in the later years of the century. In the evidence to the Royal Commission of the 1880s most of the witnesses admitted that the south-west had not suffered from any severe agricultural depression, though the admission was sometimes guarded:

> ... I do not think that we have suffered so much in the south-western counties of Scotland as they have in the centre of Scotland or in the eastern counties.
>   The part of Scotland from which you came has been under extremely good circumstances, has it not?—It has suffered less than any other, I think, although the farmers have all been losing money.[36]

From north Ayrshire, where dairying was firmly established, and was less dependent on the price of cheese because of easier access to major urban markets for liquid milk, came an even more emphatic statement, though with a bow to the need for some reduction in rent:

> As far as we are concerned, some of the farms have been rather high rented, but we have never felt the agricultural depression in our district as it has been generally felt over Scotland or England, because we have the benefit of the dairy produce. Dairy farmers have never suffered as others have; that is my opinion, and I have proof of it. Diary produce, milk and butter, has always been selling well, and the benefit to the dairy farmers of the import of grain is that the feeding for the cows is not too high. That counterbalances the lower price of the cheese, and taking it all in all, I do not know that the dairy farmer has suffered much.[37]

From the Earl of Galloway's factor came the generalisation: 'On the carse and clay lands chiefly [the depression in agriculture] has been felt; but I think that with regard to the greater part of our neighbourhood, it has not been so severely felt as in other parts of the country'.[38]

The scene was portrayed less cheerfully to the Royal Commission of the 1890s. Even then John Hannah, the highly successful tenant farmer of Girvan Mains, but still a trenchant critic of the landlords, answered laconically, 'No much' to the question 'Is there any depression in your part at all?'.[39] That was a major concession, though perhaps difficult to state otherwise from a farm which had exploited successfully the trade in early potatoes. Elsewhere conditions were not so easy as they had been. The Galloway factor explained that all were now suffering from the depression and suggested that 'the enormous imports of both cheese and butter' meant that the dairy farmers' 'prospects are not so bright as they have been'.[40]

When general economic conditions worsened, the rents to be paid became a chief bone of contention. Their real burden grew as prices fell, and the defects of a fixed rent in a long nineteen-year lease became obvious. Leases which were being renewed in the period from the mid-1860s to the mid-1870s had increased rentals as the landowners tried to gain some of the benefits of the higher prices which their tenants had appropriated in earlier years. The benefits which the tenants had gained in the period of rising prices when rents remained at their old levels were forgotten when prices fell. Those who suggested that rents were too high encountered the difficulty in the south-west that farms could be let easily and were not in hand.

There was little support from the south-west for those who held, as did the assistant commissioner reporting on southern Scotland to the Royal Commission in 1881, that there was a lack of prospective tenants at the time.[41] This view emerged only fleetingly in 1881 but was absent in the investigations of the early 1890s. John Speir had the advantage of reporting on a more restricted and coherent area than his predecessor of 1881; he also knew the south-west and its problems intimately in a way James Hope did not. He was adamant: 'There is no land idle, and no farm is in the hands of those landowners who wish to get clear of it'.[42] The three witnesses from the south-west agreed, and the evidence of rent rolls shows few farms in hand. One alleged cause of the demand, advanced generally, and resented as much by those who raised it then as by those who do so now, was the introduction of capital from outside farming, but the south-west generated its own demand from the small family farms of Ayrshire. It is not surprising that the established farmers of Wigtownshire who were finding themselves under greater pressure in maintaining their traditional enterprises and ways of working, especially in the carse and heavy clay lands, regarded with disfavour those who moved from further north in search of tenancies. They were not ready to countenance working for a labourer's wage, as Speir thought nine out of ten did in Ayrshire.[43] The slavery of the family unit there was not for them.

It was then easy to turn the willingness of some tenants to pay a higher rent into a criticism of the landowners, and to provide what was practically a repetition of the discussion of the evils of hypothec of the previous generation. It was held that the landlords should not have taken the higher rents because the willingness of some prospective tenants to offer them was taken to indicate a degree of commercial and agricultural incompetence or irresponsibility, though rarely was it recognised that the higher rents offered may have been possible by adopting different agricultural practices. Such criticisms by established farmers, especially by those in Wigtownshire, represented resentment that they were being displaced.

One defensible reason why reductions in rent were advanced so often as a remedy for the agricultural depression of the late nineteenth century was that rent represented a large part of the tenant's outgoings, and particularly of cash expenditure. Two of the witnesses from the south-west before the Royal Commission of 1881 gave details of expenditure on farms: one was of actual expenditure, the other was a representative account. Rent absorbed 24 per cent of expenditure, excluding interest, on the former, and 29 per cent on the latter. Labour costs, of 16 per cent in the former and 26 per cent in the latter, were lower in each.[44] In most farms no such accounts could have been produced and practically no farmers had any conception of the profit or loss they were making. Their entire analysis of their success was conducted in terms of the adequacy of ready cash available to meet their commitments. In the south-west labour costs were often low—even zero—because of the use of family labour. Subsistence depended so much on the produce of the farm itself that cash requirements were reduced still further and so the cash requirements of the rent seemed greater than ever. To that extent the demands for reduced rent were valid.

Whether the landlord could, or should, have granted such reductions is another matter. Reductions in rent were attractive to the tenant because they provided an immediate beneficial effect, but they did not encourage changes in agricultural practice which were essential for the long-term survival of many. Some of the criticisms which were levelled at the dairy farmers as they moved from Ayrshire to Wigtownshire may have been symptomatic of the wish to avoid change, though, as Speir recognised, the conditions under which some of the Ayrshire farmers survived were not tolerable.

Speir's writings and work in various investigations illustrate the need to recognise that the problems which had to be tackled were much deeper than anything which could have been solved by a reduction in rent. As far as the predominantly dairying interests of the south-west was concerned Speir concentrated his attention less on the traditional remedies and more on the promotion of the eradication of bovine tuberculosis as central to the advance of scientific agriculture and better marketing, and to these the landowners could make only a limited contribution.

Chapter 9

Defending the Landowners

By the early twentieth century most landowners might have had some sympathy with the view of the 11th Earl of Galloway that estate duty was the most wicked and discreditable invention ever created and only instituted and kept up by the most degraded and unprincipled men who had held the position of the Chancellor of the Exchequer.[1] They felt some need for protection as when the Small Landholders (Scotland) Bill of 1906 threatened to extend the Crofters Act of 1886 to the rest of Scotland. Various local defence associations emerged. Some included tenants, whose independence may be questioned from a dismissive comment on the meeting on 4 December 1906, which led to the formation of the Ayrshire Agricultural Defence Association, with the Earl of Galloway as chairman: 'All the resolutions were seconded by tenant farmers. Amendments were moved to two resolutions by well-known Radical farmers, but were supported by only 8 and 4 hands in a large meeting'.[2] The local associations did little and did not last. The Dumfriesshire Land and Property Association was most active of all those in the south-west but its secretary reported sadly, 'I received no subscriptions in 1913'.[3] By then the local initiative had been subsumed in the wider movement of the Scottish Land and Property Federation, founded in 1906, the name of which was changed to the Scottish Landowners Federation in 1950. The Federation could do little more than ensure some useful amelioration of the general move to undermine the position of the landowner. It helped to ensure the removal of the proposal of 1906 that tenants with rentals of under £50 should be enabled to become proprietors. It helped to gain greater relief from assessment for tax under Schedule A for certain items of expenditure. Much less successfully it tackled the provisions requiring landowners to take over bound sheep stocks at valuations which were much higher than any recognised market value. Notwithstanding these initiatives it did little to reduce the general bitterness of the complaints against the landowners.

The complaints arose because of two specific faults. The first was a failure to appreciate the different standards by which landlords and tenants approached even those problems they had in common. The second was that any suggestion that landlords should have helped their tenants more than they did, especially in the difficulties of the nineteenth century, was meaningful only if the landlords were able to meet the obligations which were thrust upon them. Tenants often failed to see benefits to them in the activities of landowners, who were remote from those everyday matters which pressed upon them. The landlords' main concern, it seemed, was often with administrative matters which took the form of imposing obligations and restrictions on the tenants. Even if justifiable as representing good agricultural practice, such provisions often chafed against the freedom of the tenant and were considered to do so even more when social pressures mounted to free the tenant from the landlord's control. Such direct improvements which the landlord did make to the living or working life of the tenants were generally confined to his accepted contribution to the provision of fixed capital of long-term benefit. Thus they seemed confined to providing remote and peripheral aids to the tenants, whose outlook was limited at best by the time-span of a nineteen year lease and at worst by his ability to meet the most importunate creditor, in contrast to the infinite time-scale imposed on the landowner by the succession to an entailed estate. The tenants were likely to be even less appreciative when they were called, as they often were, to make their own contributions to these long-term improvements.

A source which gives a more comprehensive view of the expenditure of landowners in general on their estates than can be derived from their own often fragmentary and incomplete records is the registers of improvements on entailed estates maintained in the sheriff courts. They recorded notices of intentions to improve to the heirs of entail, and subsequently information, with copies of the vouchers, on the improvements as they were carried out under the provisions of the Act of 1770, which allowed a proportion of the expenditure to be charged against the estate.

The care with which the registers were maintained varied in different sheriff courts and not all estates registered improvements, or all of them. For example, at Lochnaw expenditure on improvement was recorded carefully after the succession of the 8th baronet in 1849 but, while the figures for the 1850s in the register agree with those in the estate records, the latter has £103.6s. 0½d. for 1857: 'Irregular and not recorded',[4] and it is not to be found in the register. More revealing, as it is rarely found in the estate records, are the detailed specifications and costings which were involved. Some of the most punctilious and complete recording was from the smaller estates. Year after year the small estate of Lochryan recorded the expenditure of a few hundred pounds on improvement, the largest being £523 in 1841-2, and commonly only something over £200 each year, but the detail on each entry gave such minutiae as 4s. for a horse for one day's carting.[5] On the larger estates the extent of the information varied, depending on the combined interests of proprietor and agent. Lochnaw and Monreith, for example, were places where tree planting was given much attention, and so was well recorded.

The registers are too defective to provide a reliable record of absolute expenditure on improvements, but they show its fluctuations and distribution between different items, and being in some standard form, they allow comparison of expenditure between different estates. They confirm that expenditure was frequently on long-term capital equipment and sometimes any benefit might have seemed questionable to the tenants. An extract—the second entry from the Wigtownshire register—is representative of the balance of interests of the landowners. It was a notice given on 12 June 1799 by Col. Andrew McDouall of Logan of his intention to improve. Couched in more general terms than was often common, it was at least brief:

> I am to make additions to the Mansion House of Logan and to build offices there ... I am also to build Several farm steadings on the said Estates and am also to make enclosure thereon of Stone dykes and hedges and to improve great parts of the said Estates by draining the same and to make several Plantations thereon ...[6]

Three forms of capital investment were common from the start of the registers until their end late in the nineteenth century, all with such long-term effects that their benefits are still evident. They were dykes, farm-buildings and drainage.

Dykes and hedges appeared throughout the south-west. The reorganisation of the farms in the late eighteenth and early nineteenth centuries required new field divisions. On the lower ground they were often of thorn hedges along ditches as well as stone dykes; on the higher ground they were almost exclusively of the latter. In the upland estates expenditure was greatest in the early years of the nineteenth century as sheep farming spread. In those parts of the Galloway estates in Minnigaff most of the regular expenditure at the time was on dykes; further east on the property of R A Oswald at Cavens even larger sums were registered as having been spent. So it was with most of the £1,000 and more registered as chargeable improvements in each of the years 1808-9 and 1809-10.[7] Such expenditure often took the form of a subvention to aid the work of the tenants. As early as the 1780s the Earl of Stair recorded several sums of less than £10, one of £31. 2s. 6d. being the highest.[8] At other times a few dykers—sometimes combining the work with ditching—were engaged over long periods by the same proprietor on some contractual engagement.

Dykes were to leave a widespread and permanent legacy though accounting for only a small proportion of the total expenditure. Expenditure on farm buildings and on drainage was much more substantial. In the latter years of the Napoleonic Wars the proprietors of the Monreith and Galloway estates moved from replenishing their own mansion houses to comparable, but much more modest action for their tenants. On Monreith 'a new barn, stable and cart-shed' was the standard provision around 1813, sometimes with a byre or a straw shed added.[9] It was 'the square of offices' frequently mentioned in the records and which became a conspicuous part of the landscape of the region. Something more substantial was offered on the larger estates, such as those of the Earl of Galloway or of Horatio Murray-Stewart of Broughton and Cally, or on one where the proprietor had more extensive resources, as on R A Oswald's property in Kirkcudbrightshire. A number of the large farms on the good arable land near Galloway House were completely modernised, and not cheaply. At Penkiln a new dwelling house cost £768 and new offices and cottages cost £836 in 1811-12.[10] When more substantial expenditure began to appear again after the accession of the 9th Earl other large farms near Galloway House were reconstructed similarly after 1839. In the parish of Sorbie, Millisle was given 'a new Byre capable of containing thirty Cows and a New Stable capable of containing twelve horses'; Inch, 'a new Barn and Stable Cart shed and Granary above the Cart Shed'; a little further afield in the parish of Whithorn, Meikle Balcraig and Ardbreck were given new dwelling houses—all 'stone and lime and slated'.[11] Even some of the upland farms were reconstructed, though not so elaborately. In 1811-12 the Galloway estates in the Stewartry parish of Minnigaff recorded £1,013 spent on its many march dykes, £265 for a new barn and stable at Glenhoise, and £178 for a new square of offices at Risk. In Kirkcudbrightshire, Murray of Broughton and Cally registered £6,891 on improvements in 1811-12 and £6,740 in 1812-13: £5,380 of the former and £4,530 of the latter were on farm buildings. In 1811-12, on houses and offices at Townhead £1,153 was spent; on offices at Castramont, £702; at Disdow, £447; at Enrick, £625; at Meikle Barlay, £286; at Underwood, £811. During the year 1812-13,

£827 was spent on a dwelling house at Enrick; on offices at Balanan, £836; at Meikle Barlay, £141; at Meiklewood, £1,706 (though the sum may have included a house); at Rainton, £553; and £398 on Girthon Kirk.[12]

Lochnaw was a smaller estate chiefly in the Rhins of Galloway where dairying was pioneered. The 7th baronet, who had many other activities to take up his attention, did not register improvements with any degree of regularity, but he built farm houses during his period in possession of the estate from 1809 to 1849, as well as adding to Lochnaw Castle. His successor commented, 'He built about *forty* farms steading' but prefaced the fact rather ruefully with the remark that 'his mind went far beyond his means'.[13] The new baronet did not stop the improvement, but his careful registration of the cost of the improvements in a ledger he maintained privately, as well as in the records of his factor and of the sheriff court, show that, though steady, expenditure was not on the scale of the larger estates: an average of £625 was spent annually for the nine out of the ten years of the 1850s in which expenditure on improvements was registered.[14]

From the middle of the nineteenth century two changes in the building operations of the landowners were evident. First, attention turned from farm houses, most of which had been substantially reconstructed to the building of workmen's cottages. In 1867 his factor pointed out to the Marquess of Ailsa that the lack of suitable cottages 'has long been seriously felt' by tenants of his chief farms and, though the demand for agricultural labourers was less than it had been due to the decline in the cultivation of turnips and the increase of dairying, it was desirable to provide the labourers with more comfortable housing. Previously on the Ailsa, as on other estates, priority had been given to the erection of farm buildings, but expenditure on them was down to around £1,500 annually by the mid-1860s and drainage expenditure was expected to fall after 1870, so the factor considered adequate finance would be available both to make good old cottages attached to farms, which were often sufficient in number but deficient in accommodation, with the roofs 'which are mostly thatched ... in a dilapidated [sic] state from natural decay', and to the provision 'by way of experiment' of a few not attached to farms 'to let direct to those who will make themselves available for farming in the locality'.[15]

The same policy was adopted on other estates. At Lochnaw the 8th baronet, who had commented that his father had built about forty farm steadings, was building cottages 10 years later. In addition to improvements and repairs he built two new cottages in 1858, three in 1859, nine in 1861, four in 1862, and he was still doing so twenty years later: three in 1878, four in 1879, one in 1880, five in 1881, one in 1882, five in 1883. The building of new cottages continued though on a diminished scale until 1914.[16]

The second change in the type of building was the provision of byres, dairies, milk houses and cheese lofts, expenditure on which grew from the 1860s. Once again the records of Lochnaw show the expenditure accompanying that on cottages, often by way of addition to older buildings but with a steady stream of new byres in the early 1850s—three in 1851, two in 1852, one in 1853 and two in 1854.[17] The expenditure on byres continued as that on new cottages fell. At least nine new byres were built between 1900 and the outbreak of war, in addition to new dairies and cheese lofts and many alterations and additions.[18]

The third major contribution by the landlords towards improvement was by drainage, for which there was much need, especially in those parts of Wigtownshire which were turning to dairying. Encouragement was given to drainage in the 1840s by the provision of public funds to provide loans and by an act of 1849 to enable private companies to be formed to finance such improvements.[19] The Earl of Galloway embarked on an even bigger venture when he obtained a private act of parliament in 1839 to reclaim certain 'sleezy Ground on the shores of the said Estates, and to drain and improve the Moss of Cree'.[20] The cost was estimated at £55,000 and, while the expenditure of £15,000 on the Moss of Cree would have been a legitimate charge on the estate under existing legislation, a private act of parliament was needed to enable him to charge the balance of £40,000. By 1850, £12,451 had been recorded as an independent charge in the register of improvements for expenditure on the Moss of Cree. This was an exceptional item of expenditure in many ways, not representative of the drainage taking place generally throughout the area.

The visual evidence of drainage were the small tile works which appeared on many estates. Among them were those on the Logan estate at Terally; on the Galloway estate at Carty and Baldoon; on the Stair estate at Auchneel. On some estates—the Earl of Galloway's was a case in point—tiles were supplied to the tenants, who cut and covered the drain. Other estates employed a number of labourers on the operation, among them Monreith and Logan. An example of drainage at Logan Mains early in 1844 shows what took place.[21] On 48 days from 29 January to 23 March 1844, 26 labourers were employed, about half of them for 25 days. Four were women. From March to May 1844 only 15 men were employed and for only about

10 or 12 days. Practice was more varied on Stair estates. Tiles from Auchneel were supplied to tenants to lay, and later in the century they were given financial allowances for drainage, ranging in 1873 from £5 at Glenstockadale to £133 at High Ardwell. The estate also had a long-standing link with a certain Dan McKay, apparently illiterate, as he used his mark as a receipt, who worked on some form of contractual arrangement to drain and to build dykes over the estate for many years.

Much of the expenditure on the estates was of little direct and immediate benefit to the tenants, who gained as little indirectly from the generally stimulating effects of the expenditure, which benefited chiefly local tradesmen in the first instance. They were much more aware of the contributions they themselves were making to fixed capital formation, through carting stones to the dykes, digging drains and laying tiles, building and renovating property, and, on top of all these, of having to pay interest on borrowing to have the improvements carried out. Some more direct and immediate contribution to their needs was often felt to be more pressing, such as an allowance or reduction in rent. The difference in outlook—a difference in the temperament and in the time-period or perspective by which tenants and proprietors judged expenditure on the estate—is fundamental to an understanding of so much of the difference of opinion between landlord and tenant on what was being, or should be done. Their perspectives contrasted sharply. The consequences were noted by the shrewd John Speir when discussing attitudes to drainage and building: 'The complaints ... are more, that the landlord does it [drainage] in too thorough a way. He does it in such a way that the estate would benefit as a whole; whereas they would only do it, if they did it themselves, to benefit, say, their own time'.[22] The difference of approach was all pervasive.

A more direct and destructive criticism of the landowners' improvements was that they did not contribute directly to active agricultural improvement and may even have distracted attention from its most desirable forms. To suggest that improving proprietors may have had a retrograde influence arises because of the need to qualify the beneficial effects of their work without denying them the achievements with which they are often credited. Two qualifications may be offered, qualifications which certainly become clearer if a long-term perspective on agricultural development is adopted. First, many of those commended for their improvements grasped early and correctly that the future for much of the agriculture of the south-west lay in improving its grassland husbandry. Wight illustrated this aspect fully in his tours. The Earl of Selkirk's factor at Baldoon told him that

'The land of Galloway is entirely a grazing soil, and should never be cropped, unless the view is to improve and lay it properly down for grass'. Not all would have gone so far but among those commended by Wight for their attention to grass were Keith Stewart of Glasserton—'grass is the chief object of the ingenious operator'—and others who also had good grass as their main objective.[23] Even in 1823 after the wartime attractiveness of arable cultivation had gone, one minor proprietor, Vans Agnew of Barnbarroch and Sheuchan, was still convinced that

> ... the soil of the County of Wigtown is ... much better fitted by nature for pasture ... I have heard all the arguments in fashion during the tillage *mania*, about the kindliness of our soil, and its fitness for aration, notwithstanding the frequent interruptions to the plough, by rocks and other impediments. These arguments, however, are against reason and the obvious conclusion of common sense ... [24]

The analysis that the potential for the agriculture of the south-west lay in grassland husbandry was accurate, and it led to the success of the cattle trade, but, as has been suggested, the commercialisation of the cattle trade brought difficulties and distractions with it and led to neglect of sheep husbandry, as Wight and others who followed him recognised. Both the favourable and the unfavourable effects of the cattle trade must then be kept in mind in any assessment of the work of those improvers who promoted it.

The second qualification is that the improvers' concern with the cattle trade led them to give less attention and less encouragement to how arable cultivation should develop and so they did less than they might have done to discourage the pernicious tendency to overcrop, which, it has been suggested, was a persistent fault of much of the agriculture of the remoter south-west. The theme was taken up by the agricultural reporters with a claim that only the longer-term interests of the landowners could have forced new practices on their tenants whose 'eagerness for *immediate* profit, ... which always marks the operations of farmers of inferior rank occupying small portions of land'[25] prevented new agricultural systems from being adopted. So long as the landowners prosperity lay in the cattle trade they were unlikely to force further changes on their tenantry. It is, in any case, doubtful if some of the objectives of the critics aimed at encouraging arable cultivation were the ways towards improvement. The improvers who stressed the importance of grassland husbandry in the south-west were on the right lines. The question was the use which should be made of it. Even as the agricultural reporters were advancing their view a way to use grassland which was to prove so successful had already been shown by the moves to dairying by the small tenants and the minute proprietors of north Ayrshire. The change was not an example of acting with timidity. Their contribution to effective agricultural improvement in the south-west must be stressed as much as that of the proprietors more commonly cited.

The commendatory interpretation of the landlord as improver has to be accepted with qualification but so too must the criticism of him by the tenant, especially the criticism which arose from the short-term pressures of financial stringency at the end of the nineteenth century. It raises the question of how much help the landlord could have given the tenant, apart from the question of whether it was wise to do so. One of the most instructive ways of seeing what help was given to the tenantry is to make a detailed examination of what happened to rents during a period of decreased prosperity in the later nineteenth century. There are reasons for taking the policy on rent as a crucial test. The income from rent was a major item in the accounts of any estate and for proprietors who had no other significant sources of income, as was generally the case in the south-west, it was the major determinant of the range of actions which could be followed. It remained so even when the existence of income from other sources widened choice and supported a higher style of personal living than would have been possible from the income of the estate alone. The rents to be paid loomed even larger in the minds of most tenants, whose predictable short-term response to any financial pressure was to suggest that the landlord could cut the rent and so relieve the economic pressure the tenant faced, or even remove it entirely.

When pressure on cash flows increased for any reason, as during the depressed agricultural conditions of the later nineteenth century, the problem of the payment of rent became of even greater concern to many tenants. It is only to be expected that, whatever the explanation most favoured for the depressed conditions of agriculture—foreign competition, disease, public burdens, or simply bad weather—over-renting, however defined, was an easily accepted explanation of agricultural difficulties. It had a special attraction when any criticism of landowners was grist to the mill of their political opponents. The availability of material enables an examination to be made of the actions taken to reduce rents to assist tenants in the late nineteenth century on three estates used for other illustrations: those of the Earl of Galloway, Murray-Stewart of Broughton and Cally and Agnew of Lochnaw.[26] Comparisons of the rental of any estate over time must be made with care and with some reservations because of changes in landholdings, though, whatever the changes, the rentals show the major cash flows to the estates. Only one of the three examined recorded a major change when Murray-Stewart sold Irish estates for £47,120 and bought Rusko, a property neighbouring Cally, for £46,500 in 1878-9. The surviving factor's accounts enable Rusko to be distinguished from the other properties in the south-west. The rentals of all three estates rose in the 1870s as farms were let in the last years of general prosperity at a level of rents which was shortly to prove seemingly onerous and certainly highly contentious. The Galloway rental reached a peak of £34,324 in the year ending 31 December 1878; the Broughton and Cally rental reached its peak of £17,725 in the year ending 31 July 1880, but that year included the rental of the additional property of Rusko for the first time. Excluding its rental, the remainder's came to £16,438. On the Lochnaw estate the peak came later, of £10,542 in 1882. By 1900 all had fallen sharply from their respective peaks: the Galloway rental by 24.6 per cent; Broughton and Cally by 13.2 per cent and by 6.4 per cent if the additional property acquired in 1880 is excluded, and Lochnaw by 16.0 per cent. From the slightly different test of the payments made of rent and other miscellaneous dues, such as interest on improvements, a similar pattern emerges. The peak on the Galloway estates of £33,903 in 1878 had fallen by 24.7 per cent to £25,438 in 1900, a fall of almost the same proportion as the rental. On Broughton and Cally the peak receipts of £17,894 in 1882 had fallen by 15.7 per cent to £15,086 in 1900, a slightly greater fall than in the rental alone. On Lochnaw the peak receipts of £11,198 in 1884 had fallen by 21.5 per cent by 1900 to £8,900, again a fall greater than on the rental alone.

Reductions in rent were taking place, whatever the critics may have said about their inadequacy, but the tendency on some estates for the fall in payments to exceed the fall in rentals shows that other methods of helping the cash flow of tenants and worsening that of landlords were being followed. Financial aid generally took the forms of the granting of allowances and the acceptance, though reluctantly, of the accumulation of arrears. Tenants were given allowances for many reasons, including once-for-all reductions in rent. On the Lochnaw estate allowances in the form of a reduction in rent for a few years as a contribution towards the cost of improvements specified at the beginning of a lease were followed by small sums subsequently. On the Galloway estates allowances were trivial until the 1880s when they began to be given, as at Lochnaw, for the application of bone meal. In the same decade the Galloway estates recorded the first significant allowance of a reduction of rent—£76 out of total allowances of £147. They became substantial later in the 1880s: of the £1,070 allowed in 1888—the largest sum of any one year—£629 was for rent rebates, and £477 out of a total of £824 allowed in 1889. The Broughton and Cally estate differed from the two others as allowances as abatements of rent were more common and became regular from the mid-1880s to the mid-1890s. Aid in the form of allowances was probably given as a temporary expedient, which could be withdrawn in a way a formal reduction in rent could not be. When the leases fell due for renewal, a new rent was fixed, often at the level of the old rent less the allowances, and then the allowances ceased. The maintenance of a high nominal rent roll was attractive also because it gave the impression of better security on which the proprietor could borrow.

More substantial, though less obvious and reliable aid was given on all three estates, particularly on those of Galloway and Lochnaw, through the accumulation and subsequent writing off of arrears. (Details are in Tables 9.1, 9.2, 9.3). On Broughton and Cally, probably because of the more extensive granting of allowances as rent rebates, arrears were always less and were more easily cleared.

The position was different on the Galloway and Lochnaw estates. On the former, writing off arrears could follow the bankruptcy of a tenant, but the sums involved were not large. An exception was in 1893 when £1,886 was written off, of which £1,862 was because of three bankruptcies, each case being the balance which remained after composition had taken place. In subsequent years the death of a tenant, evidently with inadequate funds to meet obligations rather than a technical bankruptcy, led to small arrears being written off, as with £112 in 1895, £380 in 1896, and £246 in 1897. More frequently the writing off of arrears followed the general practice of a retrospective reduction in rent on the conclusion of an old lease and the negotiation of a new one. Lochnaw was the smallest of the three estates and had the sharpest increase of arrears. In the mid-1890s they were about 90 per cent of the total rental. Rent was reduced more frequently than on the three other estates and arrears appeared earlier, but their appearance and the way of dealing with them was similar. If a tenant did not pay the full rent, the arrears accumulated and were written off when the lease came up for renewal. Once again the practice was to back-date the reduction in rent as on the two larger properties.

The granting of allowances and the accumulation of arrears were often more attractive to the landlords than straightforward reductions in rent. They seemed to represent no permanent loss and, since the allowances were usually small, they held out the prospect—the over-optimistic prospect as it proved to be in many cases—that the rent would be paid in the long run through the elimination of arrears. For the same reason the methods were unattractive to the tenants. Allowances were often small, the arrears were always there to be paid if possible, and they were an unwelcome and constant reminder of the need to do so. To allow arrears to accumulate is a justifiable response to a short-run agricultural depression; in the long-run its wisdom may be doubted from the standpoint of both landlord and tenants. In the short-run it is always possible that the arrears may be paid off quickly. In the long-run, if the arrears persist, they may give the landlord a false impression of what he is about to receive one day and, on the other hand, place the tenant under a repressive burden which he could never discharge. To the one it seemed a vital financial discipline; to the other it was a failure to recognise the changing conditions over a long lease. It was certainly a policy from which the landlords were unlikely to gain any favourable publicity, especially since two additional aspects of the policy of allowing arrears to accumulate were not generally evident, or even known at all, to many who participated in the debate on over-renting. The first is the extent to which arrears were written off, usually at the end of a lease, even when the tenancy was being renewed. Often the effect was simply to back-date the reduction in rent which had been agreed as part of the new lease. The second, less evident still, even in the records, is the attitudes of tenants towards them. They were much less concerned to pay off arrears than might have been expected from some of the allegations about the power wielded by landowners. Owing arrears did not affect their readiness to claim whatever benefits or privileges they thought their landlords may have been ready to grant.

One letter from a tenant on the Galloway estates shows this attitude, which others shared though less temperately. His small arrears may have been a matter of deliberate policy, or even of principle. His letter of 2 February 1899 showed the common reluctance to pay the rent of £340 (reduced to £300 in 1900) and his expectation of additional help from the landlord:

The rent of Grange as arranged 8 years ago is out of all proportion to the price of the products; and as I said a year ago we must have a new arrangement.

The place would be fairly rented at £220 as times go. I enclose a cheque for £130 and trust you will be able to advise His Lordship to accept the same in full for past Half year.

Permit me to call attention to the drain & Pipes conveying water therefrom. The drain is leaking at the new tunnel and one or two other places; and it would be better to have it put right & the pipes serviced when theres [sic] a supply of water.[27]

The tenants may not have been satisfied with the actions of their landlords who often felt in turn that they were being pressed by importunate tenants to give aid far beyond what they felt could be justified or what they felt able to give. The ultimate key to the range of options which were open to the landlords lay in the capital resources at their command, not so much their own but those of others which they were able to tap. The problem was not new. In the south-west in the late eighteenth century the experience of the Ayr Bank showed the problems and the consequences—beneficial as well as adverse—of the limited supply of capital at a time when the landowners were becoming increasingly interested in expanding their activities. Its activities, from the standpoint of the historian of banking can easily be condensed. At best the view might be that of Adam Smith: 'The design was generous; but the execution was imprudent ...'. There was another and more beneficial aspect of the legacy of the Ayr Bank. Its inflationary policies harmed some but encouraged others to undertake agricultural improvements, even making them possible in some cases. In his account of the agriculture of Galloway Samuel Smith was critical of 'this ill-planned, and ill-conducted speculation', but, since he recognised that one of the 'chief obstacles to improvement' was lack of capital, and that,

Banks have been a powerful instrument for removing the impedi-ments arising from deficiency of capital, and of exciting the spirit, as well as of affording the means of improvement, he was not surprised at the sudden and remarkable change produced upon the state of agriculture by the Douglas, Heron Bank.[28]

A few years later, in his spirited defence of the one pound note in Scotland, Sir Walter Scott provided support for Samuel Smith's judgement: '... under its too prodigal, yet beneficial influence, a fine county [that of Ayr] was converted from a desert into a fertile land'.[29] Scott also considered a second remarkable aspect of the

Bank's history was that it met its obligations and the loss fell only on the original shareholders. This loss had the consequence that some of the property which had to be sold to meet the liabilities of the shareholders gave opportunities to purchase not normally available to new proprietors, sometimes with new ideas and with more capital to exploit them.

Landowners with resources derived from commercial or industrial interests were able to exploit the agricultural potential of an area if they chose to do so. The south-west was dependent on new landowners bringing resources in to the area from elsewhere for its development. Oswald of Auchincruive and Cavens was an early example. Later in the nineteenth century the Duke of Portland and Earl of Eglinton gained from mineral development in Ayrshire and the former was able to draw on his massive interests elsewhere. The agricultural activities on their estates were encouraged and accompanied by attempts to exploit their industrial potential. The Duke of Portland developed his mineral activities at Kilmarnock, his railway to Troon and its harbour. Eglinton's resources were less, but his mineral income grew in the nineteenth century and, when it was not being dissipated in medieval joustings, went on commercial speculation, sometimes unwise, as in the development of Ardrossan. Whether expenditure of such magnitude was wise from the individual's own standpoint may be doubted, particularly concerning its agricultural benefits. Such landowners had at least the resources to spend in the grand manner, but they were exceptional, and even an Eglinton's resources were unable to support it without harmful consequences.

Later in the nineteenth century the south-west did not have proprietors with the command of resources adequate to effect agricultural transformation or with the readiness to use them for that purpose. Ayrshire was noted for the purchase of landed property by many of the enriched industrialists of the nineteenth century, but their objective was to gain social and sporting prestige through their acquisition, and relatively few penetrated to the remoter south-west. The Bairds and the Houldsworths were families which came to Ayrshire in the first place to expand their mining and ironworking interests and became significant landed proprietors in their own right, but land ownership was incidental to their other activities and objectives. Among those who were primarily landed proprietors, few had the resources of the new industrialists to enable them to escape from the restrictions imposed by the financial restraints.

The restraint of an inadequacy of capital is an absolute barrier to much improvement, a barrier which should inhibit much criticism

of the landowner. How far an individual proprietor had the resources
for improvement and for the support of his tenants is difficult to
determine. It is easier to base criticism on the nature of the expenditure. First it is necessary to consider the possibility that any financial
stringency which the landlords experienced, and which limited their
ability to help the tenantry, was through their maintenance of a style
of life which the estate could not support. In the more improved districts of Ayrshire, William Fullarton, whose own property was later
sold to the Duke of Portland, deplored the embarrassment caused
to so many established proprietors by the 'spirit of conviviality, and
speculation, disproportioned to their income'. He went on at some
length:

> ... considering the expence, and inattention to affairs, connected
> with the situation of a country gentleman, and natural tendency
> of counting upon imaginary rentals, long before they became real
> ones; including too, the prevailing course of entertaining, drink-
> ing, hunting, electioneering, show equipage, and the concomitant
> attacks upon the purse, and misapplication of the time, it appears
> surprising that any property unentailed, should remain above two
> generations in the same succession; especially, in this part of the
> island, where the gentry have not, as in England, the resources
> of clearing from time to time, their pecuniary embarrassments, by
> large sales of timber from their woods, hedge rows, and planta-
> tions.[30]

The most notable and among the more permanent forms of conspicuous consumption was the construction or thorough reconstruction
of mansion houses, which became widespread in the nineteenth
century and continued even when agriculture was experiencing
increased competition. The assumption of the late eighteenth and
nineteenth centuries that any landed property had to have a mansion house of what was deemed to be an appropriate standard
often meant a need to improve considerably on what was already
available in the south-west. In attempts to sell land a mansion
house attached to the property being sold was deemed to be
essential for an effective sale. Its absence was considered likely
to lead to a reduction in value. Even then, as a report on the
possible sale of Dunragit House in 1875 pointed out, mansion
houses were often estimated at less than their real value. 'The
work expended from time to time in making the places what they
are would run up astonishingly high if it were carefully noted, and
the sites, the finest that could be selected, have a special value.
Everything about them requires time.'[31] Expenditure on mansion

houses was recurrent throughout the century but later, in attempts to bring the properties up to modern standards, considerable sums had to be spent and that came during the period of stagnant and even falling rent rolls at the end of the century. The survival of many of the buildings provides unusually striking evidence of what was done. Some of the best known, built in earlier years, were improved in the nineteenth century. The 5th Duke of Buccleuch, who died in 1884, added to Drumlanrig, which was perhaps the greatest house in the south-west, though on the periphery. Cally House was built between 1759 and 1765 and received later additions, particularly in the 1830s. Galloway House, dating from the 1740s, was also altered a century later.

The old house at Culhorn, which the Earl of Stair had used after the destruction of Castle Kennedy by fire, was considered inadequate for the middle of the nineteenth century. Stair, writing from Oxenfoord, formally notified Sir Hew Dalrymple, as next heir of entail other than his own issue, of 'my intention to lay out money in erecting at or near to Castle Kennedy ... a Mansion House and Offices suitable to the said Entailed Estates in Wigtownshire, and fit for the accommodation of the heirs of entail ...'.[32] The consequences were evident in the increased expenditure on improvements in the later 1860s. In the four years of heaviest expenditure recorded in the sheriff court, from 1865 to 1869, the total recorded came to £66,790, of which £42,504 or 63.6 per cent, was on the new house and its surroundings. Stables, gardens, vineries, new dignified approaches to them all, were to be expected; more unusual was a bowling alley, which alone cost over £1,250.[33] Running the new establishment required more servants: at Martinmas 1867, 21 regular indoor servants, supplemented by casual helpers were employed, though their wages were unlikely to cause great financial stringency compared with the capital expenditure on the house they ran.[34] Lochinch was exceptional only in its scale. The registers of improvements show how general the expenditure on mansion houses was. In Wigtownshire from 1868-9 £9,405 was recorded by Mrs Susannah Ommanney McTaggart in improving her house at Ardwell, and at Logan £17,956 was spent between 1874 and 1878.[35] A rueful comment by one of the contractors at the end of the construction of Logan, made when he asked for payment, may be taken to indicate that the operations were often more expensive than was anticipated: 'It is unfortunately no uncommon occurrence that the Contractor has to pay for the architect's mistake'.[36] The construction of mansion houses gave rise to related expenditure as the surrounding policies were correspondingly improved. The planting of trees was not wholly decorative—some economic gain could be made out of them, but generally, and on some estates in particular, that was not the objective. At Galloway House in 1853-4, a few years after its major overhaul, £210 was spent 'grubbing up unthriving trees and replanting in various places in & around the Policy of Galloway House'.[37] Major programmes of tree planting, much of it decorative, was undertaken at Lochnaw and Monreith. The trees planted were usually oak, ash, and birch. Alder, elm, willow and beech were less common and a whole range of other trees and shrubs less so. The scale of the work is clear at Lochnaw from a record of the trees planted annually kept by the 8th and 9th baronets from 1849 to 1923. A peak of 149,354 was reached in 1853-4 and during the years of the 8th baronet the number for any year did not fall below the 22,250 of 1884. His successor never approached these numbers but a substantial drop in planting came only in the decade before the First World War.[38]

At Lochnaw the interest and concern of the proprietors in improvement, and the financial difficulties of doing so, became evident in the time of the 9th baronet, who reduced the planting programme substantially. Under his predecessor Lochnaw Castle had been much improved and added to, but as part of a wider policy of renovation. The 9th baronet concentrated his more limited effort on the Castle and its policies. His improvements ranged from driving out the rats from the Castle soon after his succession and the installation of a bathroom and of hot water to some bedrooms in 1897-8. Thereafter some form of hot-water heating was introduced in 1899-90 followed in 1909-10 by major improvements of a new drainage system, a second bathroom, a bathroom for the servants, who were given the Castle's original bath as it had been replaced by an enamel one, a new boiler and heating system, almost total redecoration, and, perhaps most dramatic of all, the switching on of the electric light on 13 May 1910. All the time the need for economy, which had probably forced his predecessor to spend considerable periods of time on the continent, pressed on the 9th baronet. In 1896-7 he could afford no expenditure on the Castle and stables and had to let it for four months. In the year of major renovation at the Castle, when the electric light was switched on, the garden staff was reduced when old men left and in 1911-12, 'Owing to the necessity for keeping down expenses nothing has been done in the Castle during the year except a little replastering and repapering in consequence of rain having come in ...'. In the gardens also only routine work was carried on and from March 1913 to March 1914 the place was let again. There was no recovery after the war. From March 1920 to

December 1923, 'No avoidable expense incurred during this period. Only a few necessary repairs were carried out'.

Such expenditure cannot be dismissed out of hand as unproductive and unhelpful to the local community. It gave employment, helped to increase demand, and so encouraged the local economy in the same way as some modern public works. Years earlier Heron recognised these wider advantages when he contrasted improvements in Ayrshire favourably with those in Wigtownshire and offered the explanation: 'its idlers live more at home than those of many other counties'[39] and so increased local demand. Such expenditure was, or course, liable to place an estate in a more precarious financial situation unless, as was not the case with most proprietors in south-west Scotland, it could be supported by drawing on outside resources, or unless the unproductive investment was accompanied by productive investment sufficient to generate a means of supporting it.

When the various items of expenditure are brought together, the financial pressures on the proprietors, and so their ability to give tenants allowances and rent reductions and to spend on improvements is clear. Repairs and improvements were one form of expenditure which reduced the liquidity of the estate. A second burden which required even readier cash than expenditure on repairs and improvements, which were frequently carried out by local tradesmen who could be left to be paid one day, were the various public charges which fell on landed proprietors, and which, though not exceptionally heavy in Scotland, generated much opposition. The third burden was the cost of servicing debt. It was this call on liquid resources—the call of the creditors—which gravely limited the ability of the landowners to give further help to their tenants when they thought they needed it most of all. As they were bound to meet the interest payments, the proprietors felt they were unfairly hounded by suggestions that they could help still more. They had a defence, provided the examination of their position went no further than the immediate and obvious issues. A more detailed examination of why the burden of indebtedness was high is essential to provide a more substantive justification of their position and as the nature of much of their expenditure shows it is not so easy to sustain.

Tables 9.4, 9.5, 9.6, 9.7, 9.8 show the burdens as they faced the Galloway, Lochnaw and Cally estates. The extent to which these three items of expenditure absorbed the increase from rents is clear on the Cally and Galloway estates; less so in the case of Lochnaw until the 9th baronet succeeded in 1892. Earlier the only interest payment recorded is on the loans for drainage expenditure which was undertaken extensively. The extent of the interest payments,

especially before 1892, on Lochnaw must then be used with qualifications which do not apply to the Cally and Galloway estates as the
figures are probably incomplete.

The experience of the Cally estates is different from the two
others. It never allowed arrears of rent to accumulate as they
did.[40] The allowances granted to tenants were carefully regulated.
The consistency with which around two-thirds of the income from
rents was absorbed by the three items shows how little rental income
was available for other purposes. On Cally public burdens and
interest charges absorbed steady proportions. Improvements—by
their nature—were variable, but showed no sign of being cut back
even as rentals fell. The income left for other estate purposes after
meeting the three main charges was slightly less in the later 1890s.

The experience of Lochnaw was different, though the nature of
the interest charges on it are more doubtful. After the 9th baronet
succeeded and the interest charges appeared, it is then possible that
the coverage was more complete and, as on Cally, the three charges
absorbed about 60 per cent of the rent payments. Since the total
rents received were only about half of those on the Cally estate,
the absolute financial pressures on the 9th baronet increased as the
income left from rents for all other purposes in the early twentieth
century dropped below £3,000.

The Galloway estates showed the problems of financial pressure
most acutely. When rents paid were at their highest in the later 1870s,
two years of relatively higher expenditure led to the three main items
of expenditure absorbing over 80 per cent of the rents received and
leaving for other purposes only £4,211 and £5,168 from the total rents
received of £33,348 and £33,903. The situation did not improve. The
smallest amount of rent absorbed by the three main items was just
over 75 per cent in 1879, 1881 and 1896 and the highest was over 91
per cent in 1884 and 1885. The critical state of the Galloway finances,
which mark it out from Cally, and, as far as can be ascertained, from
Lochnaw as well, was due to the high level of interest charges, which
were usually around 50 per cent of the rents paid. It was this item
which was to prove catastrophic to the estate. On the succession of
the 11th Earl in 1901 arrears of rent were written off and a more
realistic rental recognised, but it was such that the interest charges
levied on the estate became crippling and left practically no income
for other purposes once the three main charges had been met. In 1907
no more borrowing was possible. The interest charges had to be met
temporarily from other sources and part of the estate sold.[41]

When all three charges are expressed as percentages of both the
rental and of the amount of rent and other charges received during

the year, their onerous effect on the cash flow to the estates becomes clear. The landlords were caught between the twin pressures of falling rentals and the burden of relatively fixed charges, conditions which explain a reluctance to agree to any permanent reduction in rents so long as some expectation could be entertained that the profitability of agriculture would improve sufficiently to enable the rent to be paid, and so long as they borrowed on the security of the nominal rental. It seemed better by far to let the arrears accumulate. The increasingly illiquid position of the estates was not appreciated by those who demanded more aid from the landowners. It is doubtful if they could have done much more without a radical reorganisation, such as came on the Galloway estates at the end of the first decade of the twentieth century, and which was not necessarily beneficial to all tenants. The landlords did cushion the blows of the agricultural depression on their tenants, and were expected to do so, often with little thanks for their pains. Some may have jeopardised the long-run survival of their estates by doing so. It was a period of adaptation and change which led to a paradox. On those estates where change took place sufficiently to allow them to continue on a new basis, the criticism of the action was often greatest. Where no, or inadequate, change took place, often to meet the desires of the tenants, short-term advantages were gained, but at the cost of the ability of the estate to survive at all in the long-run.

It is, of course, unwise, indeed impossible to make any reliable generalisation on the basis of the experience of three estates in an isolated part of Scotland, and it is even more unreliable to generalise on the basis of the conditions of the Galloway estates where several unusual conditions applied. That the same financial pressure was more general in the early years of the twentieth century was confirmed, however, in 1909 when the Scottish Land and Property Federation gathered detailed information from various estates and decreed 126 of the returns to be reliable.[42] They showed that 46.31 per cent of the income from the gross rentals was absorbed in meeting what were described as necessary outgoings (public burdens, management charges, repairs and improvements) leaving 53.69 per cent to meet all other expenditure, including interest on encumbrances. The comparable figure for the 41 returns used from the southern counties of Wigtown, Kirkcudbright, Dumfries, Peebles, Selkirk, Roxburgh and Berwick was 45.6 per cent and 47.7 per cent for the 29 estates in the western counties of Dunbarton, Lanark, Renfrew, Ayr and Bute. Not all the returns submitted from the estates in the south-west were used because of internal inconsistencies and other defects, but they showed a considerable spread. Most were in the range from

30 to 58 per cent showing that a minimum of one-third of the gross rental of the estates, and usually more, was needed to meet what were described as the necessary outgoings.

The capability of the landlords to survive in these conditions has been differently assessed by historians. Some have suggested that survival depended on the way in which proprietors changed their style of living from one of profligate, or near profligate, expenditure to a serious and responsible use of their property for the benefit of their posterity; others have concentrated less on the personal life style of the landowners and more on the resources of the estates, and on how effectively they were deployed to support whatever style of living may have been chosen. In all explanations the burden of indebtedness which fell on the estates was critical. Those who stressed the importance of the style of personal living emphasised the significance of serious, more abstemious habits as a means of ensuring that the debt did not exceed the revenue available; those who paid more attention to the resources of the estate stressed its capacity to service any debt which may have been incurred to enable its potential to be exploited more fully. Whatever the approach, the survival of the estate did not depend on the absolute amount of debt incurred but on the extent to which the resources of the estate could bear it.

Even an expensive style of living could be supported if the resources of the estate were adequate. Its potential was likely to be greatest if it had adequate mineral resources or other means of exploiting the profits to be made from industrial growth. In the south-west only a few estates in Ayrshire had such potential. Throughout a large part of the area, and especially in the remoter south-west, there were practically no industrial ventures and so estates had to depend on their agricultural potential which differed considerably. On some good land, as in the shore farms of the Marquess of Ailsa, high rents were possible, but by far the largest part of his estate was poor, low-rented, even untenantable hill land. The same contrast was evident on the property of the Earl of Galloway. In these conditions any tendency to adopt an expensive style of living was liable to lead to financial difficulties more readily than in some other parts of the country, but the variety of factors which influenced the position of an individual landowner were so many, and varied so much over time, that any generalisation is not easily maintained. When agricultural prosperity deteriorated, as it did in the later nineteenth century, the likelihood of estates being able to support a high level of expenditure diminished still more. The problems were most acute on those of the Earl of

Galloway, the sale of a large part of which before the First World War was a prelude to what became common after 1918 when the owner-occupier began to hold an increasingly influential place in rural society.

TABLE 9.1   GALLOWAY ESTATES

31/12	Arrears b/f £	Rental £	Total due* £	Paid £	Arrears c/f £	Arrears w/o £	Allowances £
1875	7,240	30,937	31,476	32,241	6,162	313	Nil
1876	6,162	32,988	33,568	32,973	6,756	Nil	35
1877	6,756	33,326	33,935	33,348	7,343	Nil	12
1878	7,343	34,324	35,011	33,903	8,130	321	Nil
1879	8,130	33,666	34,384	32,041	10,300	172	46
1880	10,300	33,185	33,790	32,585	11,318	188	147
1881	11,318	32,630	33,240	33,153	10,809	596	260
1882	10,809	32,206	32,749	32,613	10,243	701	149
1883	10,243	32,132	32,598	31,786	10,515	540	254
1884	10,515	32,091	32,567	31,902	11,032	147	113
1885	11,032	32,016	32,520	28,196	15,340	17	189
1886	15,340	31,039	31,453	30,223	16,408	162	917
1887	16,408	29,547	29,824	29,448	15,941	843	537
1888	15,941	20,022	29,299	29,871	15,123	246	1,070
1889	15,123	28,676	28,941	29,040	15,023	2	824
1890	15,023	27,993	28,249	27,940	14,942	390	430
1891	14,942	27,783	28,049	27,089	15,848	54	642
1/1/92 to 31/3/93	15,848	27,886	28,158	30,789	11,332	1,886	876
31/3							
1894	11,332	27,775	28,037	27,734	10,651	984	540
1895	10,651	27,452	27,725	27,666	10,451	259	719
1896	10,451	27,293	27,528	28,322	8,787	871	525
1897	8,787	26,445	26,676	25,852	9,354	257	491
1898	9,354	26,565	26,787	26,525	9,189	427	602
1899	9,189	26,535	26,768	26,341	8,387	1,229	354
1900	8,387	25,886	26,068	25,438	8,549	468	296
1904	718	24,859	25,030	24,806	940	3	419
1905	940	24,729	24,927	24,834	945	88	424
1906	945	24,682	24,881	24,709	1,114	4	545
1907	1,114	24,735	24,946	24,714	1,346	Nil	454
1908	1,346	24,807	25,015	25,534	743	84	361
1909	743	24,867	25,074	24,921	878	17	160
1910	878	19,665	19,848	20,052	491	185	44
1911	491	14,280	14,400	14,301	567	23	25
1912	567	14,338	14,461	14,084	749	195	14
1913	749	14,417	14,554	14,743	402	158	22
1914	402	13,778	13,918	13,860	426	34	5

* Total due = rental plus miscellaneous payments such as interest on improvements.

Source: Galloway State Books. SRO. GD 138/2/143-152.

TABLE 9.2   MURRAY OF BROUGHTON AND CALLY ESTATES

31/7	Arrears b/f £	Rental £	Total due† £	Paid £	Arrears c/f £	Arrears w/o £	Allowances £
1861	538	14,201	14,201	14,477	263		
1862	263	13,984	13,984	14,025	222		38
1863	222	14,552	14,552	14,626	148		235
1864	148	14,959	14,959	14,991	116		97
1865	116				183		
1866	183	15,186	15,186	14,936	333		255
1867	333	15,020	15,020	15,036	318		512
1868	318	15,060	15,060	14,596	782		408
1869	782	15,204	15,204	14,833	1,153		180
1870	1,153	15,218	15,218	15,736	635		224
1871	635	15,234	15,234	14,878	992		92
1872	992	15,415	15,415	15,759	649		194
1873	649	15,376	15,376	15,042	983		190
1878	379	15,908	15,969	16,335	13		72
1879	13	16,254	16,377	16,121	269		Nil
1880*	269	17,725	17,854	17,083	1,040		415
		(1,287)	(1,287)	(1,191)	(96)		
1881	1,040	17,421	17,550	17,748	842		Nil
	(96)	(1,236)	(1,236)	(1,298)	(34)		
1882	842	17,248	17,393	17,894	202	119	215
	(34)	(1,185)	(1,185)	(1,219)	(Nil)		
1883	202	16,991	17,133	17,335	Nil		116
	(Nil)	(1,135)	(1,135)	(1,135)	(Nil)		
1884	Nil	17,230	17,395	17,365	30		Nil
	(Nil)	(1,255)	(1,255)	(1,255)	(Nil)		
1885	30	17,198	17,365	16,550	846		50
	(Nil)	(1,258)	(1,258)	(1,258)	(Nil)		
1886	846	18,705	18,812	18,577	1,080		1,114
	(Nil)	(1,258)	(1,266)	(1,266)	(Nil)		
1/8/86 to 30/5/1887	1,080	8,999	9,078	9,842	317		887
	(Nil)	(796)	(804)	(804)	(Nil)		
1/6/87 to 31/7/1888	317	25,841	26,039	24,497	1,859		2,002
	(Nil)	(1,722)	(1,729)	(1,669)	(60)		
1889	1,859	17,712	17,846	17,991	1,671	43	1,500
	(60)	(1,467)	(1,475)	(1,535)	(Nil)		
1890	1,671	17,042	17,145	17,015	1,425	375	1,278
	(Nil)	(780)	(780)	(780)	(Nil)		
1891	1,425	17,125	17,212	17,492	1,145		1,702
	(Nil)	(968)	(968)	(968)	(Nil)		
1892	1,145	17,207	17,288	17,743	690		1,635
	(Nil)	(976)	(976)	(976)	(Nil)		
1893	690	16,870	16,937	16,430	1,197		1,037
	(Nil)	(976)	(976)	(976)	(30)		
1894	1,197	17,120	17,176	17,714	652	8	1,121
	(30)	(950)	(950)	(980)	(Nil)		
1895	652	16,936	16,991	16,673	970		863
	(Nil)	(922)	(922)	(922)	(Nil)		
1896	970	15,702	15,745	15,723	470	522	506
1897	470	15,487	15,518	15,661	225	102	397
1898	225	15,521	15,552	15,396	340	46	354
1899	340	15,287	15,318	15,354	304		272
1900	304	15,387	15,417	15,086	636		263

* Rusko estate added.
† Total due = rental plus miscellaneous payments such as interest on improvements.
Source: Murray of Broughton and Cally Rent rolls. SRO. GD 10/1331-59.

TABLE 9.3   LOCHNAW ESTATES

	Rental £	Due* £	Paid £	Arrears w/o £	Arrears c/f £
31/3/1863					1,535
1864	7,424	7,930	7,002	–	2,463
1865	7,474	8,004	8,869	315	1,283
1866	7,518	8,105	7,564	141	1,683
1867	7,508	8,112	8,390	–	1,405
1868	7,618	8,220	8,513	–	1,112
1869	7,905	8,424	8,912	53	571
1870	8,015	8,573	8,653	209	282
1871	8,398	8,928	9,014	–	296
1872	8,460	9,064	9,061	3	296
1873	8,454	9,092	8,921	2	465
1874	8,496	9,212	9,357	44	276
1875	8,554	9,310	9,353	–	233
1876	8,620	9,407	9,364	100	176
1877	9,255	10,056	10,013	4	215
1878	10,035	10,939	10,605	4	545
1879	10,254	11,258	11,124	–	679
1880	10,304	11,345	9,981	73	1,970
1881	10,415	11,328	10,970	157	2,171
1882	10,542	11,329	10,626	107	2,767
1883	10,440	11,259	10,923	409	2,694
1884	10,429	11,179	11,198	627	2,048
1885	10,487	11,209	11,134	121	2,002
1886	10,411	11,182	7,951	–	5,233
1887	10,113	10,618	9,457	103	6,291
1888	9,968	10,332	10,240	104	6,917
1889	9,830	10,129	9,943	411	6,693
1890	9,894	10,121	9,458	204	7,152
1891	9,900	10,136	9,453	20	7,815
1892	9,867	10,099	9,625	2	8,287
1893	9,860	10,039	9,297	241	8,788
1894	9,806	10,014	9,678	210	8,914
1895 (Mar.)	9,734	9,928	9,140	1,110	8,592
1895 (Sept.)	4,809	4,880	4,564	1,230	7,678
1896 (Mar.)	4,551	4,622	4,913	1,180	6,247
1897	9,020	9,157	9,037	917	5,450
1898	8,963	9,090	8,818	942	4,790
1899	8,924	9,032	8,786	–	5,036
1900	8,860	8,957	8,900	1,308	3,785
1901	8,734	8,821	8,673	188	3,739
1902	8,725	8,798	8,668	236	3,633
1903	8,722	8,784	8,868	444	3,105
1904	8,680	8,746	8,583	375	2,893
1905	8,637	8,703	8,516	173	2,907
1906	8,644	8,713	8,612	1,374	1,634
1907	8,626	8,669	8,406	–	1,897
1908	8,596	8,643	8,565	629	1,346
1909	8,511	8,561	8,344	152	1,411
1910	8,551	8,586	8,331	86	1,580
1911	8,580	8,617	8,519	160	1,518
1912	8,558	8,592	8,373	556	1,181

* Due = rental plus miscellaneous payments such as interest on improvements.

Source: Agnew of Lochnaw Factors' Accounts. SRO. GD 154/414-6.

TABLE 9.4   GALLOWAY ITEMS OF EXPENDITURE AND PERCENTAGE OF
RENTS RECEIVED

31/12	Improvements 1. £	Repairs 2. £	Embanking 3. £	Total (1 + 2 + 3) £	Public burdens £
1875	5,621	1,806	374	7,801 24.2%	3,910 12.1%
1876	6,564	1,934	493	8,991 24.3%	3,841 11.6%
1877	10,599	707	755	12,061 36.2%	4,076 12.2%
1878	8,276	1,047	841	10,164 30.0%	4,197 12.4%
1879	3,512	925	843	5,280 16.5%	4,254 13.3%
1880	4,448	568	764	5,780 17.7%	3,812 11.7%
1881	3,688	1,463	905	6,056 17.9%	4,013 12.1%
1882	4,441	777	718	5,936 18.2%	3,750 11.5%
1883	3,996	910	561	5,467 17.2%	4,451 14.0%
1884	8,266	1,279	481	10,026 31.4%	3,860 12.1%
1885	4,290	1,034	654	5,978 21.2%	3,739 13.3%
1886	3,363	1,076	202	4,641 15.4%	4,243 14.0%
1887	2,611	1,019	463	4,093 13.9%	4,050 13.8%
1888	2,957	1,051	266	4,274 14.3%	3,828 12.8%
1889	2,701	875	218	3,794 13.1%	4,240 14.6%
1890	5,089	1,106	340	6,535 23.4%	4,074 14.6%
1891	3,258	1,402	326	4,986 18.4%	3,930 14.5%
1/1/1892 to 1893	5,186	1,378	1,157	7,721 25.1%	6,426 20.1%
1894	3,895	1,517	441	5,853 21.1%	4,029 14.5%
1895	2,245	1,458	257	3,960 14.3%	3,448 12.5%
1896	1,850	2,056	236	4,142 14.6%	3,764 13.3%

TABLE 9.4 *continued*

	Improvements 1. £	Repairs 2. £	Embanking 3. £	Total (1 + 2 + 3) £	Public burdens £
1897	2,498	1,372	590	4,460 17.3%	3,857 14.9%
1898	1,919	1,330	509	3,758 14.2%	4,011 15.1%
1899	2,169	941	299	3,409 12.9%	3,995 15.2%
1900	3,351	1,206	259	4,816 18.9%	3,984 15.7%
1904	4,775	1,435	162	6,372 25.7%	4,353 17.5%
1905	3,353	1,722	167	5,242 21.1%	4,284 17.3%
1906	3,484	1,345	176	5,005 20.3%	4,163 16.8%
1907	3,364	1,395	194	4,953 20.0%	3,973 16.1%
1908	3,862	1,270	163	5,295 20.7%	5,464 21.4%
1909	1,934	1,196	107	3,237 13.0%	4,576 18.4%
1910	1,134	987	99	2,220 11.1%	2,984 14.9%
1911	1,559	490	257	2,306 16.1%	2,948 20.6%
1912	811	620	80	1,511 10.7%	3,061 21.7%
1913	667	884	72	1,623 11.0%	3,337 22.6%
1914	273	865	33	1,171 8.4%	3,716 22.9%

Source: Galloway State Books. SRO. GD 138/2/143-152.

TABLE 9.5   MURRAY OF BROUGHTON PAYMENTS AND PERCENTAGES OF
                        TOTAL RENT RECEIVED

31/7	Improvements 1. £	Repairs 2. £	Total (1 + 2) £	Taxes £
1866	2,872			
1867	4,096	1,476	5,572	2,354
			37.1%	15.7%
1868	2,777	1,572	4,359	2,170
			29.9%	14.9%
1869	4,585	2,110	6,795	2,363
			45.8%	15.9%
1870	2,191	1,491	3,682	2,368
			23.4%	15.0%
1871	1,541	1,912	3,453	1,981
			23.2%	13.3%
1872	1,226	2,048	3,274	2,075
			20.8%	13.2%
1873	912	2,117	3,029	3,355
			20.1%	22.3%
1878	2,565	1,087	3,652	1,665
			22.4%	10.2%
1879	1,805	1,572	3,377	1,717
			20.9%	10.7%
1880	2,127	1,177	3,304	1,913
			19.3%	11.2%
1881	2,285	1,159	3,444	1,891
			19.4%	10.7%
1882	1,486	1,537	3,023	2,063
			16.9%	11.5%
1883	3,631	2,031	5,662	1,976
			32.7%	11.4%
1884	1,685	2,399	4,084	1,879
			23.5%	10.8%
1885	1,213	2,067	3,280	2,000
			19.8%	12.1%
1886	1,538	1,458	2,996	2,324
			16.1%	12.5%
1/8/86 to 30/5/1887	566	621	1,187	1,892
			12.1%	19.2%
1/6/87 to 31/7/1888	801	860	1,661	2,246
			4.7%	9.2%
1889	446	1,301	1,747	1,860
			9.7%	10.3%
1890	1,218	1,422	2,640	1,854
			15.5%	10.9%

TABLE 9.5   *continued*

	Improvements 1. £	Repairs 2. £	Total (1 + 2) £	Taxes £
1891	1,242	2,967	4,209 24.1%	2,091 12.0%
1892	1,104	2,056	3,160 17.8%	1,967 12.0%
1893	2,490	1,577	4,067 24.8%	2,029 12.3%
1894	1,879	1,949	3,828 21.6%	1,994 11.3%
1895	1,474	1,679	3,153 18.9%	1,946 11.7%
1896	1,890	2,104	3,994 25.4%	2,004 12.7%
1897	1,877	2,069	3,946 25.2%	1,957 12.5%
1898	2,419	1,735	4,154 27.0%	1,965 12.8%
1899	998	1,607	2,605 17.0%	2,120 13.8%
1900	953	1,631	2,584 17.1%	2,105 14.0%

Source: Murray of Broughton and Cally Rent rolls. SRO. GD 10/1331-59.

TABLE 9.6   GALLOWAY INTEREST PAYMENTS AND PERCENTAGE
OF TOTAL RENT RECEIVED

	Interest				Interest	
31/12	£	%	31/3		£	%
1875	11,997	37.2	1894		14,146	51.0
1876	12,331	37.4	1895		14,144	51.1
1877	13,000	39.0	1896		13,469	47.6
1878	14,374	42.4	1897		13,494	52.2
1879	14,608	45.6	1898		13,747	51.8
1880	15,729	48.3	1899		13,492	51.2
1881	15,747	47.5	1900		12,709	50.0
1882	14,907	45.7				
1883	14,924	47.0	1904		13,675	55.2
1884	15,190	47.6	1905		14,621	58.9
1885	16,096	57.1	1906		15,004	60.7
1886	16,170	53.5	1907		15,685	63.5
1887	16,239	55.1	1908		2,055	8.0
1888	15,790	52.9	1909		272	1.1
1889	14,477	49.9	1910		4,857	24.2
1890	13,728	49.1	1911		9,286	64.9
1891	13,864	51.2	1912		9,305	66.1
1/1/92 to			1913		9,384	63.7
31/3/93	14,318	46.5	1914		9,410	67.9

Source: Galloway State Books. SRO. GD 138/2/143-152.

TABLE 9.7   MURRAY OF BROUGHTON INTEREST PAYMENTS AND
PERCENTAGE OF TOTAL RENT RECEIVED

	Interest				Interest	
31/7	£	%			£	%
1862	96	0.4	1885		5,823	35.2
1863	3,942	27.0	1886		5,745	30.9
1864	4,389	29.3	1/8/86 to			
			30/5/1887		4,403	44.7
1867	5,022	33.4	1/1/87 to			
1868	4,329	29.7	31/7/1888		800	3.3
1869	4,337	29.2	1889		5,415	30.1
1870	4,629	29.4	1890		5,425	31.9
1871	4,629	31.1	1891		5,504	31.5
1872	4,644	29.5	1892		5,583	31.5
1873	3,355	22.3	1893		5,595	34.1
			1894		5,591	31.6
1878	5,890	36.1	1895		5,421	32.5
1879	5,465	33.9	1896		4,639	29.5
1880	5,319	33.0	1897		4,413	28.2
1881	5,560	32.5	1898		4,269	27.7
1882	5,429	30.3	1899		4,512	29.4
1883	5,342	30.8	1900		4,703	31.2
1884	5,580	32.1				

Source: Murray of Broughton and Cally Rent Rolls. SRO. GD 10/1331-59.

TABLE 9.8   LOCHNAW. ITEMS OF EXPENDITURE AND PERCENTAGE
OF RENTS RECEIVED

	Improvements £	%	Public burdens £	%	Drainage £	Interest loans %	Other £	%	Total £	%
1864	1,226	17.5	1,061	15.2	722	10.3			3,009	43.0
1865	1,438	16.2	958	10.8	724	8.2			3,120	45.2
1866	352	3.5	1,000	13.2	820	10.8			2,172	27.5
1867	429	5.1	1,161	13.8	913	10.9			2,503	39.8
1868	1,239	14.6	1,012	11.9	1,100	12.9			3,351	39.4
1869	1,537	17.2	1,426	16.0	1,031	11.6			3,994	44.8
1870	1,813	21.0	1,051	12.1	1,075	12.4			3,939	45.5
1871	1,835	21.1	1,017	11.8	1,163	12.9			4,015	45.9
1872	537	5.9	1,161	12.8	1,199	13.2			2,897	31.9
1873	1,252	14.0	1,032	11.6	1,282	14.4			3,566	40.0
1874	1,460	15.6	1,020	10.9	1,500	16.0			3,980	42.5
1875	818	8.7	1,038	11.1	1,255	13.4			3,111	33.2
1876	652	7.0	1,462	15.6	1,106	11.8			3,220	34.4
1877	2,353	23.5	1,324	13.2	1,013	10.1			4,690	46.8
1878	2,390	22.5	1,202	11.3	1,005	9.5			4,597	43.3
1879	1,428	12.8	1,254	11.3	1,215	10.9			3,897	35.0
1880	463	4.6	1,123	11.3	1,022	10.2			2,608	26.1
1881	811	7.4	1,254	11.4	1,021	9.3			3,086	28.1
1882	2,077	19.5	981	9.2	911	8.6			3,969	37.3
1883	1,084	9.9	1,163	10.6	911	8.3			3,158	28.8
1884	408	3.6	1,054	9.4	712	6.4			2,174	19.4
1885	1,082	9.7	1,165	10.5	712	6.4			2,959	26.6
1886	756	9.5	1,284	16.1	711	8.9			2,751	34.5
1887	925	9.8	1,200	12.7	711	7.5			2,836	30.0
1888	698	6.8	1,104	10.8	712	7.0			2,514	24.6
1889	1,133	11.4	1,015	10.2	603	6.1			2,751	27.7
1890	714	7.5	1,170	12.4	603	6.4			2,487	26.3
1891	744	7.9	1,158	12.3	508	5.4			2,410	27.6
1892	544	5.7	1,060	11.0	414	4.3			2,018	21.0
1893	680	7.3	1,181	12.7	414	4.5	669	7.2	2,944	31.7
1894	1,692	17.5	1,063	11.0	385	4.0	2,267	23.4	5,407	55.9
1895	971	10.6	1,055	11.5	356	3.9	2,299	215.2	4,681	51.2
1895 (Sept.)	656	14.4	76	1.7	178	3.9	1,177	25.8	1,987	45.8
1896 (Mar.)	1,191	24.2	971	19.8	178	3.6	1,136	23.1	3,476	70.7
[1896	1,847	19.5	1,047	11.0	356	3.8	2,313	24.4	5,463	58.7]
1897	1,178	13.0	932	10.3	357	4.0	2,369	26.2	4,836	53.5
1898	1,120	12.7	1,066	12.1	358	4.1	2,358	26.7	4,902	55.6
1899	1,066	12.1	1,071	12.1			2,167	24.7	4,304	49.0
1900	2,804	31.5	1,676	18.8			2,197	24.7	6,677	75.0
1901	2,236	25.8	1,235	14.2			2,289	26.4	5,760	66.4
1902	1,216	14.0	1,364	15.7			2,305	26.6	4,885	56.3
1903	2,486	28.0	1,385	15.6			2,561	28.9	6,432	72.5
1904	1,185	13.8	1,238	14.4			2,848	33.2	5,271	61.4
1905	1,292	15.2	1,250	14.7			2,651	31.1	5,193	61.0
1906	1,235	14.3	1,244	14.4			2,745	31.9	5,224	60.6
1907	1,649	19.6	1,277	15.2			2,766	32.9	5,692	67.7
1908	1,241	14.5	1,247	14.6			2,821	32.9	5,309	62.0
1909	1,511	18.1	1,325	15.9			3,026	36.3	5,862	70.3
1910	1,034	12.4	976	11.7			3,132	37.6	5,142	61.7
1911	810	9.5	1,793	21.0			3,151	37.0	5,754	67.5
1912	680	8.1	1,382	16.5			3,349	40.0	5,411	64.6

Notes: Improvements include expenditure on drainage.

Source: Agnew of Lochnaw: Factor's Accounts, 1860–1912. Scottish Record Office.
GD 154/414, 415, 416.

Chapter 10

The Galloway Estates

The problems facing landowners can be seen most clearly by examining one case in detail. The Galloway estates were once among the most extensive in the south west. Their decline can be traced back to the early nineteenth century and originated in the age of improvements for which the landowners of the late eighteenth and early nineteenth centuries are often commended. In the Galloway estates, however, this was also an age when they were burdened with a degree of indebtedness from which recovery was virtually impossible.

The 7th Earl, who held the title from 1773 to 1806, contributed to the difficulties of his descendants, though one daughter and two granddaughters were considered adequate to grace Blenheim as Duchesses of Marlborough. Much of his time was spent in London in public and political affairs—he was an MP before he succeeded to the earldom—and a desire to play an even greater political role is evident in his efforts to gain a British peerage—'the wish of his Heart' as his brother-in-law, the 1st Marquess of Stafford told Henry Dundas in 1794.[1] Obsequious letters from Galloway reveal the nature not only of eighteenth-century politics but also of Galloway's mind, before the wish was granted in 1796.[2] Life on the political stage in London did not discourage expenditure on his estates, above all on Galloway House, first built by his predecessor when heir to the earldom. In 1801 he wrote to his agent: 'I must beg you to be extravagent in beautifying about Galloway House ...'. He was aware of the cost of maintaining the resulting expenditure, but hoped, with inadequate foundation as it transpired, that all would be well: 'From your uncommon exertions, & my attention, we shall have enough to keep me going ...'.[3]

Galloway House was the centre of a widespread domain which John, the 7th Earl, extended still further by purchasing the barony of Castle Stewart from Sir William Douglas and, more important, the lands of Baldoon from the Earl of Selkirk and his son Lord Daer. Indeed he was to acquire all of their lands in Wigtownshire except the tanyards at Wigtown and some superiorities.[4] The agreement to purchase was made in June 1793 and contained the unusual clause that at the end of certain leases, the Earl of Galloway had to pay an additional sum of 25 years' purchase of the excess yearly rental over £5,000. Artibrators decreed on 29 November 1805 that it should be £105,045. 3s., additional to £155,000. Several minor adjustments brought the sum to £98,560, of which £24,640 was paid and a bond issued on 7 July 1806 for similar amounts to be paid at Lammas 1806 and at Candlemas and Lammas 1807. The increased rental reflected the prosperity of landownership between 1793 and 1806 but strained Galloway's resources. The problem to be faced had been anticipated in 1804. Galloway entailed his lands in Wigtownshire and in Kirkcudbrightshire,[5] but the operation of the entail was suspended[6] as at the same time he placed his assets in trust[7] to make provision for his 'considerable' debts, to meet family encumbrances, and to pay the balances due on the purchases of the lands from Douglas and Selkirk. To do so the trustees were given authority to sell lands and, showing Galloway's attachment to the heart of his properties, they had to start by disposing those 'situated at the greatest distance from my Mansion house of Galloway House', beginning with those in the Stewartry near Dalry, next those in the parish of Mochrum, then in Kirkcolm, and lastly in Kirkcowan. A process of disposal began which was to take exactly a century before Galloway House itself was sold.

The first lands to go were at Dalry, at a public roup on 5 August 1807. Six of the 13 lots were bought by Sir William Forbes of Callendar, who proved a reluctant payer as the trustees had to take action to obtain payment and Forbes countered by disputing the title.[8] The total realised was £52,620[9] which still left debt of £275,642 on 1 March 1810. Further sales were required. Two roups followed, of lands in Mochrum, Kirkcolm and Kirkcowan in 1810 and in the upper part of Penninghame in 1813. They were bought for a total of £175,895 by George, 8th Earl of Galloway, who had succeeded his father in November 1806,[10] though he sold part of the lands in Mochrum to Sir William Maxwell of Monreith for £12,275[11] shortly afterwards. The purchase was a neat way of avoiding the disposal of more land but merely stored up trouble for the not too distant future. The trustees were discharged in 1819[12] when they made over the lands they still held to the 8th Earl[13] plus the sum of £2,325. 8s. 3d.

Though one trust deed was discharged in 1819, another had to be executed in 1823 by the 8th Earl, who held the title from 1806 to 1834, for behoof of his creditors.[14] A disposition of Galloway's lands to them was recorded on 12 February of that year. The first trustees were replaced in another trust deed of 1827 by Galloway's two brothers-in-law, Sir Arthur Paget, brother of the wife of the 8th Earl, and Sir James Graham of Netherby, his eldest sister's husband, together with John Russel, CS. It is possible to provide a more detailed examination of the expenditure of the 8th Earl partly because better records of the financial affairs of the estate have survived from their appointment and even more so because his trustees attempted to have some expenditure recognised as a charge on the entailed estate under the terms of the Montgomery Act of 1770. On his succession the 9th Earl queried if the trustees had been entitled to do so as the deed of entail, though made out by John, 7th Earl of Galloway in 1804 had not been registered until July 1823,[15] even though the expenditure had been recorded in Wigtown and Kirkcudbright sheriff courts from Martinmas 1807.[16] The action[17] showed the perilous financial state of the property which had forced the 8th Earl to execute a trust deed in 1823. At Whitsunday 1834, the first term after his death, the yearly income from the estate after deducting public burdens, life rents and interest on debt, was only about £2,024, which meant that the limit of the potential claim which could be charged under the Montgomery Act (three-quarters of the whole) was some £12,144[18]. In the words of the trustees' pleadings, the sums spent during the time of the 8th earl, even the three-quarters which could be charged on the estate, 'far exceeded' this sum. They were £18,761. 17s. 4½d. on the estate and £14,090. 5s. 3d. on the mansion house, a total of £32,852. 2s. 7½d. of which three-quarters was £24,639. 2s. As was customary, most was spent shortly after the accession, over £25,000 between 1807 and 1813 mostly on the Wigtownshire properties, and of that at least £11,355 can be identified as applicable to Galloway House and its policies.

The absolute amount of expenditure is less critical than its relation to the capacity of the estate to support it. The terms of the Montgomery Act recognised the need to ensure a reasonable proportion between the two and so did Galloway's trustees. Several signs of the financial weakness of the estate gave them cause for concern as soon as they were appointed. At Martinmas 1822, shortly before the trustees took over, the rental of the estate was £30,334 and the estate had arrears of rent of £28,688,[19] even though allowances and rebates had been given to the extent of £11,207 in the year ending 31 January 1824. Equally alarming was the heavy burden of interest payments needed to service the debts which had been incurred: £12,976 in 1824 and from then until 1834 and the accession of the 9th Earl a total of some £73,591.[20] The critical financial state may not have originated with the 8th Earl, but he did little to remedy it. The necessity for the trust deed of 1823 is obvious.

In such circumstances the trustees had little alternative but to try to sell part of the entailed estate, for which they obtained a private act of parliament on 17 June 1824.[21] A petition to the Court of Session in July 1824 and an interlocutor on 4 December 1824 initiated complex and protracted, proceedings, which lasted until 1842[22] and provide a minute account of the finances of the estate.

The first task of the accountant appointed to report to the court was to draw attention to some claims which were not in proper form and to ask the court to rule on their standing. A second report came from the accountant in 1827. These reports[23] show the nature of the debt on the estate and the action taken by the trustees to reduce it.

A definitive report in 1827 showed debts slightly different from the schedule attached to the Act of 1824. The sums in their reports also vary at different stages because of the changing status of a few marginal debts, which were sometimes allowed and sometimes not, and because the interest due on the debts was always changing, though again within fairly narrow margins. The most reliable calculation of debts incurred before 11 July 1823 with interest to 14 May 1825 gave the following:

Debts	Principal £			Interest £			Total £		
Bills	180,953.	8s.	0d.	6,723.	14s.	5d.	187,677.	2s.	6d.
Mortgages	58,400.	0s.	0d.	1,157.	15s.	11d.	59,557.	15s.	11d.
Personal bonds	53,180.	17s.	6d.	1,392.	4s.	0d.	54,573.	1s.	6d.
Open accounts	1,128.	14s.	0d.	119.	6s.	8d.	1,248.	0s.	8d.
TOTAL	293,662.	19s.	6d.	9,393.	1s.	0d.	303,056.	0s.	7d.

Other miscellaneous, or unquantifiable debts were placed aside, usually because they were too complex for even the lawyers and accountants to deal with satisfactorily. They were annuities of £390 (in return for downpayments which sometimes involved complicated arrangements on leases); a potential claim against the Earl in the Sheuchan case;[24] and a claim by Agnew of Sheuchan over the Earl's liability for teinds at Kirkinner.

The summary brought together a mass of small transactions which had accumulated over the years, often imperceptibly. The estate was financed by a wide range of creditors and often for small sums. The bills and promissory notes, which accounted for 61.6 per cent of the total debt, were held by 354 individuals, who frequently held several, generally for small amounts. Many dated in particular from

1811, when the expenditure of the 8th Earl seems to have been at its highest as he acquired land from his father's trustees,[25] and when his political and naval career were active and his family responsibilities heaviest. Many were held by local people: tenants and others. Only a few held large sums, such as Peter McCormick, who was a creditor for a total of £9,400, including £2,150 dated 9 December 1821, £1,000 dated 3 December 1822, and £3,700 dated 9 December 1822. By contrast, the heritable bonds and mortgages, which accounted for 19.0 per cent of the total debt, were few. Two advances from the British Linen Bank of £25,000 each, on 16 July and 11 December 1822, were secured by the Earl of Galloway disponing to the British Linen Bank 'heritably but redeemably' lands which were part of Upper Penninghame. Two mortgages held over the Sussex property Coalhurst, which the Earl owned, were security for loans from members of the family: of £6,400 from Edward Richard Stewart, the Earl's younger brother, and the Rev Dr Spencer Madden, father-in-law of another brother, James Henry Keith, who had himself loaned £2,000 on a mortgage. Twenty-seven creditors shared the personal bonds, which accounted for 18.1 per cent of the debt. The open account was to John Russel, CS, Galloway's Edinburgh agent, and one of the trustees appointed in 1827. Four others, for sums totalling £98. 2s. 6d. included in the schedule to the act of parliament, were disallowed subsequently through lack of evidence.

The sale of part of the entailed estate, for which the private act was obtained, did not take place until a considerable time after the succession of the 9th Earl. More immediate steps to reduce the indebtedness were taken by the realisation of personal effects and non-entailed property. The real estate held by the Earl was chiefly Upper Penninghame and Coalhurst in Sussex. He also held Corsbie House, the old cotton mill at Newton Stewart, and various superiorities. Corsbie House and the cotton mill were transferred to Lord Garlies, the heir, for £1,100 and £500 respectively, and the superiorities were also sold to him, and to Sir Alexander Muir Mackenzie, Bt., who had inherited nearby Cassencarie, for £3,187.

The two major properties of Upper Penninghame and Coalhurst were soon sold. Upper Penninghame went to James Blair for £96,000 on 11 May 1824.[26] Blair repaid the two advances of £25,000 which the Earl had been given by the British Linen Bank, which then assigned the lands it held 'heritably but redeemably', to Blair. Coalhurst was sold on 13 September 1824 to Arthur Chichester for £8,040 and £2,468. 19s. 6d. for its timber. He took over the existing mortgages totalling £8,400.

The personal effects of the Earl, distributed among Galloway House, Coalhurst and 12 Grosvenor Square, London, were modest and valued at:

	Household £	Wines £	Plate £	Books £	Horses £	Total £
Galloway House	1,318	140	317	1,000	47	2,822
Grosvenor Square	136	186	578	(Paintings – 52)		952
Coalhurst	2,000			223		2,223
Plate at Coutts			1,415			1,415
TOTAL	3,454	326	2,310	1,223	47	7,412
plus debts due to the Earl £1,388						8,800

The Earl retained some of the effects but others were sold. The paintings from Grosvenor Square realised £27. 11s. 3d. at Christie's compared with the estimate of £52. 10s.; the plate at Coutts sold better, at £1,582, compared with the £1,415 of the estimate. Most of the contents of Coalhurst were auctioned and brought in only £1,665. The final sum available from the disposable of the personal effects was £8,383, including debts of £1,388 due to the Earl (£1,138 of which was from the road funds of Penninghame, Kirkcowan and Sorbie).

With various minor adjustments, chiefly because of interest received, and perhaps including arithmetical errors, the trustees reckoned the assets realised gave them £120,782 for the reduction of the debt, which they applied as follows:

Debts	Principal £	Interest £	Total £
Bills	43,307. 15s. 0d.	6,030. 14s. 0d.	49,338. 9s. 0d.
Mortgages	58,400. 0s. 0d.	1,157. 15s. 11d.	59,557. 15s. 11d.
Personal bonds	9,350. 0s. 0d.	1,287. 15s. 8d.	10,637. 15s. 8d.
Open accounts	1,128. 14s. 0d.	119. 6s. 8d.	1,248. 0s. 8d.
TOTAL	112,186. 9s. 0d.	8,595. 12s. 4d.	120,782. 1s. 4d.

In addition the Earl and the trustees proposed further payment to the representatives of deceased creditors who had failed to exhibit legal titles:

Debts	Principal £	Interest £	Total £
Bills	280. 0s. 0d.	165. 7s. 2d.	445. 7s. 2d.
Personal bonds		7. 7s. 1d.	7. 7s. 1d.
TOTAL	280. 0s. 0d.	173. 4s. 4d.	453. 4s. 4d.

A saving in interest payable of £372. 8s. 3d. reduced the liability of the trustees further and left the net liabilities of the estate after all the payments and before any sale of entailed land permitted by the Act of 1824:

Bills:	£137,365.13s.0d.;
Personal bonds:	£43,830.17s.6d.;
Interest:	£251.16s.1d.;
Total:	£181,448.6s.7d.

In addition the Earl had to meet annuities of £390 and the uncertainties of his liabilities under the Sheuchan case.

The beneficial effect on current interest payments was obvious once the trustees were able to repay debts after 1825, but, though reduced, the interest payments remained high, especially when compared with the rental from the estate and the continuing high level of arrears. The interest payments[27] of £12,976 in the year ending 31 January 1824 had fallen, however, to £7,931 in the year ending 30 April 1826 and from then until 1834 fell steadily: 1827, £7,351; 1828, £7,348; 1829, £7,481; 1830, £6,272; 1831, £6,353; 1832, £6,766; 1833, £6,228; 1834, £5,944; 1835, £5,869.

The rental of the estate which was over £30,000 in the early 1820s was over £28,000 ten years later. The percentage absorbed by interest charges fell from 40 per cent when the trustees took over to 22 per cent in 1833 before the death of the 8th Earl. In one other respect the finances were healthier; arrears of rent were lower, though in part only through writing them off. The huge sum of £21,512 in arrears, two-thirds of the year's rental, in the trustees' first year was down to £14,388 in the following year, reached £7,823 at Martinmas 1830 and £4,422 at Martinmas 1832.

In these circumstances it is not surprising that the 9th Earl, when he succeeded in 1834, resisted the attempts to saddle the estate with a proportion of the expenditure on improvements made by his predecessors. Nor is it surprising that the trustees had soon to make a major sale of the entailed land which they had been authorised to do. When they did so in 1839, the liabilities of the estate had changed from those outlined in 1827. A report of 1841[28] gave a sum currently due of £162,436, made up as follows: capital sum unpaid in 1827, £181,196 (£181,448 less £252 interest), to which had been added an additional liability of £5,252 in connection with the Sheuchan case, giving a record total of £186,448. A sum of £24,012 had been paid to creditors since then, leaving £162,436 to be paid. To achieve this end, it was decided to sell a large area of land in the Machars of Wigtownshire. James Cumming, factor for Sir William Maxwell of Monreith, suggested a sale in five separate lots. Their combined existing rental was £3,729—almost 15 per cent of the entire estate rental—which Cumming thought might be increased to £4,136. He suggested an upset price of £118,892 which was changed because of various alterations in feu duties to £118,857. At the roup of the land held on 24 June 1840 only the fifth lot, of land in Penninghame and Wigtown, experienced competitive bidding and all five went eventually to Sir James Gibson-Craig, acting for the Earl of Stair, for a total sum of £119,359,[29] which had been increased by interest payments to £120,520 when it was paid on 21 January 1841. By the time the accountants and lawyers had completed their calculations for final approval by the Court in 1842, the payment of further interest had increased the sum to £120,981, which was the sum available to help meet the debts incurred before 1823. The sum proved sufficient to repay debts of £117,928, interest of £1,331, expenses of £1,674, leaving a surplus balance of £47. 3s. 9d.

Two minor debts which it had been hoped to pay of £120 and £265 were carried forward. The creditors for the remainder—£44,123 were willing to leave their debt as a charge on the estate, together with a bond for £10,000 for the benefit of the younger children of the 8th Earl. The debt of the estate had been greatly reduced, though at the cost of the alienation of substantial parts of the property. The creditors who remained were different from those the trustees paid off. The debts were few in number, almost all held in trust in twelve debts spread among the extended Galloway family. Of these creditors the trustees of James Stewart of Cairnsmore held £15,283 (James Stewart held £2,000 personally) and the trustees of the Widows' Fund of the Ministers of the Church of Scotland had £9,920. The next highest was a debt for £15,000.

By the early 1840s the debts incurred before 1823 had been cleared apart from those debts charged on the entailed estate, the minor debts of £325, and the £10,000 bond for the younger children. There still remained, but in a different and uncertain category, annuities of £390, the claim by the Earl of Stair and others for £5,262 following the Sheuchan case, and the claim of Agnew of Sheuchan for the teinds of Kirkinner.

The further reduction in interest charges which followed the sale to Stair improved the financial position of the estate, though the charges still absorbed a significant part of the rental, which was itself affected adversely by a resurgence in arrears.[30]

Year ending	Interest payments £			Rental £			Interest as percentage of rental	Arrears £		
31/3/1841	7,007.	17s.	7d.	26,920.	13s.	2d.	26.0	7,757.	6s.	5d.
31/3/1842	2,227.	0s.	2d.	22,973.	3s.	6d.	9.7	7,925.	15s.	10d.
31/3/1843	3,366.	0s.	8d.	22,933.	9s.	10d.	14.7	9,713.	5s.	3d.
½ year to
31/10/1843	1,952.	12s.	1d.	11,021.	5s.	8d.	17.7	11,615.	15s.	11d.
31/10/1844	3,289.	14s.	1d.	22,895.	10s.	5d.	14.4	13,710.	0s.	1d.
31/10/1845	3,229.	9s.	9d.	23,021.	13s.	2d.	14.0	13,340.	12s.	2d.
31/10/1846	3,624.	9s.	10d.	23,052.	17s.	5d.	15.7	13,465.	2s.	9d.
31/10/1847	3,762.	3s.	9d.	23,512.	17s.	3d.	16.0	14,238.	12s.	11d.
31/10/1848	4,169.	8s.	9d.	23,676.	0s.	2d.	17.6	15,376.	8s.	1d.
31/10/1849	4,771.	10s.	8d.	23,628.	1s.	7d.	20.2	15,529.	3s.	9d.
31/10/1850	4,162.	8s.	5d.	23,420.	5s.	5d.	17.8	17,202.	1s.	2d.

Though the financial position of the estate was improved, all problems had not been removed for the 9th Earl, yet his activities show little of the financial stringency or prudence which he should have followed. Even before he succeeded Cumloden was purchased after the death of his uncle and he embarked on a major phase of expenditure there in the 1840s.[31] The register of expenditure on entailed estates in Wigtownshire, where most of the property was located, in the eight years from Martinmas 1841 to Martinmas 1849 gives expenditure of £30,106, of which £17,427, or nearly 58 per cent of the total, was on Galloway House and its policies. Just over half of it occurred in three years from 1843 to 1846. Expenditure fell soon after this. Comparison with the record of expenditure kept in the General Ledgers of the estate is difficult because it does not cover the same period as the registers in the sheriff court, and not all expenditure was allowed as a charge against the heirs of entail in any case. Six nearly comparable years from both show that the expenditure which was registered was more restricted but that on Galloway House figured largely in both. From Martinmas 1845 to Martinmas 1850 the Register has total expenditure on improvements of £15,144, made up of £12,744 in Wigtownshire and £2,400 in Kirkcudbrightshire and the General Ledgers from 1 November 1845 to 31 October 1850 give a total of £22,171. It is reasonable to assume that the Register shows three-quarters of the expenditure, which is the sum the Montgomery Act allowed to be charged to the estate.

The most interesting feature of the expenditure is that it took place when the estate was so heavily indebted. The sale of land to the Earl of Stair was a prelude to the construction of the magnificent terraces south and east of Galloway House, to the miles of stone wall surrounding it and to marble work brought from Kendal for its interior. The policy was hardly wise, but the estate survived without further major disruptions in the second half of the nineteenth century though a financial situation was evolving by then which could not easily support the additional strains which brought about a collapse in the early twentieth century and greater sales than ever, including the splendour of Galloway House itself.

By the time of the death of the 9th Earl in 1873 the financial burdens on the estate were little different from what they had been when he succeeded. The 10th Earl petitioned to have debt of £315,000 charged against the estate, which was done. Thereafter it is possible to detect signs of increasing financial pressures which were to come to a head in 1907, by which time the succession had passed to his brother, the 11th Earl. The same long-term difficulties already outlined which had affected the estate earlier prevailed. The rental had reached its peak in 1878 at £34,324, but had fallen by 24 per cent by 1900; the rent and miscellaneous dues such as interest on improvements actually paid had fallen from a peak of £33,903 in 1878 by almost the same proportion, to £25,438 in 1900. Arrears of rent were as common as earlier and reached a peak of £16,408 or 53 per cent of the nominal rent roll of £31,039 in 1886. Most important, as it affected the liquidity of the estate, threatening a major crisis, was the old problem of the interest charge, which rose from absorbing under 40 per cent of the rents received in the mid-1870s to over 50 per cent in the later 1890s.

It is not surprising that there were signs of possible difficulties before the death of the 10th Earl. That he recognised them in his last years is evident. He made his allegedly final, testamentary disposition on 30 November 1891 but in the space of a little over nine years until his death he managed to add six codicils and a memorandum of explanation. The theme of them is explained in the codicil of 29 October 1900, when '… in respect of the heavy falls in rents, and great depreciation of landed property, and consequent reduction of my Executry Estate, I find it necessary to revoke and recol [sic] and reduce certain legacies …'.[32] On 15 January 1901 a petition was submitted to disentail the estate with a view to a new deed of entail,[33] but the 10th Earl died before the legal process had made much progress. A recognition of the need for stringency facing the new 11th Earl, came in 1902 with a petition to restrict the jointure of Mary, Countess of Galloway, his sister-in-law and widow of the 10th Earl to not more than one-third of the free yearly rental of the entailed lands and estates, which it was suggested was then only

£2,113. The case was taken to the House of Lords, to the indignation of the 11th Earl. By the time of the final interlocutor in 1904 the widow was already dead.[34]

Later the 11th Earl was to look back on his succession with mixed feelings. His factor gave him little encouragement to think otherwise:

> ... we cannot put the position from us, for it is not the result of a year, or 10 years, but far more ... I must again seriously implore your Lordship to consider these financial matters on the basis that you inherited an Estate which was merely nominal, and that, if there is to be any hope for those dear to you in the future, you would I fear require to turn your back upon the least benefit you can get out of the Estate in anyway for a time and thereafter that everything be done to make the most that was possible out of it.[35]

These comments followed a financial crisis which had engulfed the estate in 1907. It had then standing overdraft facilities with the British Linen Bank to finance improvements on the understanding that a petition would be presented to the Court of Session in due course to allow, firstly, a temporary rent charge, and secondly, a permanent bond to be charged on the estate. Generally, an insurance company—often the Scottish Provident Institution—took over the bond at first. Later various trust funds were invested in them, almost in perpetuity, and it was to these bondholders that the increasing sums of interest payments were due. The permanent debt of £315,000, which the 10th Earl had charged against the estate when he succeeded in 1873, and which he reduced marginally by some minor sales was £390,505 when he died, and £411,821 by 1907.

The precise origins of the crisis of 1907 are not clear though the general problem was simply the old one of the inadequacy of liquid funds caused by the heavy burden of interest charges on a stagnant rental. The details were not made any clearer by the death on 6 May 1907 of the factor who had run the estate for many years on traditional lines and practically none of whose records have survived. A crisis was brewing in 1906. Authority to issue a bond for improvements of £9,305 was given on 1 October 1906,[36] but the factor could not place it with an insurance company in the usual way. As his successor exaplained,

> Under the old method of things, everything appears to have been done in order to keep up the traditions of the past, and to spend money freely to the last so as to keep up the financial credit of the Estate. But ... this policy had come to its natural conclusion

immediately before Mr Drew's death, as he had discovered he could
borrow no more money and he had no money to go on with.

More to the point, in an explanation to new Edinburgh agents, he
added, 'there was then such a large proportion of Bonds and Rent
Charges compared with the amount of Rents received that Mr Drew
could not get the last Rent charge placed'. The British Linen Bank
took over the temporary rent charge, but on further investigation
found that the overdraft it allowed to finance capital improvements
had also been used for current expenditure and so that part of its
advances was unsecured.[37]

From then onwards the financial problems of the estate had to be
dealt with at two levels. The first was the immediate, short-term
problem of finding sufficient cash to enable the estate to continue,
and meet the personal expenditure of the Earl and of his family.
The second was the long-term reduction and reorganisation of the
capital burden. The two were to interact constantly in the years that
followed and were constant themes of many letters from the factor
to the Earl. The immediate problem of the bond which could not be
placed was dealt with by the Edinburgh agents, Russell and Dunlop,
obtaining a loan from their own bankers, the Bank of Scotland, for
£8,500, though the British Linen Bank had also been willing to grant
one. The Edinburgh agents were then in a key position to control
the finances of the estate and it was to them that some of the most
urgent appeals for funds went from the perpetually illiquid factor
in Newton Stewart. They went almost daily in June 1907. On the
Monday of one week (17 June) he wrote to Edinburgh: 'My great
difficulty here for the last week has been the want of money and
it would not serve much good merely paying the interests if we get
into difficulties here'. On the Wednesday (19 June): 'You will ...
see that we are in immediate need of a considerable sum of money
here in order to carry on for wages and other urgent payments before
the August rents come in, and we would require at least £1,000 soon
else I fear it will be as bad in matters of publicity as if we had failed
to pay interests ... We will have our hands full of actions if this is
not attended to soon'. On Thursday (20 June): '... you will see how
impossible it will be for us to carry on unless you can provide us
soon with a considerable sum of money'. On Friday (21 June): '...
the position here is practically an impossible one till we are, at least,
instructed what answers we are to give to those who cannot longer
lie out their money ... It is of first importance to retain the credit of
the Estate for a few months, for without it we should simply be in no
end of actions and probably have Sales interfered with ...'.[38]

The factor's objective was to make sure that no inkling of this position spilled out to the public in Galloway. He stressed the need not to risk 'exposure'. '… if once the Estate here gets into disrepute, there will I fear be no means of managing finances at all.'[39] That all was not as it had been was becoming evident more widely. A sale of furniture from Galloway House was held in July 1907, though the factor resisted Lord Galloway's suggestion that some carriages should also be sold on the grounds that they were not likely to bring in much revenue. Nor did the furniture. Its realisation of less than £40 justified Lady Galloway's suggestion that a 'very strong advertisement' about the sale should not be inserted in the *Galloway Gazette* 'in case we are blamed for bringing people of the class who might not get what they expected'.[40] The most likely sign to outsiders that matters were not as they had been lay in the imposition of more stringent control of expenditure on farms and the more expeditious exaction of payment of rents. With understandable feeling the factor wrote to the Edinburgh agents a month later: 'I do not think you know what I have had to pass through almost every day with tenants and others here in consequence of the absolutely necessary reversal of management, and what it may be, if it comes out that we cannot meet our engagements, it is not difficult to see'.[41]

Such immediate pressing distractions were peripheral to the main task of dealing with the bondholders whose grip on the estate limited much action. The possibility of making over the property to them was considered but rejected, and a decision was made to sell the Wigtownshire estates. Lord Galloway stressed, 'the Kirkcudbrightshire Estates are not to be sold unless it is absolutely necessary for the balance of the accounts'.[42] Col R F Dudgeon, formerly factor to the Earl of Selkirk and then an independent land agent, toured the property in late June 1907 to suggest how to effect the best sale and, as the factor reported to the Edinburgh agents, the tour was indicative of another change which was also to transform the social and economic life of Galloway: 'We had the benefit of Lord Galloway's Motor Car and we were on our rounds from 9 in the morning till about 8 at night every day and in consequence of this we finished the work in six days, which, without the Car and with ordinary time, would have taken, I should say, from three weeks to a month'.[43] Dudgeon thought that an attempt should be made to sell the whole of the Wigtownshire property centred on Galloway House, since splitting it would have left large blocks without the accompanying mansion houses which were thought essential. It was, however, on the basis of the smaller units that the sale went ahead.

The formal move to sell came in August 1907 with a petition to the Court of Session for permission to sell parts of the entailed estate.[44] In November authority was given for the sale by public roup or private bargain at an upset price of £487,000 and, if not sold in one lot, then it was to be offered in four blocks at the following prices:

1. Lands in Sorbie and Kirkinner at £255,000;
2. Lands in Wigtown land Penninghame (lower division) at £130,000;
3. Lands in Penninghame (upper division) at £77,000;
4. Lands in Whithorn at £25,000.

When the sale took place at Dowell's auction rooms in Edinburgh on 18 December 1907 there were no bidders.

The failure to sell deepened the short-term liquidity crisis. Both Lord Galloway and his factor in Newton Stewart felt let down by the Edinburgh agents, who doubtless were as annoyed at the repeated demands for more ready cash which came to them. Lord Galloway and his factor felt the demands from Edinburgh for economies were unreasonable and the factor considered he was unduly restricted in the supply of funds. He complained:

> When you remember that during the last 66 years, of which I have a return, there was regularly expended on the Estate an annual sum averaging £4,676, and … that … the annual sum spent … in the last ten years averaged £4,807, you will realise what I have suddenly been called upon to face when that £4,807 has at once been pulled down to £2,580 ….[45]

Lord Galloway began to doubt the wisdom of following the policy of the Edinburgh agents and to wonder if it might not be wiser to try to obtain an alternative source of funds in London, or even to give up the struggle altogether and let the bondholders deal with the situation as best they could, as might have happened at his succession.[46] The factor advised restraint, arguing that there was really no alternative but to continue with the existing policy because 'the fortunes of your estates are hanging in the balances'.

> Your Lordship naturally complains of certain steps proposed, turning you and yours out of the County for a time, but it is a question of choosing the least of two evils, and my feeling is that it is better to do that temporarily than permanently. Supposing you had faced difficulties at your succession would not this have been the usual

course in order to save money provided that, along with it, the local arrangements had been conducted on the same lines.[47]

The desperate outlook of the factor was summed up to Lord Galloway on 20 February 1908:

> ... in view of the peremptory letters which I am receiving from Edinburgh I am at my wits ends to know what to do between so many fires ... your Lordship must see that the position of anyone placed as I am here is practically an impossible possible [sic] position between Edinburgh Office, Rate Collectors, Tradesmen, Ministers' Stipends, Tenants' repairs, etc., without which they will refuse to pay their rents, and especially as your Lordship does not fall in with the arrangements which the Edinburgh Agents, who are financing the matter, consider necessary in order to carry on the Estate. There is evident not a day's time to be lost in order to get on to a solid foundation, and we cannot put the position from us, for it is not the result of a year, or 10 years, but far more ... My objective from the beginning was to save from the wreck the residue of the Estate, if it came to be sold, and that is what we have to fight for, whereas, if it falls into the hands of Creditors that will probably be gone for ever.[48]

As is often the case the great issues are brought home in more detailed, and sometimes even in trivial examples. On 16 January 1908 the factor advised the Edinburgh agent that Lord Galloway could cover his own personal expenditure provided the estate could meet the fees for his two sons at Harrow. The factor sent the sum of £134. 12s. 3d. for fees which were due at the end of the month, to find his action countermanded by the Edinburgh agents. Lord Galloway had to raise the money elsewhere as well as £20 for assessed taxes still unpaid on the last day for payment.[49]

Keeping the news of the financial difficulties of the estate from becoming known locally became still more difficult. The position was explained to the London solicitor, who had been brought in to try to find additional funds, on 14 March 1908.

> As to Rates ... we have at this office so managed financial matters that there is not at this point anything known outside the Office to hint to weakness, excepting that the rates are not paid and overdue to the extent of nearly £1,500. My anxiety, however, is that some of the Collectors come down upon us without further notice, and, on the other hand, I do not wish to approach any of the collectors to ask for time as that would be sure to indicate a weakness which I dont desire to confess ... any approach to compulsion on the part of anyone to whom we owe money would I fear bring upon us an avalanche ...

> Should things come to grief, I know the principal regret of those who
> will afterwards investigate matters will be to discover how much has
> been done during the last eight months which was never attempted
> before ....[50]

In July 1908 the situation seemed to become more desperate with
the calling in of some bonds at Martinmas 1908. Ruefully the factor
reflected, '... their position today is much stronger than it was a
year ago, and the future prospects immensely improved. If, however, the lenders insist upon ending these methods, just when good
fruits are likely to be reaped from them, it is not difficult to see what
the result will be'.[51] A possible solution, or at least a palliative, was
in sight. A possible purchaser, Sir Malcolm McEacharn, appeared
in July 1908 to view Galloway House.[52] In August 1908 a meeting
took place at the Angel Hotel, Doncaster, and by missives of 8 and
14 August 1908, Sir Malcolm McEacharn agreed to purchase for
£229,500, or 10 per cent below the upset price, the first and most
attractive part of the estate which had been offered for sale, the area
around Sorbie and Kirkinner including Galloway House, with entry
at Whitsunday 1909, though with the right to Galloway House once
the tenant left on 25 March 1909. On 27 August the Court of Session
agreed to the sale. On 16 November 1908 McEacharn paid £11,475 or
5 per cent of the purchase price, the balance to be paid on delivery of
the disposition, which was registered on 15 May 1909.[53]

There was a general feeling of relief, tinged with regret at this sale
of land at the heart of the Galloway property. Galloway went off to
Russia with his family later in August and returned to the Grand
Hotel, Harrogate in September. The factor wrote:

> I can enter very fully into the mixed state of your feelings at present,
> but, one thing must satisfy you that you have done your best for all
> concerned under very difficult circumstances and, that now your
> Lordship may hope to see some little light in the distance ... [54]

To the widow of a younger brother of Lord Galloway he wrote:

> ... Sir Malcolm has purchased Galloway House with the land up to the
> river Baldnoch. It is a great regret to Lord Galloway, but there never
> lately was almost any hopes of keeping the whole, and I trust that the
> sale of the most expensive part may lead to greater happiness. I quite
> understand your feelings, but Lord Galloway is not to blame for the
> present position of matters.[55]

Hopes that the problems were greatly changed were too high, but that was realised only after more immediate issues were tackled of how the funds from the sale of the property changed the indebtedness of the estate, which was the root of all the troubles.[56] McEacharn's payment of £229,500 was used first to meet legal fees of £7,314, a sum which annoyed Lord Galloway, and £8,500 to pay for improvements and especially for the installation of electric light at Galloway House because 'Lord Galloway had no funds wherewith to pay the amount, and that, but for the Electricity, which was there for the benefit of the Entailed Estate, nothing like so much money would have been got from Sir Malcolm'.[57] The balance of £213,686 was available to meet the debt. The debt, however, was, of course, much greater. Just how much more was not always completely clear because of emerging claims and changing liabilities but identifiable claims brought the total to £442,321 plus an annuity of £250 and various family provisions. It was possible to analyse the total debt under five sub-headings.

1. The permanent debt, which consisted of:
    a. the two sums of £281,000 and £30,000, which had been secured on different parts of the estate at the succession of the 10th Earl and were held by trusts, often testamentary funds or marriage contracts. The four largest bondholders—of £50,000 each—showed the variety: the trustees of the late Earl of Moray, the Scottish Provident Institution, the trustees of the Church of Scotland Ministers' Widows' Fund, and the trustees of the marriage contract between the Hon. Ronald and Mrs Grenville.
    b. Annual rent and debt charges which had been converted since the succession of the 10th Earl into bond charges on the whole estate, totalling £49,686 and all held by the University Court of the University of Edinburgh.

2. The annual rent and debt charges, totalling £51,135 of which the Scottish Provident Institution held £45,830 and the British Linen Bank the remainder, the loan it had given in 1906 when the liquidity crisis had first become acute.

3. Debt charges, *inter alia*, on Lord Galloway's life rent of the estate, totalling £30,500, of which £22,000 was held by the Scottish Provident Institution, the remaining £8,500 being the emergency credit arranged with the Bank of Scotland in 1907.

4. An annuity of £250 to Lady Isobel Stewart.

5. Family provision of £1,500 for the Countess and £20,000 for the children if the Earl predeceased them.

Of the debt of £442,321, £117,830 or 26.6 per cent of the total, was held by the Scottish Provident Institution. It was proposed to use the free balance of £213,686 from the sale of the land to McEacharn to reduce the permanent debt (items 1a. and 1b. above) from £360,686 to £147,000. The annual rent and debt charges and the debt on Lord Galloway's life rent (item 2 and 3 above) remained unchanged, with the result that the major groups of liabilities listed had fallen from £442,321 to £228,635.

Among the minor liabilities two others had to be recorded: a stipend of £31. 7s. 2d. for the new parish of Bargrennan and a bond of relief for £8,500 to the Edinburgh agent who had provided security for that loan from the Bank of Scotland. The annuity to Lady Isobel Stewart remained at £250, but the provision for the Countess and the family should they survive the Earl, was reduced from £1,500 and £20,000 to £1,000 and £10,000 respectively.[58]

The creditors showed the same pattern as before the change. The Scottish Provident Institution held £67,830 or 29.7 per cent of the total debt, a slightly larger share than before the reorganisation. The next largest creditors were the University of Edinburgh for £50,000, the Church of Scotland Ministers' Widows' Fund for £32,000, and, a new name, the Scottish Society for the Prevention of Cruelty to Animals for £20,000. The six remaining creditors—three for £10,000 and three for £5,000—were mainly trust funds.

The financial situation had been improved but it was soon obvious that it had not been transformed. The debt was reduced, but so too was the rental, especially as the best parts of the estate had been sold and particularly the part which with Galloway House might have been most attractive to someone seeking a large residential property. The continued precarious finances of the estate was obvious in one simple illustration. The permanent debt after the repayment and reorganisation stood at £228,635; the price at which the remaining property had been offered for sale in December 1907, and not sold, was £232,000. Though Lord Galloway held property in Kirkcudbrightshire as well it was not the most valuable. On a simple test the estate may have been marginally solvent, but it did not have adequate liquidity to enable it to operate easily. The interest charges, which had exceeded £15,000 in 1906 and 1907, were reduced to over £9,000 in the years before the war, but the proportion of the reduced rental which they absorbed was, if anything, slightly higher, still around two-thirds of the total.

In these circumstances it is not surprising that the tenor of the letters from the factor to Lord Galloway continued to raise the same spectre of illiquidity as before the sales. On 26 October 1908 he predicted 'a small credit balance of over £200 for the next year instead of the former large debit balances. That is a wonderful change in the short time ... but it is not enough'.[59] Exactly a year later, on 27 October 1909, the message was the same:

> Your Lordship will remember how very anxious I have been about the outcome of our financial position for a long time because I saw what we were coming to ... the question is now very pressing and immediate how we are to carry on, for though we have not the apparently hopeless annual deficit of two year's ago we have an immediate and regular deficit to face whether anything is drawn from the Estate funds or not, and we have to face it at once.[60]

In February 1910 a particularly ominous event loomed. To Lord Galloway, the factor wrote on 4 February 1910:

> ... we will soon be unable to carry on for want of funds. The Fiars Court is held this month, and, as soon as it is past, the Ministers collect their Stipends, and we cannot delay payment of these without affecting our credit or causing serious difficulties, and I have no money wherewith to pay them and other things.[61]

A collection of rents the same day did not produce enough to meet the income tax. The London solicitors, who were clearly considered less informed on such intricacies, were warned on 12 February 1910 that funds had to be produced by the 22 February, when the Fiars Court met at Wigtown, since 'we are forced to pay the Clergymen within a day or two thereafter, else the condition of our finances will be published everywhere'.[62] As one financial requirement was met, another took its place. Lord Galloway was told on 26 February 1910:

> I had however so far looked before me to prevent a collapse this week as was bound to have been the case if we did not pay the Clergymen, and the way I did it was to delay payment of Income Tax which would have more than swamped the whole. I have been able to pay the Clergymen this week and only hope that Financial agreements may be made on Tuesday or Wednesday of next week to let me get wages and other things paid and have enough to pay the Income Tax regarding which no time will be allowed when once the collectors have legal power to act.[63]

Two months later further postponement seemed impossible. '... we will very soon be forced to pay the Income Tax, and there will be no mercy shown in recovery ...'[64]

Two contrasting examples may be cited to show the financial extremities of the estate even after the major sale of property. First, all of the voluntary grants made to pensioners were stopped after 1 January 1909. The circular, which went to all recipients on 25 November 1908, explained that the change was 'In consequence of the provision of the "Old Age Pension Act 1908", and also of other circumstances known to you ... As you are aware, Lord Galloway, like other similar Rate-payers, had to contribute largely to the funds to be raised to pay the Public Pensions after 1st January next'. That was the formal position; informally the pensioners were told they would be given 'a present' so long as Lord Galloway was able to do so to make up their income to what it had been.[65] Second, in the following year, when Lord Galloway's unmarried sister fell ill, the factor wrote to two other sisters and suggested on Galloway's behalf, that the three should contribute twenty guineas each to the additional cost: 'I dare say you know that his Lordship is not in a position at present to do as much as it would be his desire to do'.[66]

Life was a hand-to-mouth existence for the factor and for Lord Galloway. In the few years that followed the failure to sell off about half of the Wigtownshire property, attempts were made to exploit fully what remained, especially by the local factor, attempts which did not always meet with Galloway's approval, as he felt he was being deprived of the use of his property. The factor persuaded a reluctant McEacharn to offer £4,000 for the properties held in fee simple in the village of Garlieston at the end of 1908.[67] More difficult to tackle were attempts to let the sporting rights, not only in part, as had been the case hitherto, but more generally. As the factor wrote to Lord Galloway, these were 'the two departments upon which I see you and I are not of the same mind'.[68] On the sale of the properties in Garlieston, the Earl thought the price was not high enough, though he was persuaded to agree on the grounds that only McEacharn would buy, and he would pay no more. The loss of sporting rights was resisted more vigorously, though Galloway was warned that 'it looks hopeless to make ends meet, if any substantial sum goes off for sporting rights' and the factor assured the Countess that a small credit balance was possible next year only if all remaining shootings and houses were let, and so, in effect, if the Galloways were turned out of their houses to make way for the shooting tenants.[69] The factor reversed one sporting plan. An attempt had been made about 1904 to turn part of the Glentrool area into a deer forest. Tenants in nearby farms complained strongly about the depredations of the deer and demanded such compensation that the factor pressed the Earl to give up the venture and duly obtained his agreement.[70] From one economy, or more accurately from one way of raising more revenue, the factor recoiled with horror. New Edinburgh agents took over and raised the possibility of levying feudal casualties which had fallen into disuse. The factor warned:

> ... the collection of casualties in this district, and I rather think in much of the South of Scotland has for long years been practically departed from. I know cases where it was tried and given up in despair in consequences of the near approach of a revolution in the district if brought about ... I would not like the record to remain, whether I live to see it or not, that our action now with reference to Casualties had done much to alienate the people from a family with such a record as that of our clients.[71]

A year later the factor had been replaced.

The new administration was no more able to save the estate than the old. The financial position was such that more land had to be sold. A further petition went to the Court of Session on 31 May 1913.[72] The objective was to sell the block of land in Wigtown and the lower part of Penninghame (the second block of the original plan of sale) with some 26 acres of upper Penninghame. The lack of a mansion house was thought to impede a profitable sale of the block as one unit. Accordingly, it was sold in individual lots, so opening up the way for a very different type of landownership. In almost every case the purchasers were the existing tenants or working farmers from elsewhere who meant to take the farms in hand.[73] In December 1913 sufficient sales had taken place to enable repayment of the loan of £32,000 from the Church of Scotland Ministers' Widows' Fund and one of several loans of £3,955 from the Scottish Provident Institution. It was the beginning of the piecemeal disposal of the estate, to which its disentailing in 1916 was a prelude.[74] In the early 1920s another bout of sales, usually to the tenants, came as part of a general move of landowners from unprofitable landownership as occupiers became owners of their land. The disposal of Galloway land was not as exceptional as it had been and, perhaps the greatest irony of all, the McEacharns also disposed of the holdings which the family had acquired less than a quarter of a century before.

Notes

INTRODUCTION pp ix to xx

1   J H Clapham, the Study of Economic History' in N B Harte (ed), *the Study of Economic History* (London, 1971), p 61.
2   M M Postan, 'The Historical Method in Social Science', *ibid.*, p 132.
3   C J Brown, *The Soil of Carrick and the Country Round Girvan* (Edinburgh, 1973), pp 243 and 251.
4   Ian Carter, *Farmlife in Northeast Scotland 1840-1914* (Edinburgh, 1979), p 179.
5   Malcolm Gray, 'Farm Workers in North-East Scotland' in T M Devine (ed), *Farm Servants and Labour in Lowland Scotland 1770-1914* (Edinburgh, 1984), p 15.
6   John Wilson, 'The Farming of the East and North-Eastern Districts' in *Report on the Present State of Agriculture in Scotland* (Highland and Agricultural Society of Scotland, Edinburgh, 1878), p 35.

CHAPTER 1 pp 3 to 12

1   Ian Donnachie, *The Industrial Archaeology of Galloway* (Newton Abbot, 1971), pp 162-7.
2   General estimate and observations on the proposed road from the River Sark to Portpatrick, 24 October 1757. Scottish Record Office [SRO]. Murray of Broughton and Cally MSS. GD 10/546/2.
3   Report of the Tidal Harbour Commissioners of the Harbours of Scotland, etc, *British Parliamentary Papers* [BPP]. 1847. XXXII.
4   Report from the Select Committee appointed to consider Mr Telford's Report and Surveys on communication between England and Ireland by the North-West of Scotland. *BPP*. 1810-11. III. 789; Report from the Select Committee on the Glasgow and Carlisle Roads. *BPP*. 1814–15. III. 331; Report from the Select Committee of the Northern Roads. *BPP*. 1830. X. 189.
5   Report from the Select Committee on the Glasgow Port-Patrick Roads, etc. *BPP*. 1823. V. 153 and 1824. VII. 151.
6   *BPP*. 1824. VII. 151, p 5.
7   Quoted in W Taylor, *The Military Roads of Scotland* (Newton Abbot, 1976), pp 106-7.
8   See below, chapter 4.

CHAPTER 2 pp 13 to 28

1 *Old Statistical Account (OSA)*, iv, 270 (1791).
2 *Ibid*. ii, 259 (1790-1).
3 *Ibid*. ii, 138 (1790); ix, 339 (1792).
4 *Ibid*. xi, 312 (1792).
5 *Ibid*. xx, 178 (1797).
6 *Ibid*. vii, 47 (1791-2).
7 *Ibid*. ii, 80 (1791).
8 *Ibid*. vi, 106 (1791).
9 James Shaw to Henry Dundas, 17 June and 10 September 1895. Melville Castle MSS. SRO. GD 51/1/32/1 and 4; Submission and history of Douglas and Shaw, 1823. SRO. Abercromby of Forglen MSS. GD 185/Box 40. See also Boxes 38 and 39.
10 *OSA*, i, 361 (1791)
11 *Ibid*. i, 248-9 (1790-1).
12 *Ibid*. xiv, 485-6 (1793).
13 *Ibid*. xv, 554 (1794).
14 *Ibid*. ix, 333 (1792).
15 *Ibid*. ii, 255 (1790-2). See also p 25.
16 *Ibid*.
17 *Ibid*. xv, 90 (1794).
18 *New Statistical Account (NSA)*, Ayrshire, 201 (1837), 233 (1836), 627 (1841), 827 (1842), 460 (1837), 850 (1842).
19 *Ibid*. 405 (1837).
20 *OSA*, vii, 150-1 (1791-2).
21 *NSA*. Ayrshire, 716-7 (1840-1).
22 *NSA*, Kirkcudbrightshire, 168 (1841-4).
23 *NSA*, Wigtownshire, 98 (1839).
24 *Ibid*. 47 (1836-38).
25 *NSA*, Kirkcudbrightshire, 340 (1840-4).
26 *NSA*. 261-2 (1844). See p 25.
27 *Ibid*. 310 (1844).
28 *OSA*, xi, 37 (1793); *NSA*, Kirkcudbrightshire, 60 (1841-3).
29 *OSA*, i, 249 (1790-1); *NSA*, Wigtownshire, 32 (1838).
30 *NSA*, Kirkcudbrightshire, 251 (1840-4).
31 *NSA*, Wigtownshire, 74 (1839).
32 *NSA*, Dumfriesshire, 336 (1835).

CHAPTER 3 pp 29 to 44

1 *OSA*, ix, 321 (1792).
2 The information which follows is from the censuses from 1801 onwards. See also M W Flinn *et al.*, *Scottish Population history* (Cambridge, 1977).
3 Alexander Webster, *An Account of the Number of People in Scotland in 1755* in J G Kyd, *Scottish Population Statistics* (Scottish History Society, Edinburgh, 1952).
4 Places of birth are taken from the censuses of 1851, 1871 and 1891.
5 *OSA*, x, 48 (1792).

6 *Ibid.* iii 321 (1790-1).
7 *Seventh Report of the Commissioners for inquiring into the opportunities of Public Religious Worship, and means of Religious Instruction, and the Pastoral Superintendance afforded to the People of Scotland. BPP.* 1839. XXV. 1, p 362.
8 *Royal Commission on the Poor Laws in Scotland. BPP.* 1844. XXV. p 517.
9 *Royal Commission on the state of the Irish Poor.* Appendix G. Report on the State of the Irish Poor in Great Britain, 1835. *BPP.* 1836. XXIV. 427.
10 *Ibid.* Appendix, p 150 and p 152.
11 *Ibid.* p 148.
12 *Ibid.* p 143.
13 *Ibid.* p 143.
14 *NSA,* Wigtownshire, Sorbie: 30 (1838); Old Luce: 72 (1839); Penninghame: 179 (1838); Whithorn: 60 (1839); Kirkcolm: 115 (1837).
15 *Poor Laws in Scotland. BPP.* 1844. XXII. p 444, p 525, p 529, p 535, p 533.
16 *Fourth Report of the Commission on the Employment of Children, Young Persons, and Women in Agriculture.* Report by J H Tremenheere on Dumfriesshire, Kirkcudbrightshire, Wigtownshire and Ayrshire, para. 81. *BPP.* 1870. XIII.
17 *Third Report of Select Committee on Agricultural Distress BPP.* 1836. VIII. Q. 12,254-5 (William Brown).
18 Canon Lord Archibald Douglas, 8 August 1918. Housing conditions of migratory workers, 1916-26. SRO. AF 59/64.
19 Captain Hardy M Hardy, 12 January 1911. Housing conditions of migratory workers, 1910-1916. SRO. AF 59/63.
20 Educational statistics are from the census of 1871.

CHAPTER 4 pp 47 to 69

1 *Notebook of family history of AH, c.1500-1736.* Heron of Heron and Kirroughtree MSS. SRO. GD 307/15.
2 *OSA,* xii, 341 (1792).
3 *OSA,* vii, 299 (1792-3).
4 *OSA,* i, 154 (1790).
5 Estate Management, 18th/19th centuries. Galloway MSS. SRO. GD. 138/3/15/8 and 14.
6 *OSA,* xvii, 589 (1794-5).
7 *OSA,* i, 248 (1790-1).
8 Bryce Johnston, *General View of the Agriculture of the County of Dumfries* (London, 1794), 109.
9 Samuel Smith, *General View of the Agriculture of Galloway* (London, 1810), 74-5.
10 A Wight, *Present state of Husbandry in Scotland.* Fifth Survey. (Edinburgh, 1778), iii, 92-6.
11 Robert Heron, *Observations made in a Journey through the Western Counties of Scotland in the autumn of MDCCXCI* (Perth, 1799), ii, 206-7.
12 *OSA,* i, 351 (1790-1).
13 W Fullarton, *General View of the Agriculture of the County of Ayr* (Edinburgh, 1793), 26-7.
14 James Webster, *General View of the Agriculture of Galloway* (Edinburgh, 1792), 11-2.
15 Smith, *Agriculture of Galloway* (1810), 49 and 108.

16 Johnstone, *Agriculture of Dumfries* (1794), 20.
17 William Singer, *General View of the Agriculture of the County of Dumfries* (Edinburgh, 1812), 169-70, 195, 179, 192.
18 Wight, *Husbandry in Scotland*, iii, 127.
19 *OSA*, Anwoth: xii, 348 (1792); Buittle: xvii, 129 (1793); Colvend: xvii, 103 (1794); Kirkgunzeon: vii, 190 (1791-2); Borgue: xi, 37 (1793); Kelton: vii, 299 (1792-3); Lochrutton: ii, 41 (1790); New Abbey: ii, 127 and 130 (1790); Kirkbean: xv, 122 (1793); Crossmichael: i, 181 (1791); Kirkmabreck: xv, 545 (1794).
20 *OSA*, Sorbie: i, 250 (1790-1); Glasserton: xvii, 589 (1794-5); Mochrum: xvii, 566 (1794-5); Wigtown: xiv, 477 (1793).
21 *OSA*, Glasserton: xvii, 590 (1794-5); Wigtown, xiv, 478 (1793); Kirkinner: iv, 143 (1791); Whithorn, xvi, 280 (1794); Kirkcolm: ii, 47 (1791); Kirkoswald: x, 490 (1792); Girvan: xii, 341 (1792); Kirkmichael: xii, 341 (1791).
22 Fullarton, *Agriculture of Ayr* (1793), 24, 25.
23 Webster, *Agriculture of Galloway* (1794), 12 and 6.
24 Smith, *Agriculture of Galloway* (1810), 49 and 50.
25 Singer, *Agriculture of Dumfries* (1812), 215.
26 Wight, *Husbandry in Scotland*, iii, 134, 124, 158, 161.
27 Fullarton, *Agriculture of Ayr* (1793), 20.
28 Webster, *Agriculture of Galloway* (1794), 12, 6-7.
29 Smith, *Agriculture of Galloway* (1810), 151, 154.
30 *NSA*, Dumfriesshire, 85 (1834).
31 *NSA*, Kirkcudbrightshire, 57 (1841-3).
32 *Ibid*. Borgue: 58 (1841-3); Buittle: 205 (1836-44); Kirkbean: 243 (1844); Crossmichael: 197 and 198 (1844); Balmaghie: 187 (1844); Twynholm: 43 (1838-44); Urr: 353 (1843).
33 *NSA*, Ayrshire, Kirkoswald: 785 (1842); Girvan: 401 (1837).
34 *NSA*, Wigtownshire, Stoneykirk: 165 (1839); Kirkinner, 19 and 21 (1838).
35 Wight, *Husbandry in Scotland*, iii, 148.
36 David Archibald, 'The Blackfaced Breed of Sheep', *Transactions of the Highland and Agricultural Society of Scotland* (*THAS*), fourth series, xvi (1884), 228.
37 James Biggar, Agriculture of Kirkcudbrightshire and Wigtownshire (1876), 33.
38 James Drennan, 'The Farming of the West and South-western Districts' in *Report on the Present State of Agriculture in Scotland* (1878), 93-5.
39 *NSA*, Kirkcudbrightshire, 310 (1844).
40 *NSA*, Ayrshire, 680 (1841).
41 *Ibid*. Beith: 590 (1839); Dreghorn: 526 (1838); Largs: 802 (1842); Stevenston: 464 (1837).
42 *Ibid*. 283 (1837).
43 A Sturrock, 'Report of the Agriculture of Ayrshire', *THAS*, i (1866), 66.
44 *OSA*, ix, 537 (1792).
45 *Ibid*. xii, 97-8 (1791-3).
46 *NSA*, Ayrshire, Dalry: 226 (1836); Stewarton: 735 (1840-2).
47 *Ibid*. 301 (1836-7).
48 *Ibid*. Dalrymple: 283 (1837); Dundonald: 680 (1841).
49 *Ibid*. Dunlop: 299 (1836-7); Stewarton: 735 (1840-2).

50 *Ibid.* Monkton and Prestwick: 178 (1832-37); St Quivox: 121 (1831-7); Tarbolton: 758 (1842); Dreghorn: 526 (1838); Coylton: 659 (1841).

51 Sturrock, 'Agriculture of Ayrshire', *THAS*, i (1866), 47 and Drennan, Report on Agriculture (1878), 61-2.

52 *OSA*, Dalry: xii, 96 (1791-3); Dreghorn: iv, 281 (1790-1); Stevenston: vii, 30 (1791); Craigie: v, 371 (1790-1); Monkton and Prestwick: xii, 400 (1791-3); Galston: ii, 77n (1719); Symington: v, 398 (1792).

53 *NSA*, Ayrshire, Dalry: 227 (1836); Dunlop, 299 (1836-7); Coylton: 658 (1841); Auchinleck: 327 (1837); Stair: 646 (1841).

54 *Ibid.* 227 (1836).

55 *Ibid.* Tarbolton: 759 (1842); Dreghorn: 526 (1838); Dundonald: 680 (1841); Kilmarnock: 551 (1839); Monkton: 121 (1832-7); St Quivox: 175 (1831-7); Stewarton: 734-5 (1840-2); Coylton: 658-9 (1841).

56 *Ibid.* 227 (1836).

57 *Ibid.* Dalry: 226 (1836); Dunlop: 299 (1836-7); West Kilbride: 263 (1837); Tarbolton: 759 (1842); Galston: 186 (1837).

58 *OSA*, vi, 106-7, 105 (1791).

59 *Ibid.* x, 491 (1792).

60 *Ibid.* Glasserton: xvii, 584 (1794-5); Mochrum: xvii, 567 (1794-5).

61 Webster, *Agriculture of Galloway* (1794), 22-3; Wight, *Husbandry in Scotland*, iii, 146-7.

62 *NSA*, Ayrshire, Ballantrae: 420 (1836); Colmonell: 531 (1838); Girvan: 399 (1837); Dailly: 386 (1837); Maybole: 370 (1837); Kirkoswald: 785 (1842).

63 *Ibid.* Wigtownshire, Kirkcolm: 116-7 (1837); Glasserton: 45-6 (1836-8); Whithorn: 57 (1839); Old Luce: 72-3 (1839); Penninghame: 183 (1838); Kirkmaiden: 211 and 210 (1839); Inch: 91 (1839).

64 *Ibid.* Dumfriesshire, Closeburn: 85 (1834); Holywood: 563 (1837); Keir: 469 (1836); Kirkconnel: 318 (1835); Morton: 98 (1834); Tynron: 478 (1836).

65 *Ibid.* Kirkcudbrightshire, Tongland: 95 (1843); Balmaclellan: 105 (1840-4); Balmaghie: 187 (1844); Crossmichael: 194-5 (1844); Kirkbean: 240 (1844); Kirkmabreck: 318 and 337 (1840-4).

66 *Royal Commission on Agricultural Depression.* BPP. 1896. XVII. Q. 55,336 (William McConnell). The complaint stretched back well into the nineteenth century. See *Royal Commission on the Law relating to the Landlord's Right of Hypothec in Scotland in so far as regards agricultural subjects.* BPP. XVII. 413. Evidence, p 278 (William Sproat).

67 *Royal Commission on Agricultural Depression.* BPP. 1895. XVII. Report on south-west Scotland by John Speir, para. 18.

CHAPTER 5 pp 70 to 84

1 The Highland and Agricultural Society of Scotland carried out a pioneering survey of the agricultural statistics for East Lothian, Roxburgh and Sutherland in 1853 and a national series for Scotland from 1854 to 1857. They were published in BPP. 1854-5. XLVII. 637; 1857. LIX. 369; 1857 (Sess. 1). XV. 1; 1857-8. LVI 33. The official series begins in 1866, but, because of changes in coverage and dates to the returns, the series is comparable only from 1869. The minimum size of holding from which returns were made was 1/4 acre, which was increased to 1 acre in 1882.

Information on all livestock was obtained and is on an additional sheet. The original returns were destroyed but parochial summaries, which are used extensively in this chapter are available in the SRO for 1866 to 1911 in AF 39.

Ayrshire:	1866–97	– AF 29/3/1
	1898–1911	– AF 39/3/2
Dumfriesshire:		– AF 39/9
Kirkcudbrightshire:	1866–1891	– AF 39/19/1
	1892–1900	– AF 39/19/2
	1901–1911	– AF 39/19/3
Wigtownshire:	1866–97	– AF 39/32/1
	1898–1911	– AF 39/32/2

2   The compilers of the earliest agricultural statistics recognised the imprecise distinction between temporary and permanent grass. The distinction made in 1854 between 'grass under rotation' and 'permanent pasture' was eliminated in 1855, when only tillage was taken into account—i.e. no permanent pasture – and all land which was in the ordinary course of rotation, or which would be broken up sooner or later, was classified as being under rotation. Much which had been classified as permanent pasture in 1854 (especially in the dairying districts) was transferred to that category. The same difficulty of classification explains the sharp increase in temporary grass in 1885, which, as was stated at the time, 'appears to give significance to the statements in the reports of many of the officers that some confusion of mind has been occasioned by the sub-headings reintroduced into the Schedule this year to distinguish for both temporary and permanent grass the acreages used for hay and for fodder'. (BPP. 1884-5. LXXXIV. 16. p 9) The report which accompanies the statistics for 1886 made further reference to the problem: 'The acreage of Clover and Rotation grasses was discovered to have been overstated though not so largely in proportion to the increased acreage than sown'. (BPP. 1886. LXX. 23. p 13) Though the distinction between permanent and temporary grass is inexact—it often lies only in the eye or mind of the beholder—any move to place more land under permanent grass in the agricultural returns can be taken to show at least a move to rotations where the years under grass were so long that their use was considered to be permanent. This is especially so in any area, such as the south-west, where truly permanent grass was unusual.

3   Archibald MacNeilage, 'Farming Methods in Ayrshire', *THAS*, xviii (1906), 3.

4   Sturrock, 'Agriculture of Ayrshire', 66.

5   John Gillespie, 'Report on the Agriculture of Dumfriesshire', *THAS*, Fourth series, iv (1869), 303.

6   Drennan, *Report on the Present State of Agriculture* (1878), 79-80.

7   John Speir, 'Dairying in Scotland', *THAS*, Fourth series, xviii (1886), 304-5; MacNeilage, 'Farming Methods in Ayrshire', 3-4.

8   Sturrock, 'Agriculture of Ayrshire', 33.

CHAPTER 6 pp 85 to 93

1 *Select Committee on Agricultural Distress.* BPP. 1836. VIII. Q. 12,103 (William Brown).

2 *Royal Commission on Agricultural Depression.* Report on south-western Scotland by John Speir, para. 101. BPP. 1895. XVII.

3 Report showing the number of occupiers of farms (whether owners or tenants) in each County and Parish in Scotland with the Gross Rental, according to the valuation roll, for the year ending at Whitsunday 1906. BPP. 1907. LXXIII. 411. The similar return for 1881 (BPP. 1882. LII. 5070) does not have information for the whole of Ayrshire.

4 John McCulloch. 'On Dairying Management as Pursued in Galloway', *THAS*, fourth series, vii (1875), 267; Thomas MacLelland, 'On the Agriculture of the Stewartry of Kirkcudbright and Wigtownshire', *THAS*, fourth series, vii (1875), 52; William H Ralston, 'The Agriculture of Wigtownshire', *THAS*, fourth series, xvii (1875), 120.

5 *Royal Commission on the Employment of Children, Young Persons, and Women in Agriculture.* Fourth Report on Women in Agriculture. BPP. 1870. XIII. Evidence to the Assistant Commissioner on Ayr, etc., pp 7, 10, 12, 13.

6 *Report on the present state of agriculture in Scotland, THAS,* (1878) p 88.

7 Sturrock, 'Agriculture of Ayrshire', 81.

8 MacNeilage, 'Farming Methods in Ayrshire', 6.

9 *Royal Commission on Agricultural Depression.* BPP. 1896. XVII. Qs. 46,986 and 47,001-3 (John Speir).

10 MacNeilage, 'Farming Methods in Ayrshire', 7.

11 Thomas Farrell, 'On the Ayrshire Breed of Cattle', *THAS*, fourth series, viii (1876), 141.

12 Quoted in Ralston, 'The Agriculture of Wigtownshire', 121.

13 John Drysdale, 'The Management of a Dairy Farm', *THAS*, fifth series, xxv (1913), 72.

14 *Select Committee of the House of Lords on the Law of Hypothec in Scotland.* BPP. 1878-9. IX. Q. 1,892.

15 Sturrock, 'Agriculture of Ayrshire', 83.

16 MacLelland, 'Agriculture of Kirkcudbright and Wigtown', 52.

17 Sturrock, 'Agriculture of Ayrshire', 84.

18 John Gillespie, 'Report on the Agriculture of Dumfriesshire', *THAS*, fourth series, iv (1869), 309.

19 Sturrock, 'Agriculture of Ayrshire', 89.

20 Ralston, 'Agriculture of Wigtownshire', 129.

21 Sir John Sinclair, 'Hints regarding cattle', *Farmers' Magazine*, iii (1802), 161.

22 *Royal Commission on Labour.* Report by H Rutherford on Ayr, Renfrew, Bute, para. 26 and on Wigtown, Kirkcudbright and Dumfries, para. 34. BPP. 1893-4. XXXVI.

23 *Royal Commission on Agricultural Depression.* BPP. 1896. XVII. Q. 465,884-5 (John Speir).

24 I am grateful to Mr Lee for supplying information on employment on a county basis.

CHAPTER 7 pp 97 to 107

1 *Return of Owners of Land, 1872-3*. Part III (Scotland). BPP. 1874. LXII.
2 John Bateman, *The Great Landowners of Great Britain and Ireland* (4th edn, London, 1883).
3 *Ibid*. x-xi.
4 A comparison of the Return and Bateman for the 63 landowners in the south-west who had over 10,000 acres of land or £5,000 gross annual value shows 31 to be the same. Of the remaining 32, four were not included by Bateman; four in the Return were combined into two by Bateman; four had changes in the succession; ten had the same acreage but a slightly different rental; seven had various very minor differences; leaving three where the differences were more substantial. However, in the one where the differences were greatest (in the gross annual value) the explanation is almost certainly that, unusually, Bateman did not distinguish mineral rentals in that case (Oswald of Auchincruive) and the potential of the minerals on the estate had probably increased. The two others (Agnew of Lochnaw and Jardine of Castlemilk) were not sufficiently different to cause the general comparability of the Return and Bateman to be rejected as far as the south-west is concerned.
5 Of the five excluded as the test rose from £1,000 to £2,000, one landowner —Ferguson of Craigdarroch—did not have land of £2,000 value even in one county; the landowner with land in three counties—Carrick-Moore of Corsewall—moved into holding land of the higher valuation in only two.
6 As the values beyond the south-west are taken from Bateman, his figures have also been used for the south-west in this case. The differences from those for the south-west in the Return are negligible, except in the cases of Eglinton and Portland. On the Portland succession in 1878, the Ayrshire property was split between the late Duke's sisters and his successor, leading to a reduction in the new Duke's still considerable interest in the south-west.
7 Register of Deeds. SRO. RD 2/311/416, 18 February 1811.
8 Five who succeeded to property in the years between the Return and Bateman's work are excluded.

CHAPTER 8 pp 108 to 128

1 Acts of the Parliaments of Scotland, viii, 477 (1685).
2 Detailed information is in SRO. RT1. The SRO's copy of Samuel Shaw, *An Alphabetical Index of the Registered Entails in Scotland 1685 to 1784* (Edinburgh, 1784) has been updated in manuscript to 1833.
3 Adam Smith, *An Inquiry into the Nature and Causes of the Wealth of Nations* (1776) II, ii, 6.
4 10 Geo. III, c.51 (1770); 11 and 12 Vict. c.36 (1848); 4 & 5 Geo. V, c.43 (1914).
5 *First Report of Select Committee on Scotch Entails*. BPP. 1828. VII. 151, p 9, p 7, p 17.
6 *Second Report on Scotch Entails*. BPP. 1828. VII. 315.
7 *First Report on Scotch Entails*, pp 87f.
8 *Ibid*. p 69.

9   *Ibid*. p 56 and p 65.
10 *Ibid*. pp 84-5.
11 G J Bell, *Commentaries on the Laws of Scotland* (7th edn by J McLaren, Edinburgh, 1870), ii, 46-7; E D Sandford, *A treatise on the History and Law of Entails in Scotland* (Edinburgh, 1822), 260-1; *First Report on Scotch Entails*, p 86.
12 *Second Report on Scotch Entails*, p 56.
13 30 & 31 Vict. c.42 (1867); 43 Vict. c.12 (1880) abolished agricultural hypothec for most practical purposes.
14 Sir J C Dalrymple Hay to Disraeli, 11 March 1876. Quoted in I G C Hutchison, *A Political History of Scotland, 1832-1924* (Edinburgh, 1986), p 104.
15 *Report and Evidence of the Royal Commission on the Law relating to the Landlord's Right of Hypothec in Scotland in so far as regards agricultural subjects*. BPP. 1865. XVII, 413. Report, p xii.
16 *Ibid*. Evidence, p 279.
17 Miscellaneous papers, Dunragit estate, Cunninghame of Craigends MSS. SRO. GD 148/406.
18 See below pp 138-9.
19 *Royal Commission on Hypothec*. Evidence, p 113.
20 *Ibid*. p 131.
21 *Ibid*. p 212.
22 *Ibid*. p 276 and p 277.
23 *Ibid*. p 298.
24 *Ibid*. p 273.
25 *Ibid*. p 284.
26 *Ibid*. p 128.
27 Register for sequestrations for rent. Wigtown Sheriff Court (1867-1909), SRO. SC 19/15/1; Stranraer Sheriff Court (1871-93), SRO. SC 18/15/1.
28 Rent Ledgers. Galloway MSS. SRO. GD 138/104-134.
29 *Royal Commission on Agriculture*. BPP. 1881. XVII. Qs. 36,967-36,994 (George Cowan).
30 *Ibid*. Q. 43,594; also 43,651-3 (George Kynoch).
31 *Royal Commission on Hypothec*. Evidence, p 278 (Thomas Biggar).
32 Miscellaneous papers, Dunragit estate. Cunninghame of Craigends MSS. SRO. GD 148/406.
33 *Royal Commission on Agriculture*. BPP. 1881. XVII. Q. 44,636 (James Hope).
34 *Royal Commission on Agricultural Depression*. BPP. 1895. XVII. Report of Assistant Commissioner (John Speir) on south-west Scotland, paras. 50 and 52.
35 *Ibid*. BPP. 1896. XVII. Q. 55,239 (William McConnell).
36 *Royal Commission on Agriculture*. BPP. 1881. XVIII. Q. 37,208-9 (George Cowan).
37 *Ibid*. Q. 37,823 (Andrew Allan).
38 *Ibid*. Q. 44,227 (James Drew).
39 *Royal Commission on Agricultural Depression*. BPP. 1896. XVII. Q. 51,275 (John Hannah).
40 *Ibid*. Q. 53,716-7 (James Drew).
41 *Royal Commission on Agriculture*. BPP. 1881. XVII. Q. 44,557 (James Hope).
42 *Royal Commission on Agricultural Depression*. BPP. 1896. XVII. Q. 46,765 and Q. 46,777 (John Speir).
43 *Ibid*. Q. 47,071 (John Speir).

44 *Royal Commission on Agriculture*. BPP. 1881. XVII. Q. 42,366 (Thomas Biggar); Q. 37,066 (George Cowan).

CHAPTER 9 pp 129 to 159

1 Codicil to trust disposition and settlement, 17 September 1914. SRO. RD 5/4682/495.
2 James Fergusson to Col. Dundas, 4 December 1906. Scottish Landowners' Federation MSS. SRO. GD 325/1/2454.
3 From J R Macdonald, 13 February 1914. GD 325/1/244.
4 Factor's accounts, 1850-59. Agnew of Lochnaw MSS. SRO GD 154/412.
5 Register of improvements for entailed estates, Wigtown Sheriff Court. SRO SC 19/65/3, 24 February 1823.
6 *Ibid*. SRO. SC 19/65/1. 12 June 1799.
7 *Ibid*. Kirkcudbright Sheriff Court. SRO SC 16/64/3, 1809-13.
8 Factor's Accounts. Stair MSS. SRO GD 135/40.
9 Register of improvements for entailed estates, Wigtown Sheriff Court. SRO. SC 19/65/2, 30 April 1813.
10 *Ibid*.
11 *Ibid*. SRO. SC 19/65/4, 4 April 1829.
12 *Ibid*. Kirkcudbright Sheriff Court. SRO. SC 16/64/3. pp 162f. and 242f.
13 Journal of improvements, 1849-1892. Agnew of Lochnaw MSS. SRO. GD 154/762.
14 Register of improvements for entailed estates. Wigtown Sheriff Court. SRO. SC 19/6555/9. 1852-65; Factors Accounts, 1850-59. Agnew of Lochnaw MSS. SRO. GD 154/412.
15 Information for Lord Ailsa on the subject of Cottage for Agricultural Labourers, 30 January 1867. Ailsa MSS. SRO. GD 25/9/78/7/5.
16 Journal of improvements, 1849-92. Agnew of Lochnaw MSS. SRO. GD 154/762.
17 Factor's Accounts, 1850-59. Agnew of Lochnaw MSS. SRO. GD 154/412.
18 Lochnaw Estate Book, 1892-1918. Agnew of Lochnaw MSS. SRO. GD 154/766.
19 Government grants in the 1840s and the promotion of private companies for land drainage were used extensively.
20 2 & 3 Vict. c.36, 19 July 1839.
21 Register of improvements for entailed estates. Wigtown Sheriff Court. SRO. SC 19/65/6, 10 March 1845: for Monreith see SRO. SC 19/65/5, 2 March 1843.
22 *Royal Commission on Agricultural Depression*. BPP. 1896. XVII. Q. 46,931 (John Speir).
23 Wight, *Husbandry in Scotland*, iii, p 109, p 124, p 129, p 158, p 161.
24 Letter to the farmers of Wigtownshire by John Vans Agnew, 4 December 1823. Vans Agnew of Barnbarroch MSS. SRO. GD 99/228/22.
25 Smith, *Agriculture of Galloway*, 53.
26 When no other source is cited, the following are used—Galloway: State Books, 1873-1915 (except 1901-3). SRO. GD 138/2/143-52; Murray of Broughton and Cally: Rent Rolls, 1861-1900 (except 1865, 1874-7); SRO. GD 10/1331-59; Agnew of Lochnaw: Factors' Accounts, 1860-1912. SRO. GD 154/414-6.

27   The letters are loose sheets inserted at the entry for the farm in the Rent Ledgers, from 1818. SRO. GD 138/2/104-34.

28   A Smith, *Wealth of Nations*, II.ii.73; S Smith, *Agriculture of Galloway*, 350-2.

29   Sir Walter Scott, The Letters of Malachi Malagrowther (Edinburgh, 4th edn, 1826), 24.

30   Fullarton, *Agriculture of Ayr*, 91-2.

31   Report by James Drennan. Cunninghame of Craigends MSS. SRO. GD 148/409/1/21.

32   Register of improvements for entailed estates. Wigtown Sheriff Court. SRO. SC 19/65/9, 19 October 1861.

33   *Ibid*. SRO. SC 19/65/10, 11 March 1869.

34   Factor's Accounts, 1867-70. Stair MSS. SRO GD 135/205.

35   Register of improvements for entailed estates. Wigtown Sheriff Court. SRO. SC 19/65/10, 11, 12.

36   *Ibid*. SRO. SC 19/65/12, 28 January 1879.

37   *Ibid*. SRO. SC 19/65/9, 10 March 1855.

38   Journal of Improvements, 1849-92 and Lochnaw Improvement Book 1892-1893. Agnew of Lochnaw MSS. SRO. GD 154/762 and 763.

39   Heron, *Journey through the Western Counties*, ii, 381.

40   See above, chapter 8.

41   See below, chapter 10.

42   Scottish Landowners Federation MSS. SRO. GD 325/1/246.

CHAPTER 10 pp 160 to 180

1   Dated 9 August 1794. Melville Castle MSS. SRO. GD 51/1/26.

2   Earl of Galloway to Henry Dundas, 16 August 1793 and 2 May 1795. SRO. Melville Castle MSS. SR. GD 51/1/22 and 31.

3   Earl of Galloway to James Nish, 4 December 1801 and 25 December 1801. Estate papers, 1801-2. Galloway MSS. SRO. GD 138/3/21/5 and 6.

4   Register of Deeds. SRO. RD 3/338/170; RD 4/278/974; RD 5/174/430. Register of Sasines. SRO. RS 61/8/257; RS 3/1093.

5   SRO. RD 3/314/405.

6   SRO. RT 1/62/30, 3 July 1804.

7   SRO. RD 3/314/995.

8   SRO. RD 2/311/416; RD 5/86/59; RS 3/1020.

9   SRO. RD 3/340/621.

10   SRO. RD 5/74/325, 305 and 342.

11   SRO. RD 5/252/100.

12   SRO. RD 5/174/403 and 430.

13   SRO. RS 3/1148/139; RT 1/54/335, 1 December 1819.

14   SRO. RD 5/238/549, 628; RD 5/251/472; RD 5/279/317.

15   SRO. RD 3/3144/405, 21 January 1807, but not in RT 1/62/30 until 11 July 1823. The deed is dated 3 July 1804. See also RT 1/102/183.

16   SRO. SC 19/65/1 and SC 16/64/3.

17   Earl of Galloway v. Galloway Trustees. Extracted processes. SRO. CS 46/38 of 16 May 1837.

18   Calculated as four years of free rent for expenditure on the estate and two years of free rent for expenditure on the mansion house.

19 General ledger, 1823-26. Galloway MSS. SRO. GD 138/2/74.
20 General ledgers, 1823-34. Galloway MSS. SRO. GD 138/2/74-76 and 78.
21 5 Geo. 4 c.17.
22 Extracted processes. SRO. CS 46/163 of 16 July 1842.
23 Reports in process to sell entailed lands: 1825, CS 96/3665; 1827, CS 96/3712, ex unextracted processes: CS 44 of 9 July 1825 and CS 44 of 15 July 1827.
24 See above p 111.
25 See above p 161.
26 SRO. RS 3/1366/239, 23 May 1824.
27 General ledgers. Galloway MSS. SRO. GD 138/74-76, 78-79.
28 Extracted processes. SRO. CS 46/163 of July 1842.
29 Extracted processes. SRO. CS 46/27 of December 1840.
30 General ledgers. Galloway MSS. SRO. GD 138/2/82-85.
31 *Ibid.* SRO. GD 138/2/75.
32 Disposition and settlement by Alan Plantaganent, Earl of Galloway. SRO. RD 5/3094/472, 15 February 1901.
33 SRO. RD 5/3094/472, 15 February 1901.
34 SRO. CS 272/2/225, 21 January 1902.
35 Dated 20 February 1908. Letter book, 1907-8. Galloway MSS. SRO. GD 138/2/25.
36 Extracted process. SRO. CS 46/42 of January 1907.
37 Factor to Russell and Dunlop, Edinburgh agents, 9 July 1908; factor to Cowan and Stewart, 5 July 1910. Letter Books, Galloway MSS. SRO. GD 138/2/26 and 29.
38 Letter books, Galloway MSS. SRO. GD 138/2/24.
39 Factor to Russell and Dunlop, 24 July and 22 June 1907. Letter books, Galloway MSS. SRO. GD 138/2/24.
40 Factor to Lord Galloway, 27 June and 2 July 1907. Letter books, Galloway MSS. SRO. GD 138/2/24.
41 Factor to Russell and Dunlop, 20 July 1907. Letter books, Galloway MSS. GD 138/2/24.
42 *Ibid.* 20 June 1907.
43 *Ibid.* 4 July 1907.
44 Register of Acts and Decreets. SRO. CS 45/106 of June 1909. Extracted processes CS 46/106 of January 1909 and CS 46/11 of November 1914 were conjoined. They were retransmitted to the Court and returned to the SRO much later. They are the key papers but are difficult to trace.
45 Factor to George Dunlop, 20 February 1908. Letter books, Galloway MSS. SRO. GD 138/2/25.
46 Factor to Lord Galloway, 30 October 1907 and 31 January 1908. SRO. GD 138/2/25.
47 *Ibid.* 31 January 1908.
48 *Ibid.* 20 February 1908.
49 *Ibid.* 31 January 1908 and to Russell and Dunlop, 16 January 1908. Letter, books, Galloway MSS. SRO. GD 138/2/25.
50 Factor to H. Weller Richards, 14 March 1908. Letter books, Galloway MSS. SRO. GD 138/2/26.
51 Factor to Russell and Dunlop, 9 July 1908. Letter books, Galloway MSS. SRO. GD 138/2/26.
52 Factor to Russell and Dunlop, 2 December 1907, 'Lord Galloway asks me

if I can tell him about an Australian (a name like Sir Malcolm Maclaughlan) who is supposed to be thinking of Estate and who has got particulars'. SRO. GD 138/2/25. MacEacharn was born at Bridgend, Islay, in 1852. He was in a shipping business in Ayr with Andrew McIlwraith before they went to Australia in 1879. McEacharn pioneered the trade in frozen meat, was engaged extensively in pastoral farming and with McIlwraith was a shipowner, coal contractor and general merchant. His second wife was the daughter of John Boyd Watson, who owned gold mines in Bendigo. MacEacharn died at Cannes in March 1910, a year after he acquired Galloway House.

53   SRO. RS 122/160.
54   Dated 24 August 1908. Letter books, Galloway MSS. SRO. GD 138/2/26.
55   Factor to Mrs Adela Anstruther, 21 August 1908. Letter books, Galloway MSS. SRO. GD 138/2/26.
56   The detailed financial arrangements which follow are taken from the sources cited in note 44 above.
57   Factor to Russell and Dunlop, 26 August 1908. Letter books, Galloway MSS. SRO. GD 138/2/26.
58   SRO. RS 122/160/98 and RS 122/161/109.
59   Letter books, Galloway MSS. SRO. GD 138/2/27.
60   *Ibid*. SRO. GD 138/2/28.
61   *Ibid*.
62   *Ibid*.
63   *Ibid*. SRO, GD 138/2/29.
64   Factor to Cowan and Stewart, 23 April 1910. Letter books. Galloway MSS. SRO. GD 138/2/29.
65   Letter books, Galloway MSS. SRO. GD 138/2/27; see also letter to N Matthews, 25 November 1908.
66   Factor to Lady Henrietta Turnor, 5 August 1909. Letter books, Galloway MSS. SRO. GD 138/2/28.
67   Factor to Lord Galloway, 20 October 1908. Letter books, Galloway MSS. SRO. GD 138/2/27.
68   *Ibid*. 26 October 1908.
69   *Ibid*. 20 and 29 October 1908; to Countess, 3 December 1908.
70   Factor to Craig and Henderson, Glasgow, 20 December 1909; to Lord Galloway, 7 and 27 August 1909. Letter books, Galloway MSS. SRO. GD 138/2/28.
71   Factor to Cowan and Stewart, 31 October 1910. Letter books, Galloway MSS. SRO. GD 138/2/29.
72   Extracted process. SRO. CS 46/11 of November 1914.
73   SRO. RS 122/180.
74   SRO. RT 1/234/163, 29 November 1916; RS 106/277/91, 22 December 1916.

Index